Shirley Clarke

Visionaries: Thinking Through Female Filmmakers
Series Editors Lucy Bolton and Richard Rushton

Titles in the series include:

The Cinema of Marguerite Duras: Multisensoriality and Female Subjectivity
Michelle Royer

Ana Kokkinos: An Oeuvre of Outsiders
Kelly McWilliam

Gillian Armstrong: Popular, Sensual & Ethical Cinema
Julia Erhart

Kathleen Collins: The Black Essai Film
Geetha Ramanathan

The Cinema of Mia Hansen-Løve: Candour and Vulnerability
Kate Ince

Céline Sciamma: Portraits
Emma Wilson

Shirley Clarke: Thinking Through Movement
Karen Pearlman

Shirley Clarke

Thinking Through Movement

Karen Pearlman

EDINBURGH
University Press

Edinburgh University Press is one of the leading university presses in the UK. We publish academic books and journals in our selected subject areas across the humanities and social sciences, combining cutting-edge scholarship with high editorial and production values to produce academic works of lasting importance. For more information visit our website: edinburghuniversitypress.com

We are committed to making research available to a wide audience and are pleased to be publishing Platinum Open Access ebook editions of titles in this series.

© Karen Pearlman, 2025, under a Creative Commons Attribution-NonCommercial licence

Grateful acknowledgement is made to the sources listed in the List of Illustrations for permission to reproduce material previously published elsewhere. Every effort has been made to trace the copyright holders, but if any have been inadvertently overlooked, the publisher will be pleased to make the necessary arrangements at the first opportunity.

Edinburgh University Press Ltd
13 Infirmary Street
Edinburgh EH1 1LT

Typeset in 12/14 Arno and Myriad by
IDSUK (DataConnection) Ltd.

A CIP record for this book is available from the British Library

ISBN 978 1 3995 0143 9 (hardback)
ISBN 978 1 3995 0144 6 (paperback)
ISBN 978 1 3995 0145 3 (webready PDF)
ISBN 978 1 3995 0146 0 (epub)

The right of Karen Pearlman to be identified as the author of this work has been asserted in accordance with the Copyright, Designs and Patents Act 1988, and the Copyright and Related Rights Regulations 2003 (SI No. 2498).

Contents

List of Figures — vi
Preface and Acknowledgements — xi

Introduction — 1
1. Biography and Context — 13
2. Distributed Cognition and Creative Practice — 44
3. Dancing Cognitions — 70
4. Editing Thinking — 107
5. Directing Enaction — 138
6. Conclusions and Continuances — 187

Index — 199

Figures

Frontispiece	Shirley Clarke circa 1960, photo by George Amberg. Shirley Clarke collection, M91-052, Box 26, Folder 4, Wisconsin Center for Film and Theater Research	xv
Figure 1.1	Montage of selected images of Felix the Cat found in Shirley Clarke's archives at the Wisconsin Center for Film and Theater Research. Shirley Clarke collection, U.S. Mss 145 AN, various boxes, Wisconsin Center for Film and Theater Research	13
Figure 1.2	Bert and Shirley Clarke setting up a shot together in 1959, photographer unknown. Shirley Clarke collection, M91-052, Box 25, Folder 9, Wisconsin Center for Film and Theater Research	17
Figure 1.3	Narration of 'Artistic Accomplishments' by Shirley Clarke for grant application to the Guggenheim Foundation, circa 1960, page 1. Shirley Clarke collection, U.S. Mss 145 AN, Box 12, Folder 6, WCFTR	20
Figure 1.4	Narration of 'Artistic Accomplishments', page 2	21
Figure 1.5	Narration of 'Artistic Accomplishments', page 3	22

Figure 1.6	Narration of 'Plans' by Shirley Clarke for grant application to the Guggenheim Foundation, circa 1960, page 1. Shirley Clarke collection, U.S. Mss 145 AN, Box 12, Folder 6, WCFTR	27
Figure 1.7	Narration of 'Plans', page 2	28
Figure 1.8	Narration of 'Plans', page 3	29
Figure 1.9	Narration of 'Plans', page 4	30
Figure 1.10	Narration of 'Plans', page 5	31
Figure 1.11	Shirley Clarke, Wendy Clarke, Jonas Mekas and others at a twelve-hour marathon of reading of a Lionel Zippens book, circa 1965, photographer unknown. Shirley Clarke collection, M91-052, Box 26, Folder 17, Wisconsin Center for Film and Theater Research	34
Figure 2.1	Shirley Clarke thinking in motion. Date unknown (circa 1950s–60s), photo by Gideon Bachman. Shirley Clarke collection, M91-052, Box 25, Folder 6, Wisconsin Center for Film and Theater Research	44
Figure 2.2	Shirley Clarke thinking with place and collaborators (and cigarettes!) on the set of *The Connection*, circa 1960. PH 7162, *The Connection*, Box 107, Folder 4, WCFTR	60
Figure 3.1	Shirley Clarke in full flight, circa 1950. Shirley Clarke collection, M91-052, Box 25, Folder 5, Wisconsin Center for Film and Theater Research	70
Figure 3.2	Shirley Clarke with cinematographer Peter Buckley directing *Bullfight* (1955). Credit: Halcyon Pictures. WCFTR Name photograph file, PH 7163, Box 52, Folder 1, Wisconsin Center for Film and Theater Research	72

Figure 3.3	Collage of production stills from *Bullfight* (1955) and *Dance in the Sun* (1953). Shirley Clarke collection, U.S. Mss 145 AN, Box 12, Folder 1, Wisconsin Center for Film and Theater Research	78
Figure 3.4	Daniel Nagrin in *Dance in the Sun*, promotional flyer annotated by Shirley Clarke with notes on screenings and prizes for the film, circa 1954–5. Shirley Clarke collection, U.S. Mss 145 AN, Box 13, Folder 5, Wisconsin Center for Film and Theater Research	88
Figure 3.5	Diagram of three overlapping 'genres' of screendance: dancefilm, dance on camera, and videodance	98
Figure 4.1	Shirley Clarke in the edit suite. Photos by Peter Buckley, 1958. Shirley Clarke collection, M91-052, Box 26, Folder 7, Wisconsin Center for Film and Theater Research	110
Figure 4.2	Shirley Clarke editing with splicer and Moviola, circa 1966. Shirley Clarke collection, M91-052, Box 25, Folder 9, Wisconsin Center for Film and Theater Research	118
Figure 4.3	Shirley Clarke on the street in Harlem during the shoot of *The Cool World*. Photo by Leroy McLucas, circa 1963. WCFTR film title photograph file, PH 7162, *The Cool World*, Box 108, Folder 32, Wisconsin Center for Film and Theater Research	120
Figure 5.1	Shirley Clarke on the phone, circa 1960, presumably finding a way to get a film made. Photographer unknown. WCFTR film title photograph file, PH 7162, *The Connection*,	

List of Figures   ix

Figure 5.2 Some of the cast and crew of *The Connection* on set. Photo by Gideon Bachman, 1960. WCFTR film title photograph file, PH 7162, *The Connection*, Box 107, Folder 1, Wisconsin Center for Film and Theater Research   150

Figure 5.3 Directing *The Cool World*, with Baird Bryant, cinematographer, using a wheelchair as a dolly. Carl Lee and Bryant's first assistant, and wife, Jane, also pictured. Photo by Leroy McLucas, 1960. WCFTR film title photograph file, PH 7162, *The Cool World*, Box 108, Folder 32, Wisconsin Center for Film and Theater Research   155

Figure 5.4 Clarke has written in pencil on the back of this photo: 'Setting up C.U. frame for opening shot of "The Cool World", Carl Lee – leading actor and co-author with Clarke, street speaker – Richard Ward –, photo by Leroy McLucas, p.s. I love this photo – looks like I'm about to "pee".' Shirley Clarke collection, M91-052, Box 25, Folder 9, Wisconsin Center for Film and Theater Research   162

Figure 5.5 Carl Lee and Shirley Clarke at a press conference for *The Cool World* at the Venice Film Festival. Photo by Giacomelli, 1963. WCFTR name photograph file, PH 7163, Shirley Clarke collection, Box 52, Folder 1, Wisconsin Center for Film and Theater Research   164

Figure 6.1 Shirley Clarke and members of the Video Space Troupe: notes on the backs of photos in this folder indicate that this is the first   175

	performance of the Troupe and that it is taking place at The Kitchen, May 1973; and that the photos are 'taken by Margarite Journalist from Caracas Venezuela'. Shirley Clarke collection, M91-052, Box 27, Folder 16, Wisconsin Center for Film and Theater Research	192
Figure 6.2	A complex set up of multiple video monitors at the Chelsea Hotel, circa 1973. WCFTR name photograph file, PH 7163, Shirley Clarke collection, Box 52, Folder 3, Wisconsin Center for Film and Theater Research	192
Figure 6.3	Ornette Coleman and Shirley Clarke in Fort Worth for the shooting of *Ornette: Made in America*, circa 1983. Shirley Clarke collection, M91-052, Box 25, Folder 16, Wisconsin Center for Film and Theater Research	194

Preface and Acknowledgements

Shirley Clarke (1919–1997) set out to be a modern dancer in New York in the 1940s. She then used the kinaesthetic intelligence accrued through dance training to master the choreographic art of film editing. From there, she built on the strategic intuitions of an editor to catapult herself into directing.

I had never heard of Shirley Clarke when I set out to be a dancer in New York, then used those skills to bounce myself into film editing, and then cut my way into directing films. When I did finally start to learn about Shirley Clarke, I felt was discovering the ground I'd been walking on for years.

As Dall'Asta and Gaines write: 'As we are undertaking this research, we come to align ourselves with the women we study. Forming a constellation with them, we locate ourselves historically ... what we 'find' when we locate one of these figures is that, actually, we are discovering and locating ourselves in our own historical moment'[1]. Shirley Clarke's major film works were all about the lives of Black men, and mine are, so far, all about the lives of overlooked women filmmakers. Nonetheless, the plan is to draw on our common embodied experiences with dance, editing and directing to think through her work – to form a 'constellation'[2] with her, and to give more film scholars and filmmakers the opportunity to align with her in their own scholarship and creativity.

In this process, many, many thanks and acknowledgements are due, starting with my immense gratitude to Wendy Clarke, Shirley Clarke's daughter, whose generosity, insight, humour and staying power have buoyed the process of writing this book for many years. Dennis Doros and Amy Heller of Milestone Films are the chief instigators of the wave of interest in Shirley Clarke's films that this book is riding. I would never have found the films or understood their significance without their years of scouring the archives to bring together and preserve the DVD/Blu-Ray/Streaming collection of films directed and edited by Shirley Clarke, plus outtakes, interviews, home movies and more. With one exception, every film discussed in this book can be found in that collection, now distributed by Kino-Lorber. The skilled and dedicated archivists at the Wisconsin Center for Film and Theater Research (WCFTR) who collected the films, papers and photographs on which this book relies include Mary Huelsbeck, current guardian of the collection, Amanda Smith, keeper of the moving image components, and the person who originally took custodianship of Shirley Clarke's archives, Maxine Fleckner Ducey (who was colourful in her encouragement of Dennis Doros, who, in turn, was gorgeous in his encouragement of me). Thank you all, and everyone who helped us on our visits to the WCFTR.

Thanks are also due to everyone at Edinburgh University Press who has helped this book through the years long process of ideation, proposing, writing, editing and production. I particularly thank Lucy Bolton and Richard Rushton, editors of the 'Visionaries' series for – well, I'm just going to say it – your vision in steering the series. The 'Visionaries' series is making a major impact on the historiography of film and it was the original inspiration for this book: thank you. EUP publisher Gillian Leslie, your insight and acuity have been so significant to the realisation of this project. Senior assistant editors Sam Johnson and Kelly O'Brien, desk editor Grace Balfour-Harle and copy-editor Gill Cloke, your work in guiding and producing the book has been invaluable. As I argue throughout this book, the work of editing is not to be under-estimated in its contribution to the creative and intellectual process of authoring, and I am indebted to all of you at EUP for yours.

Closer to home, I'd like to thank my colleagues John Sutton, Iqbal Barkat and Peter Doyle, who have inspired and provoked ideas in the book and the ways they are expressed, and everyone in the 'Interiors' gang – your collegiality and creative community make such a big difference to the working process. I also extend warm thanks to Kate Rossmanith and Eve Vincent for convening the workshop on Fact, Fiction and Narration where parts of this book were pulled apart and put back together, better. Thanks are due to research assistants/interns Desmond Bravo, Lana Chryssavgis and Timothy Sharp, whose curiosity and enthusiasm for the subject helped to bring a renewed sense of purpose to the task. I warmly acknowledge the support of Macquarie University, particularly Deputy Dean, Research and Innovation in the Faculty of Arts, Professor Louise D'Arcens, current and former managers of the Arts Research Office Dr Christine Boman, and Dr Jan Zwar, Director of the CDRC Professor Tom Murray, and head of the department of Media, Communications, Creative Arts, and Literature, Professor Hsu-Ming Teo; all of whose material support in the form of resources and grants, and moral support in the form of mentorship has been invaluable.

An earlier version of the discussion of *Brussels Loops* in Chapter 4 was commissioned by Alix Beeston and Stefan Solomon for their groundbreaking volume, *Incomplete: The Feminist Possibilities of the Unfinished Film*. (See: Pearlman, K. (2023). 'One Long Electrical Cord: Dance, Editing and the Creative Unfinished'. In A. Beeston and S. Solomon (Eds.), *Incomplete: The Feminist Possibilities of the Unfinished Film* (pp. 211–225). University of California Press.)

In the same chapter, a version of the discussion of *The Cool World* was first crafted for the 2021 special issue of *Textual Practice* edited by Paul Sheehan and James Alexander Mackenzie. (See: Pearlman, K. (2021). 'Editing and Authorship: Writing, Choreographing, Conducting Cinematic Movement in *The Cool World* and Beyond'. *Textual Practice*, 35 (10), 1587–1605.) Reprinted by permission of the publisher (Taylor & Francis Ltd, https://www.tandfonline.com/doi/full/10.1080/0950236X.2021.1965291

My profound thanks to all of these editors – Alix Beeston and Stefan Solomon, Paul Sheehan and James Alexander Mackenzie – for the insights, skills and creative intelligence you applied to these contributions to your excellent publications.

To the incredibly patient and skilled workers at St Jude Café in Redfern, thank you for the 'desk' in the sun and endless cups of tea that made writing possible.

Finally, Richard James Allen, archive hound, producer, poet and creative collaborator in pretty much all of my work: saying 'thank you' doesn't really cover it, but my hope is that, over the long durée, you know what I mean and how much you mean to the realisation of this book.

Notes

1 Dall'asta, M. and Gaines, J. M. (2015). 'Prologue: Constellations: Past Meets Present in Feminist Film History'. In C. Gledhill, J. Knight, M. Dall'Asta and J. Gaines (eds.), *Doing Women's Film History: Reframing Cinemas, Past and Future*. University of Illinois Press. https://doi.org/10.5406/illinois/9780252039683.003.0002 p. 19.

2 Ibid. p. 19.

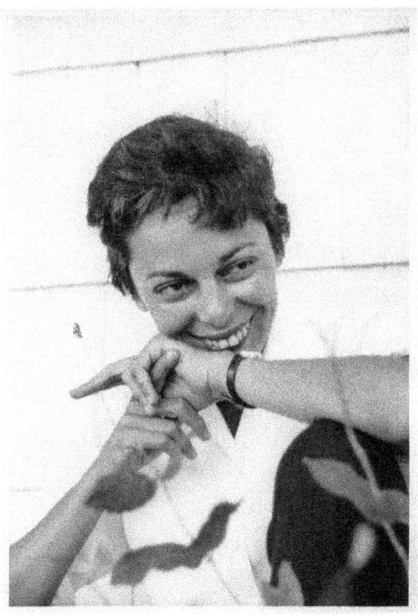

Frontispiece: Shirley Clarke circa 1960, photo by George Amberg. Shirley Clarke collection, M91-052, Box 26, Folder 4, Wisconsin Center for Film and Theater Research

Introduction

Shirley Clarke: Thinking through Movement is a creative practice and distributed cognition account of Shirley Clarke's cinematic innovations and provocations. It is the first film-philosophy book on 'pioneer, radical, visionary'[1] filmmaker Shirley Clarke and the films she edited and directed. The book draws on film analysis, archival research, dance and film theory, and creative practice expertise, to think through Clarke's work as a dancer turned multi-award-winning editor and director of dancefilm, fiction, documentary and video art.

In the context of the New American Cinema movement of the 1960s, where Clarke's 'fierce campaigns for independent cinema'[2] were core, Clarke was eventually marginalised by her male contemporaries' self-mythologising of independent filmmaking as 'a succession of Great Men wrestling with genius'.[3] One of my key aims in writing this book is to correct these erasures of Clarke and contribute a research framework specifically designed to be used to address similar erasures in film history and theory. This framework synthesises creative practice, distributed cognition and feminist film historiography approaches to ask about Clarke's embodied practices in dance, editing and directing, and the ways they are embedded and enacted in her particular social, political and creative contexts. This synthesis is designed to illuminate Shirley Clarke's particular distributed expertise as the source of narratives, aesthetics and dynamics in the diverse and radical body of work she directed and edited.

My creative practice and distributed cognition framework also aims to be useful in a larger task: providing a novel pathway through the feminist conundrum of auteur theories that have historically excluded women but now are racing to embrace us. The objective is to rewire, in a sense, auteur theories so that they can recognise distinctive abilities of unique individuals, but also understand that these abilities do not reside solely inside the individual's skull and skin. They are *distributed* through the bodies, tools, contexts and collaborators as led by that individual.

This creative practice and distributed cognition framework offers a feminist alternative to authorship theories. It is not trying to say that authors don't exist. It is, rather, proposing that we can recognise them by the unique ways in which they integrate and activate their worlds, interactions and bodies in a distributed creative practice. It repositions filmmaking creativity as distributed without diminishing the profound effects of the role of directors' standpoint, skill, expertise, perseverance and presence in manifesting films with voice and vision.

This contribution to the Edinburgh University Press Visionaries series will argue that Clarke's distinctive films arise from her distributed kinaesthetic intelligence and imagination. These manifest via her embodied expertise in dance and editing; her embedded fluency with technologies and aesthetics; and her enactive and responsive engagement with political and artistic movements of her times. Thus, a distributed cognition account of Clarke's visionary directing and editing can both recognise her distinctive authorial approach and understand that vision does not 'spring fully-striped / from the head like tigers'.[4]

Shirley Clarke: Thinking Through Movement begins with a chapter on Clarke's biography, followed by a chapter on my theoretical framework for thinking through her methods, subjects, experience, context and the films she edited and directed. The framework is then applied to chapters that consider Clarke's early work in dancefilm; her creative editing expertise on her own and others' films; and the impacts of her cultural context, dancing and editing on her directing.

Overview of chapters

Chapter 1: Biography and Context

Chapter 1 begins with Clarke's family life in New York, in the 1920s and 30s, as daughter of a 'rage-aholic',[5] Jewish, self-made millionaire, father. It briefly chronicles Clarke's key rebellions, including escape from her father's controlling rage by slipping out to jazz clubs, and navigating and finding voice in modern dance. The modern dance world's affordances[i] and constraints are considered, briefly, alongside the expectations of white women's social, political, personal and professional lives that were normative in America in the 1950s and 60s. Discussion of the ways that Clarke did and did not choose to challenge these forms and cultures could be sub-titled 'a camera of one's own'. In the 1950s, technological autonomy and self-sufficiency with filmmaking gear galvanised Clarke's creativity and capacity to manifest cinematic ideas. She was independent, technologically adept and outspoken, all of which challenged the norms of femininity in her times and afforded her access to filmmaking scenes that were almost exclusively male. Clarke influenced and challenged various independent film movements, such as observational cinema, New American Cinema and experimental film. Key figures and ideologies of these movements, and Clarke's dynamic interactions with them, will be discussed in this chapter, as they incited important themes in Clarke's filmmaking. These themes in her creative practice included: her fierce commitment to addressing racism; her dedication to the art of editing as central to the conception and realisation of film ideas; her fascination with technologies and their affordances; and the expanded freedoms of working with untrained people – social actors, doing what she calls 'life-dancing'.[6] Cumulatively, this chapter will set up discussion to come, in subsequent chapters, of Clarke's complex, fluid 'dances' with film movements and social movements and the ways they were significant in her creative processes.

---

[i] An 'affordance', as defined by the interaction design foundation, is 'what a user can do with an object based on the user's capabilities'. See: Interaction Design Foundation (IxDF) (2016). 'What are Affordances?' IxDF, September 13. https://www.interaction-design.org/literature/topics/affordances.

True to Shirley Clarke's own credo that editing is where films are made, this chapter presents Clarke's biography primarily as a montage of her own words about herself, and others about her. Over the course of her career, Shirley Clarke generated a number of self-narratives: short documents, usually appended to grant applications or unfurled as parts of interviews, where she describes key events, projects, and, towards the later stages of her career, reflections on her feelings. Given that these are available in the archives that Clarke herself donated to the Wisconsin Centre for Film and Theater Research (WCFTR), it is possible to centre my account of her life on her own testimony by reproducing one of these documents herein. It could certainly be argued that Clarke is not the most objective source of information (in spite of the factual tone most of these documents present), but objectivity was not particularly seen as a virtue by Clarke. Her documentary films, by her own account, are questions about the 'voice of God' approach to documenting the world. Voice, who gets to speak and who is heard, is a key concern of Clarke's oeuvre and the idea of an omniscient narrator is something she considers a problem to be solved. So, as much as possible, I am leaving space for Clarke to speak about herself in her own voice. This approach to Clarke's biography is augmented by sources close to her, particularly that of her novelist sister Elaine Dundy, on whom I rely for the account of Clarke's childhood/teenage years, family and education. My own unobjective voice enters the account in relation to the films and filmmaking contexts. Here I rely on evidence embedded in the visual, aural forms Clarke generated and the place these have in context of forms and ideas being generated around her – the dance, film and music cultures in which Clarke directed and edited.

Chapter 2: Distributed Cognition and Creative Practice

This chapter articulates the premises of the creative practice and distributed cognition framework. It outlines how this framework challenges theories of authorship and offers a distinctive cognifeminist perspective from which to do film analysis. The distributed cognition framework postulates that the work of mind is not exclusively taking place inside individual brains, rather, that complex cognitive processes are *distributed* across 'material, symbolic, technological, and cultural artifacts and objects as well as other people'.[7] Applying this premise to Clarke's filmmaking practice and augmenting it with her own film editing and directing expertise, I will think through the ways that Clarke's distributed creativity with tools, collaborators and communities generated her film's innovations in subject matter, style and form.

In so doing, I will also make a cognitively grounded challenge to the 'auteur theory'. Auteurism is frequently debated.[8] However, the heated discussions of authorship in film studies mask what I would consider to be a more serious problem with calling a director an author: it misconstrues what a director's actual work is. This book aims to think through Shirley Clarke and her working processes, to arrive at a more nuanced and accurate understanding of the cognitive complexities of creative process and the fluidity of their distribution, and to contribute to global efforts to 'fundamentally reconceive authorship'.[9]

My aim is not to sub-divide Clarke's voice and iconoclasm into percentages and reallocate credit points. Rather, I intend this analysis of her embodied, embedded and enactive creativity to reveal the ebb and flow of her 'thinking', the ways her ideas form through and with interactions of bodies, tools and contexts. Thinking through the work of Shirley Clarke in this way will posit that filmmaking, far from being the competitive, militarist operation it is often described as, is in fact an unpredictable, complicated, creative instance of distributed cognising, and that when it is actively practised in this way, as it is by Clarke, film forms are invigorated.

Chapter 3: Dancing Cognitions

Clarke's first film was a dancefilm. Since then, almost nothing ever written about her fails to mention that she was a dancer, but the question of how the particulars of American modern dance aesthetics and processes impact on her approach to and execution of films remains open. Batson (2014) describes the kind of dance in which Clarke was involved as 'mid twentieth century western contemporary dance ... destined for display' and goes on to say that this intention (display) 'shapes cognitive processes uniquely'.[10] Drawing on Batson and other scholars of 'choreographic cognitions'[11] and dancers' 'lived experience' (as I understand it from having lived it myself, in the same New York City milieu and often with the same teachers or influences as Clarke), this chapter will lay the groundwork for the theoretical framing of the hybrid dramas, documentaries and dancefilms Clarke directed and edited, as choreographic, kinaesthetic, embodied and rhythmically distinctive.

Clarke's training and professional career in mid-century American modern dance offers a highly visible, theorised and aesthetically structured instance of development of embodied cognition, or a 'thinking body'.[12] Drawing on theory of expressive dance contemporary to Clarke, and more recent theories of kinaesthetic empathy and kinaesthetic imagination, close analysis will be made of the qualities of gesture and the methods of framing, cutting and structuring movement in Clarke's early short films to articulate some principles of style which Clarke sustains when she turns her gaze away from dance and towards experimental, hybrid and narrative filmmaking. The film I will give the most attention in this chapter is Clarke's first film, *Dance in the Sun* (1953), about which Clarke says, 'all the kinds of things I discovered about the choreography of editing and the choreography of space/time came from making that very first film'.[13] I follow an extended analysis of passages in this film with much briefer looks at key moments, influences and formal innovations in the short films Clarke directed and/or edited from 1953 to 1959.

Chapter 4: Editing Thinking

Editing theory will be the primary framework of this chapter, which will propose that Clarke's signature kinaesthetic cognitions are visible through her edited patterns of movement, her juxtapositions and associations, and her spatial and temporal compositions. Her edits are her thoughts. That she is able to 'think' these thoughts into and through film form in a context when few women had the opportunity to make films arises, at least in part, from her editing ability. Unusually for a feature film director, Clarke edited the films she directed. Study of Clarke's 'editing thinking' (creative cognising with tools and materials of editing processes[14]) offers the opportunity to further develop theory of her editing as an instance of kinaesthetic intelligence and distributed cognition.[15] Clarke's creative editing is a clear example of cognition distributed through the tools and practices whereby editors 'generate ideas in response to material, with the material, and through their actions in relation to the material'.[16] The feminist implications of Clarke's editing are also significant, so I consider how her embedded mastery of the 'physical objects and epistemic tools'[17] of editing afforded Clarke a creative agency in writing and directing films that her position as a marginalised minority in the film industry would have otherwise made difficult, even in the independent film movements she helped to generate and sustain.

The chapter offers a close analysis of editing that Clarke did on short 'experimental' films. One of these, *Brussels Loops* (1957), is a sequence of fifteen short montage 'loops' produced by Willard van Dyke for the 1958 Brussels World's Fair. Clarke was the only woman of the nine directors employed on the project. She edited the segments she directed and also edited some sequences shot by other directors, creating a diverse set of short études in juxtaposition and flow. Her 1958 solo project, *Bridges-Go-Round*, arose from the *Brussels Loops*, and continues her experimentation with choreographic composition of non-human images into rhythmically and spatially dynamic phrases. *Bridges-Go-Round* is best known for its two versions, each with a different score, and the vivid illustration Clarke created with these of how music influences perception. Finally, the chapter looks at the opening sequence from one of Clarke's long-form works, *The Cool World* (1963). This film mixes documentary footage with semi-scripted/

improvised drama and was, therefore, necessarily finally 'written' in editing. This analysis aims to show what that means as a creative process for coming up with and realising ideas.

Chapter 5: Directing Enaction

The long-form films directed and edited by Clarke all focus on the lives of Black men. In the 2020 scramble by film festivals and streaming services to demonstrate solidarity with the Black Lives Matter movement, there was a sudden flurry of attention to these films. This was inevitably followed by a backlash, as white women came under scrutiny for their part in systemic racism.[18] Clarke was a white woman,[ii] performing a white man's role in a white man's world. However, compared to racism, she said, 'my personal woman's experiences seemed unimportant'.[19] Before intersectional feminism, this position was not a common theme for feminist women in film theory, and for men in film theory it was just another reason to disregard her work. In the current era of intersectional feminism, it is also creating complex viewing of her films. Is she a (white) 'oppressor' telling a story that is not her own? Or is she a member of an oppressed, marginalised and excluded group (women) working closely, and in solidarity, with community stakeholders to tell their stories? Like her films, which tend to defy categories, Clarke most likely would have eschewed compartmentalisation in either way and preferred to be understood as an 'ally', working from a complex position of having certain kinds of access and power, and not others.

Clarke's films about marginalised cultures were so far outside mainstream Hollywood fare that they, 'might' as Dargis

---

[ii] She was actually a Jewish woman, which complicates the question a little bit. In Clarke's lifetime, Jews were despised much more publicly/unashamedly than now, were subject to quotas and excluded from many roles in America, but Clarke generally enjoyed 'white privilege' (money, education), if not white experience.

says about the star of *Portrait of Jason* 'as well have been from another planet'.[20] This chapter examines Clarke's 'improvisation'[21] with these communities as instances of an ally's 'enactive cognition' (thoughts and ideas developing and being realised through active engagement in and with the social and material environment). It synthesises the discussion of embodied dance expertise and embedded fluency with editing and applies the distributed cognition framework to the study of film directing. Investigating Clarke's filmmaking practices as instances of this kind of socially shared 'participatory sense-making'[22] develops a better understanding of directing creativity as 'coordination of intentional activity in interaction, whereby ... new domains of social sense-making can be generated that were not available to each individual on her own'.[23] By approaching Clarke's work with Black men on devising films, and by analysing the films themselves for evidence of this enactive cognising, this chapter lays the groundwork for my novel approach to understanding directing that is distinct from 'authorship' and at the same time recognises the director's agency, voice and vision in the creative shaping of cinematic experiences.

Chapter 6: Conclusions and Continuances

Chapter 6 considers, briefly, the choices, circumstances, affordances and issues precipitating Clarke's shift from film to video art. Her video artwork will not be analysed in depth in this film theoretical book; however, brief discussion of the ways it returns Clarke to the performance principles of her early artistic pursuits will round off the book's discussion of Clarke's oeuvre and its impact.

Clarke anticipated participatory filmmaking, LGBTQ+ filmmaking and hybrid filmmaking. She pioneered in video art, social activist filmmaking and dancefilm. *Shirley Clarke: Thinking Through Movement* considers each of these aspects of her work and argues that mid-century modern dance methods and aesthetics uniquely shaped her thinking; that her edits are at least one visible instance of her thoughts; that her creative cognitions arose through working with collaborators, communities and the affordances of her technology and her times. Thinking through the work of Shirley Clarke in this way makes the case that her embodied, embedded and enactive filmmaking cognitions are the site of her voice and vision and it is through this distributed creativity that she disrupts and invigorates film form.

Notes

1 Dargis, M. (2013). 'One Man, Saved From Invisibility'. *The New York Times*, 30 January (p. 14). https://www.nytimes.com/2013/04/14/movies/shirley-clarkes-portrait-of-jason-back-in-circulation.html, accessed 15 July 2023.
2 Rabinovitz, L. (2003). *Points of Resistance: Women, Power and Politics in the New York Avant-garde Cinema, 1943–71*. University of Illinois Press, p. 8.
3 Rich, B. R. (1998). *Chick Flicks: Theories and Memories of the Feminist Film Movement*. Duke University Press, p. 103.
4 Allen, R. J. (1995). 'Tigers'. In *The Air Dolphin Brigade*. Paper Bark Press and Shoestring Press, in association with Tasdance, p. 40.
5 Dundy, E. (2012). *Life Itself! An Autobiography*. Little, Brown Book Group, p. 11
6 Shirley Clarke, as quoted in the interview transcript: 'My life is one long electrical cord (with me crawling around on the floor trying to make a connection)'. Interviewer unknown, circa 1975 (Wisconsin Center for Film and Theater Research, Shirley Clarke collection, Box 12, Folder 2).
7 Sutton, J. (2008). 'Remembering'. In *The Cambridge Handbook of Situated Cognition* (pp. 217–35). Cambridge University Press, p. 227.
8 See, for example: Kael, P. (1963). 'Circles and Squares'. *Film Quarterly*, 16(3), 12–26. Gaut, B. (1997). 'Film Authorship and Collaboration'. In R. Allen, & M. Smith (Eds.), *Film Theory and Philosophy* (pp. 149–72). Johnston, C. (1999). 'Women's Cinema as Counter-Cinema'. In S. Thornham (Ed.), *Feminist Film Theory* (pp. 31–40). Edinburgh University Press. https://doi.org/10.3366/j.ctvxcrtm8.7. Grant, C. (2001). 'Secret Agents: Feminist Theories of Women's Film Authorship'. *Feminist Theory*, 2(1), 113–30. https://doi.org/10.1177/14647000122229325. Meskin, A. (2008). 'Authorship'. In P. Livingston and C. Plantigna (Eds.), *The Routledge Companion to Philosophy and Film* (pp. 12–28). Routledge. https://doi.org/10.4324/9780203879320. Callahan, V. (2010). 'Re-writing Authorship'. In V. Callahan (Ed.), *Reclaiming the Archive: Feminism and Film History*

(pp. 1–7). Wayne State University Press. Bacharach, S. and Tollefsen, D. (2010). 'We Did It: From Mere Contributors to Co-authors'. *Journal of Aesthetics and Art Criticism*, 68(1), 23–32. Livingston, P. (2011). 'On Authorship and Collaboration'. *Journal of Aesthetics and Art Criticism*, 69(2), 221–5. https://doi.org/10.1111/j.1540-6245.2011.01463.x. Polan, D. (2001). 'Auteur Desire'. *Screening the Past*, 11, 1–9. http://www.screeningthepast.com/2014/12/auteur-desire/. Wexman, V. W., Keil, C., Luhr, W., Kozloff, S., and Langford, D. (2018). *Directing* (vol. 5). Rutgers University Press. Pearlman, K., and Sutton, J. (2022). 'Reframing the Director: Distributed Creativity in Filmmaking Practice'. In M. Hjort and T. Nannicelli (Eds.), *A Companion to Motion Pictures and Public Value*. Wiley, pp. 86–105.
9 Stamp, S. (2015). 'Feminist Media Historiography and the Work Ahead'. *Screening the Past*, 40, 1–11.
10 Batson, G. (2014). *Body and Mind in Motion: Dance and Neuroscience in Conversation*. Intellect, p. xv.
11 Stevens, K., McKechnie, S., Malloch, S., and Petocz, A. (2000). 'Choreographic Cognition: Composing Time and Space'. In *Proceedings of the 6th International Conference on Music Perception and Cognition*, pp. 297–326.
12 Todd, M. E. (1937). *The Thinking Body: A Study of the Balancing Forces of Dynamic Man*. P. B. Hoeber, Inc.
13 Shirley Clarke, as quoted in Rabinovitz, L. (1983). 'Choreography of Cinema: An Interview with Shirley Clarke'. *Afterimage*, December, 8–11. https://www.vasulka.org/archive/4-30c/AfterImageDec83(300), p. 8.
14 See Pearlman, K. (2016). *Cutting Rhythms: Intuitive Film Editing*. New York; London: Focal Press. https://www.routledge.com/Cutting-Rhythms-Intuitive-Film-Editing/Pearlman/p/book/9781138856516.
15 See also: Pearlman, K. (2017). 'Editing and Cognition Beyond Continuity'. *Projections (New York)*, 11(2), 67–86. https://doi.org/10.3167/proj.2017.110205; Pearlman, K. (2018). 'Documentary Editing and Distributed Cognition'. In C. Brylla and M. Kramer (Eds.), *A Cognitive Approach to Documentary Film*. Palgrave/MacMillan, pp. 303–19.
16 Pearlman, K., MacKay, J., and Sutton, J. (2018). 'Creative Editing: Svilova and Vertov's Distributed Cognition'. *Apparatus. Film, Media and Digital Cultures of Central and Eastern Europe*, 0(6). http://www.apparatusjournal.net/index.php/apparatus/article/view/122/306.
17 Sutton, J. (2006). 'Distributed Cognition, Domains and Dimensions'. *Pragmatics and Cognition*, 14(2), 235–47. https://benjamins.com/catalog/pc.14.2.05sut, p. 237.
18 Cowan, S. (2020). 'The Complicated Camera of Filmmaker Shirley Clarke'. *New York Review of Books*, 10 October, 1–11. https://www.nybooks.com/daily/2020/10/10/the-complicated-camera-of-filmmaker-shirley-clarke/.

19 Shirley Clarke, as quoted in Robinson, L. (1992). 'Ellipsing Time and Space'. *Daily Californian*, 9 October. https://cinefiles.bampfa.berkeley.edu/catalog/9662.
20 Dargis, 'One Man, Saved from Invisibility'.
21 See Millard, K. (2014). *Screenwriting in a Digital Era*. Palgrave Macmillan. https://link.springer.com/book/10.1057/9781137319104.
22 See De Jaegher, H., and Di Paolo, E. (2007). 'Participatory Sense-making: an Enactive Approach to Social Cognition'. *Phenomenology and the Cognitive Sciences*, 6(4), 485–507. https://doi.org/10.1007/s11097-007-9076-9.
23 Ibid., p. 497.

1

Biography and Context

Figure 1.1 Montage of selected images of Felix the Cat found in Shirley Clarke's archives at the Wisconsin Center for Film and Theater Research. Shirley Clarke collection, U.S. Mss 145 AN, various boxes, Wisconsin Center for Film and Theater Research

Shirley Clarke was born in 1919. Felix the Cat was also 'born' in 1919. Since Clarke included the Felix the Cat image in her collages, featured him on her notebook covers, and even had a favourite Felix the Cat pin regularly adorning her lapel, it is tempting to elaborate on their shared sensibilities and traits. For example, his 'Magic Bag of Tricks' that could assume an infinite variety of shapes, and Clarke's restless shapeshifting in creative forms; or his affinity for jazz and staying in motion, and hers. In a 1987 catalogue essay about her exhibition at the Whitney Museum of

Modern Art, Clarke writes that as a child 'I had a 16mm film by Otto Messmer called *Felix Out of Luck*. So, I would sit watching my Felix film in my Felix the Cat costume, surrounded by my entire collection of Felix the Cats'.[1] But Clarke, proficient as she was with all manner of filmmaking gear, did not have a tail that could magically transform into tools. So, rather than try to map Clarke's temperaments and exploits to those of her mascot, much as she might have liked that, I turn instead to other sources.

This chapter begins with Clarke's childhood and some of its most salient features. Here I draw on the account provided in the autobiography written by Clarke's sister, novelist Elaine Dundy. I then insert a scan of a biography Clarke wrote about herself, and later, a grant proposal or 'Plan', that sheds some light on both her biography and her thinking about film. Laced in between and through these accounts, I provide a bit of context on the films she lists in her self-narrative up to 1960 and those which come after. My precis places Clarke in various cultures and 'scenes' within which she was defined and those that she was a significant force in defining. With this necessarily brief view of Clarke in context, I hope to illuminate some of the ways she enacts creativity and disruption, and invents herself through and in opposition to the times in which she lived and the movements with which she is associated.

The opposition is as important as the alignments with these movements, in many cases. Opposition is core, in the first instance, to Clarke's relationship with her controlling father, and the ways she defines herself from her youth onwards. (It also explains some of her affinity for Felix the Cat, who was known for creatively slipping around rules and boundaries in his animated world.) Beyond biography and affinities though, opposition is central to many choices Clarke makes about form and subject matter for creative work. It is also salient to the ways that Clarke has been treated by history. She was a leader in dancefilm, creative documentary, observational documentary, New American Cinema, montage filmmaking, civil rights activism and video art. Yet she is not historicised as such in any canon that focusses on just one of these areas. Her participation is often noted, but rarely is she accorded acknowledgement for her influence and ideas.

So, the aims of the chapter are twofold: to lay the groundwork for seeing how the rhythms and movements of Clarke's times and cultural constellations are embodied, embedded and enacted in the directing and editing of her films, and to notice those places where her ideas and influence could be more equitably observed in film history and theory.

I begin with Clarke's youth in New York, and the specific aspects of her family life and access to Black culture that formed her sensibility. Much of this part of the story is drawn from Clarke's sister Elaine Dundy's autobiography. A bestselling novelist, Dundy may have been prone to exaggeration, or a romantic perspective, but given that Shirley Clarke wrote little about her childhood, Dundy's account, including aspects of personality and perspective injected into facts, offers some useful contextualising markers concerning the family culture in which Clarke was raised.

Dundy narrates the ways that the family into which Clarke was born, particularly her Jewish immigrant, self-made millionaire, 'rage-aholic' father,[2] seemed to force Clarke's attitudes and creativity into particular directions through her acts of rebellion. Her rebellion manifested as immersion in jazz music and modern dance. She would, according to Dundy's autobiography, *Life Itself* (2012), slip out to the jazz clubs of Harlem at night. Jazz improvisation and Black culture became central to her sensibility at that time and are both central to her later filmmaking. Dundy writes: 'she genuinely worshipped black genius (we all did growing up in the nightclubs and dance circles in New York). A political activist from her teens, the injustices suffered by American blacks had always been a cause close to her.'[3]

About their early childhood, before the stock market crash of 1929, Dundy writes:

> we ... were part of the Jewish new rich who in the twenties had staked out the concrete towers of Central Park West. In this respect we were very much like the rest of our cliff-dwelling neighbors. My sisters and I all went to the Ethical

> Culture School, two blocks down from us on Central Park, and were togged by Tots Toggery, Fifth Avenue's most expensive children's store.[4]

Wealth was worn lightly with those 'Tots Toggery' clothes throughout the 1920s, it was taken for granted by them as kids born into it, but as Dundy says: 'my sisters and I grew up in the great American tradition that decrees wealth, luxury and opportunity be counter-balanced by fear, unhappiness and repression.'[5] Shirley Clarke would have been ten (her sister only seven) on Black Tuesday. In the life of rich kids, the crash become a marker of change:

> it seemed to me that only after the Crash did we become a dysfunctional family – a phrase that covers rather than exposes what was going on, just as describing my father in the current term as a rage-aholic covers but does not expose him.[6]

Their father lost money, but they were not destitute by any means, and within a few years he had found a new position and recovered their lifestyle, but not found any equanimity.

Years later the rage that Clarke and her sisters had experienced as children had not abated. Both sisters write about their father's rage as motivating them to get out of the house. In Shirley Clarke's case, it motivated her to go to college first. But her only interest in college, she says, was in dance departments and she writes that she attended a number of them, including Bennington in Vermont, and Stephens College in Missouri. She took all the dance classes or workshops they had to offer, and then moved on to the next one.

Rather than return home, Clarke (née Brimberg) married Bert Clarke in 1943. After her divorce in in 1963, Clarke claims that the marriage was motivated solely by her desire to get away from her tyrannical father, but the home movies (see Milestone DVD *Project Shirley: The Magic Box*) and photos don't corroborate that story. Shirley and Bert Clarke are, in these images, loving, playful and physical with each other in ways that demonstrate a substantive attraction and affection. In Clarke's diaries and interviews later in the 1970s and early 1980s it is not unusual

Figure 1.2 Bert and Shirley Clarke setting up a shot together in 1959, photographer unknown. Shirley Clarke collection, M91-052, Box 25, Folder 9, Wisconsin Center for Film and Theater Research

to come across notes that could be read as expressing a sense of loss about Bert, possibly even regret; certainly, a lot of goodwill towards 'a kind, talented, and very handsome man'.[7]

Shirley and Bert Clarke's daughter Wendy (b.1944) is an independent video artist so richly deserving of her own book as to make writing a paragraph about her in a book about her mother seem almost disrespectful. What can be said, briefly, is that Shirley Clarke took immense pride in her daughter's achievements, brought her into the rhythms and responsibilities of her own professional practice early in Wendy's life as a member of casts and crews, made three films that feature Wendy as a key character (*In Paris Parks, Rose and the Players* and *Butterfly*), and worked with her steadily as a collaborator in the video work of the 1970s. Archival documents in the WCFTR reveal the full array of feelings and complexities of a mother/daughter relationship, including deep love, companionable friendship, professional respect and, from Shirley Clarke, a measure of rivalry. In the catalogue for a

New York Museum of Arts and Design retrospective of Shirley and Wendy Clarke's work, Wendy is quoted as saying:

> People have asked me if I found it difficult to be in the art world as a woman artist. My answer has been: Since I was a little girl I remember my mother taking me to dance rehearsals where I would quietly sit and watch, then watch her making her dance films (even being in some), then being a gofer and assistant on all aspects of The Cool World, then dressing the set for Portrait of Jason and finally collaborating with her at The Tee Pee Video Space Troupe. So, from my point of view, my mother could do anything. She gave me the gift of gender confidence that she had to fight for. We had a very special relationship, one that not many artists that I know experienced. She was completely supportive of my work and we had long conversations about the potential of the video, film, dance, and painting mediums. My mother wanted us to show our work together and it has taken until the MAD retrospective for this to happen.[8]

Wendy Clarke's work is described, in the same brief catalogue essay on their retrospective, as 'a cinema of listening, quiet beauty and devastating emotion'.[9] These are not qualities generally ascribed to Shirley Clarke's work, however, unlike Shirley Clarke's relationship to her father, Wendy's approach to creative work doesn't seem to be a rebellion against her mother's world view. Rather, it nuances that view with qualities of a different temperament and a different generation's insights into the creative conversation.

By contrast, Shirley Clarke does describe her creative work's rebellions as reactions to her father. In an article reporting on a symposium in which Clarke, Louise Nevelson and Vivian Gornik spoke, journalist Mary Haryse quotes Clarke, on the subject of what makes her art happen, as saying: 'I was going to show my father'.[10] However, while Shirley Clarke and her sister Elaine both make this connection between the rage and their creative choices, for Shirley Clarke rebellion, dance, music and activism are more than aesthetic interests or lifestyle choices. The formal methods of social activism, dance and jazz contemporaneous with Clarke are methods that become thoroughly embedded and uniquely enacted in her films and filmmaking processes.

Clarke's immersion in jazz is particularly salient. As cognitive philosopher Joel Krueger notes about music: 'we actively engage with – and indeed use – music to animate behaviour, cultivate and refine affective experiences, and orient ourselves to others and the world more generally'.[11] For Clarke, who was dyslexic and did not learn to read and write until very late in her primary school years, music and dance were profoundly entangled with who she was and the films she conceived and created.

Dance, as connected to identity and to music, was intrinsic to Clarke's personal and creative development. When she was out dancing in clubs she was, as her colleague contemporary dancer/ choreographer Daniel Nagrin described it, filling a 'profound reservoir' of creative fuel. He wrote:

> The dance floor is the birthplace of much of what we dancers do. On it, we can encounter some parts of what we really are, unexpected truths, joy and a profound reservoir of what makes us dance. Many dancers make a habit of this experience. Too many do not.[12]

Nagrin certainly made a habit of this experience, and when I met him, he was teaching Jazz Styles – complexly rhythmic forms of social dance that were as structured and as improvised as the music they swung to. The rhythms of that music were in Nagrin's and Clarke's bodies in a deeply habituated way, and this is palpable in the films she directs and edits.

The first film Clarke directed and edited, on which she collaborated with Nagrin, begins with a shot of a piano player and a dancer collaborating. Clarke's first feature film is centred on a few hours in the life of junkies and a quartet of jazz musicians waiting for a dealer. Its rhythms are implicitly and explicitly those of the quartet's jazz. Her last feature-length film is a creative collaboration with jazz composer Ornette Coleman (a long-time friend), and in between there is *The Cool World* (1963), on which she collaborates with Mal Waldron; *A Portrait of Jason* (1967), an extraordinary film composition drawn from the rhythms of a man who would be a cabaret singer; and a series of other short films each with a distinctive score, rhythm and, as Clarke wrote, a concern with time and space and film's unique ability to 'alter and control temporal and spatial sequence'.[13]

Once she began making films in 1953, with a camera that she received as a wedding present, Clarke started to narrate her own life story in interviews and grant applications. Figures 1.3, 1.4 and 1.5 comprise a scan of one such narration, a professional bio of

> Shirley Clarke
>
> ARTISTIC ACCOMPLISHMENTS   (page 1)
>
> After graduating, from the Lincoln School of Teachers College, New York, and studying evenings and Saturdays with Martha Graham, I went in 1940 to Stephens College, Columbia, Missouri. There I majored in modern dance and theatre, and was Maude Adams' dance director. Summer 1940 spent at Bennington School of the Dance. I left college to study dance with Hanya Holm and in the Summer of 1941 joined her Company. In 1942 I spent the winter in Chapel Hill as a "Playmaker" and toured the South with Elizabeth Waters' dance company. I married that summer and subsequently directed for the Children's Theatre in Baltimore and taught dance at Johns Hopkins University, Teachers College (1943-45). I had a daughter in February, 1944, and in 1946 returned to New York. There I studied choreography with Doris Humphrey and as her protege performed under her direction my own works at Carnegie Recital Hall, the Dance Theatre of the YM-YWHA, Hunter College, etc. in 1947, I formed the Contemporary Dance Company with Pearl Lang, Daniel Nagrin, Donald McKayle, Herbert Ross, Annabel Lyon and Beatrice Seckler. We performed in concert together for several years. In 1950 I studied mime with Etienne Decroux, in Paris. 1951-52 I danced with Anna Sokolow's Dance Company. Back in 1949 I was Chairman of the Board of the National Dance Association, an organization which brought prominent ballet and modern dancers together to benefit the dance field; it also sent dancers and dance films to represent America at festivals abroad. It was at this

Figure 1.3 Narration of 'Artistic Accomplishments' by Shirley Clarke for grant application to the Guggenheim Foundation, circa 1960, page 1. Shirley Clarke collection, U.S. Mss 145 AN, Box 12, Folder 6, Wisconsin Center for Film and Theater Research

```
                                                      Shirley Clarke

ARTISTIC ACCOMPLISHMENTS            (page 2)


time that I first saw dance films and became aware of the potentialities

of dance and film and the need for them.  In 1953 I gave up dancing and

began to make dance films.  Since 1953 I have made approximately one

film each year.  They are the following:

      DANCE IN THE SUN, 1953.  7 minutes, black and white, sound.
      With Daniel Nagrin.  Music by Ralph Gilbert.  A dancer performs
      both on stage and on a beach a dance in the sun.  Best Dance
      Film of 1954, presented by New York Dance Film Society at The
      Museum of Modern Art, New York, 1954.  Selected for screening
      at Zurich International Film Festival, 1954.

      IN PARIS PARKS, 1954.  13 minutes, color, sound.  Music by
      LaNoue Davenport.  A nostalgic film about children playing in
      the parks of Paris.  Preview performance at Cinema 16, April,
      1955.  Ran four months at Paris Theatre, New York, 1955.
      Selected for screening, Golden Reel Film Festival, 1955.

      BULLFIGHT, 1955.  9 minutes, color, sound.  With Anna Sokolow.
      Music by Norman Lloyd.  A dancer, through her dancing, re-
      captures her feelings while watching a bullfight.  Certificate
      of Acceptance, Edinburgh Film Festival, 1955.  Diploma of
      Participation, Venice Film Festival, 1955.  Screened, Cinema 16,
      1955.

      A MOMENT IN LOVE, 1957.  9 minutes, color, sound.  Music by
      Norman Lloyd.  A boy and girl and their moment in love.  Special
      Citation, Creative Film Foundation, 1957.  Silver Reel, American
      Film Assembly, 1957.  Selected as one of the best 10 non-
      theatrical films of the year by The New York Times, 1957.  Chosen
      as one of 40 documentaries and shorts for showing in the American
      Documentary Festival at the World's Fair, Brussels, 1958.

      "LOOPS", 1958.  Fifteen 2-1/2 minute loop films, color, silent.
      Photographed and/or edited for the American Pavillion at the
      World s Fair, Brussels, 1958.  These films covered many aspects
      of American life.  To be preserved in the archives of The
      Museum of Modern Art Film Library.
```

Figure 1.4 Narration of 'Artistic Accomplishments', page 2. Shirley Clarke collection, U.S. Mss 145 AN, Box 12, Folder 6, Wisconsin Center for Film and Theater Research

Clarke's 'Artistic Accomplishments', written for a Guggenheim Foundation grant application. It is undated, but from the chronology of the films mentioned, it is possible to deduce that it was circa 1959–60.

It is interesting that in this 'Artistic Accomplishments' narrative Clarke does not mention studying film formally. Chronicler of *The Downtown Pop Underground* of New York City in the 50s and 60s,

22 Shirley Clarke: Thinking Through Movement

```
                                              Shirley Clarke

ARTISTIC ACCOMPLISHMENTS                (page 3)

     BRIDGES-GO-ROUND, 1958-59. 3-1/2 minutes, color, sound. Music
     by Teo Macero. An abstract dance of the bridges around Man-
     hattan. Selected for screening at the International Experi-
     mental Film Festival, Brussels, 1958, and the Design Conference,
     Aspen, Colorado, 1959. Special Citation, Creative Film Founda-
     tion, 1959. Scheduled to play Paris Theatre, 1960.

     SKYSCRAPER, 1959. 20 minutes, 35mm black and white and color,
     sound. With William Van Dykes and Irving Jacoby. Music by
     Teo Macero. Songs and dialogue by John White. A new sky-
     scraper takes its place in the changing city. First prize
     (category: Peoples, Places, Folklore), Venice, 1959.

     Golden Mercury, awarded by Venice Chamber of Commerce for best
     short subject, 1959. Honorable Mention, Flaherty Award, 1959.
     Award of Special Merit, Edinburgh, 1959.

My films have played in many American universities, film societies and
museums, and at special screenings in Paris, Brussels, Berlin, Edinburgh,
London, Zurich. Prints have been pruchased by libraries and film
archives including the Eastman House Archives at Rochester, Australian
Federation of Film Societies in Melbourne, Canadian Federation of Film
Societies, Cinematheque de Belgique, Cinematheque Francaise, public
libraries in New York, Boston and Chicago, museums in Boston, San
Francisco, Los Angeles, Minneapolis, Seattle and others.
I have lectured on film at Teachers College, Columbia University, College
of the City of New York, Museum of the City of New York, Rochester
Public Library, Northwestern University, University of Chicago,
Minneapolis Institute of Fine Arts, New York Public Library, Franklin
Institute, Pratt Art Institute, and for many film societies.

                            # # # #
```

Figure 1.5 Narration of 'Artistic Accomplishments', page 3. Shirley Clarke collection, U.S. Mss 145 AN, Box 12, Folder 6, Wisconsin Center for Film and Theater Research

Kembrew McLeod writes: 'Mekas and Clarke were classmates in 1950 at City College of New York, where she studied film with Dadaist Hans Richter'.[14]

Both figures mentioned by McLeod – Jonas Mekas (1922–2019) and Hans Richter (1888–1976) – are salient to Clarke's developing sensibility in film, and the film movements through which her active period of work as a filmmaker winds. However, Clarke is not a disciple of either of them, and it seems that rather than being simple influences on Clarke, the relationships are complex and, on both sides, wary.[i] Richter and Mekas perhaps each exemplify a pattern that will repeat, as Clarke continues defining her distinctive creative perspectives in a complex brew of absorption with, and opposition to, the creative cultures swirling around her.

This resistance to joining movements and becoming clearly affiliated with their manifestos is something Clarke observes in herself as an internalised contradictory desire to be an art filmmaker and to be a maker of popular films.[15] It is beyond the scope of this short biography (and my capacities), to psychologise the source of this ambivalence, however it is certainly worth noting as a likely reason why Clarke's work has remained so resistant to histories. She is not categorisable by any single movement, she moves through many.[ii]

In the first instance, Clarke is affiliated with 'cine-dance' forms. However, although Clarke enters the 1950s and 60s avant-garde and experimental film movement via dance filmmaking, her work is rarely taught in dancefilm classes or discussed in dancefilm books or journals. In Chapter 3, I argue that this is, in part, because of her blend of Hollywood styles

---

[i] For Clarke's account of the uneasy negotiations she and Mekas had around the running of 'The Filmmaker's Co-op' see Rabinovitz, L. (1983), 'Choreography of Cinema: An Interview with Shirley Clarke'. *Afterimage*. December, 8–11. https://www.vasulka.org/archive/4-30c/AfterImageDec83(300).pdf, p. 10.

[ii] Clarke also expresses some scepticism about the idea of film movements in a 1964 interview with Harriet Polt who asks if she considers herself part of the 'New York School'. Clarke is quoted as saying: 'I'm not sure there is such a thing. Both in New York and on the Coast there is a renaissance of films being made by individuals. These individuals come in two varieties: the young men who are trying to get to Hollywood, and the kind who want to remain personal and keep costs down. This is the only common ground.' (Polt, H. (1964). 'Interview: Shirley Clarke'. *Film Comment*, Spring, pp. 31–2.)

and abstract expressionist ideas and moves. I make my case through extended analysis of *Dance in the Sun* (1953), Clarke's first dancefilm.

The highly lauded *Dance in the Sun* seamlessly blends a clear character journey with an abstract, expressive dance form, and a tension that runs throughout Clarke's career becomes evident here. Clarke's approach to filmmaking, established in *Dance in the Sun*, can't be absolutely categorised with Hollywood or with the avant-garde. It is, uniquely, both, and as such is a form of rebellion within and against an arts movement that defines itself by its rebelliousness.

In spite of my own early interest in dancefilm and dance on film, I didn't grow up admiring Clarke and wanting to emulate her. In fact, I never even heard about her when I was dancing or making my early dancefilms. She was also absent from the syllabi of the film history and theory classes I later attended. I never even encountered Clarke until the second decade of the twenty-first century, when I began looking at film history through a feminist lens.

In dance this is explicable, perhaps, because she was competing with the stellar self-mythologiser, Maya Deren. In film history, it may have just been because of the relentless focus on men in the twentieth century. But there is also something else that may have contributed to Clarke's slipping through the pages of books that identify authorial achievement with consistency of form, style and thematic concerns, and that is her restless shifting across forms, and what could almost be called reactivity to what she sees as pretension when colleagues establish and claim their mannerisms as forms. The creative transgression of forms and norms (stated and implied) causes her to be hard to classify, which I contend is a significant factor in whether and when her work is theorised.

With *In Paris Parks* (1954), the second work she directs and edits, Clarke makes a dancefilm with no dancers in it. In doing so, she steps outside of the culture that warmly embraced her first film. *In Paris Parks* is imagined as a kinaesthetically driven film. It is created from a 'choreographic sensibility',[iii] but is not often featured on the syllabi of studies of dancefilm form, perhaps because at the time it was not understood as dance. Forty-six years later, David Hinton will win the coveted IMZ Dance Screen Award and spark a community wide debate about 'What is dancefilm?' by doing the same thing in *Birds* (2000). But Clarke's radical refutation of the necessity of involving dancers for something to be understood as dance has been more or less ignored.

After *In Paris Parks*, and Clarke's next dancefilms, *Bullfight* (1955) and *A Moment in Love* (1956),[iv] Clarke was invited by Willard van Dyke to work on *Brussels Loops* (1957), a series of short montage films for exhibition in the American pavilion at the 1958 Brussels World's Fair. On this project, Clarke also got to know D. A. Pennebaker and Richard Leacock. They set up a shared workspace. As Clarke notes, it is through association with them and 'like-minded Canadian and French film makers we found ourselves developing hand-held sound cameras and techniques of using experimental and documentary techniques to tell stories'.[16]

Clarke's association with this filmmaking movement sometimes known as 'direct cinema' is, again, ideologically dynamic. These dynamics incite important themes in Clarke's filmmaking. These include: her dedication to the art of editing as central to the conception and realisation of film ideas; her fascination with technologies and their affordances; and the expanded freedoms of

---

[iii] The term 'choreographic sensibility', meaning an approach to film directing and editing, was first articulated to me by Richard James Allen in a conversation at the American Dance Festival Screendance conference of 1996, when the gathering of academics and artists were trying to find ways of describing some of the diverse forms that could be called screendance. More on this in Chapter 3.

[iv] Some online sources give a date of 1956, which is when it was made; some 1957, when it was released. Since the year of production and year of first distribution are frequently different, I have, where possible, used the year of production (and copyright) to date films.

working with untrained people – social actors, doing what she calls 'life-dancing'.[17] Clarke's kinaesthetically vibrant montage work is as far as can be from Drewe's hallmark observational filmmaking, and, in spite of their multiple creative collaborations, including the Academy Award nominated *Skyscraper* (1959), Clarke is not substantively featured in the historiographic narratives of the 'direct cinema' pioneers' development, either.

She and these documentary collaborators eventually part ways when Clarke moves on in 1959–60 to directing narrative drama, by making an adaptation of *The Connection*, a play originally staged by The Living Theatre.

I pause here, before moving into the 1960s, to insert another document written by Clarke: this one, from the same Guggenheim Foundation grant application, is called 'Plans' (see Figures. 1.6, 1.7, 1.8, 1.9, 1.10). In it, Clarke begins with a manifesto about her approach to film through a dance sensibility. This view of her core ideals as a filmmaker changes little throughout her lifetime. In interviews and other self-narrativising that she does, Clarke sticks to the story that her films are kinetic, and that they deal with movement, time and space in a way that is integral to their forms and narratives. I insert this particular plan, at this juncture in this chapter on biography, because it also includes a rough scenario for a film Clarke never created but which contains, she writes, 'dramatic narrative passages recalled from my own life' (see Figure 1.8).

Clarke never made the film described in this document: instead she directed and edited *The Connection* (1961). *The Connection* was originally a controversial, but ultimately very successful, off-Broadway play staged by Judith Malina of The Living Theater. Clarke's sister, Elaine Dundy (who was married to theatre critic Kenneth Tynan and therefore very well connected and au fait with theatre) writes:

> One day in '59 Shirley announced she was going to take a big step. Up till then she had only made short films; now she felt ready to take the plunge and do a feature film. Could I help her? Could I think of any book I'd read, any play I'd seen, a short

For 1st Guggenheim application

Shirley Clarke

PLANS   (page 1)

I call myself a film-maker rather than a producer, director, editor or cameraman because I firmly believe in the role of the individual, independent film-maker in contrast to the division of labor and single skills necessary in the purely commercial film. I believe that film is much more than an industry, that it is the new art form of the twentieth century and should be practiced as an art, just as a painter paints, or a composer composes. The problems are great in this medium in which the technical difficulties are so vast, where the machine stands between the artist and his work, and the field is generally regarded as an "industry" or "business". But for film to progress as an art there must be film-makers willing and equipped to conquer these obstacles.

Happily, with the new developments in lightweight, easily maneuverable cameras and portable sound equipment (thanks to the age of the transistor), it is daily more feasible for the independent film artist to control his medium successfully. Progress will come from the individuals who have mastered the total craft (total film-makers), who have energy and imagination, and who believe in film as an art.

It is my ultimate purpose to play an active part in this new period in the growth of film, helping to free it to develop in realms not yet conceived but sure to be individual, personal, and truly cinematic.

As a film-maker I have been especially interested in investigating and understanding the particular relationships of time and space in film.

Figure 1.6 Narration of 'Plans' by Shirley Clarke for grant application to the Guggenheim Foundation, circa 1960, page 1. Shirley Clarke collection, U.S. Mss 145 AN, Box 12, Folder 6, Wisconsin Center for Film and Theater Research

story, or anything that could be adapted for this purpose. I didn't even have to think. Something that would suit her right down to the depths of her avant-garde soul was the off-Broadway play *The Connection*. It was written by a new playwright, Jack Gelber, and stunningly performed under the direction of Judith Malina at the Living Theatre.[18]

> Shirley Clarke
>
> PLANS   (page 2)
>
> It is the ability to alter and control temporal and spatial sequence that is the unique contribution of film to all the arts. Along these lines I have experimented, finding new ways for film to tell a story, impart ideas, concepts, emotions. All my films have concerned themselves with this time-space continuum:
>
> | | |
> |---|---|
> | Dance in the Sun | Instantaneous flashback |
> | Bullfight | Three levels of time and place |
> | A Moment in Love | One moment shattered into many pieces so that the instant lasts forever |
> | Bridges-Go-Round | Perpetual motion, and motion within motion |
> | Skyscraper | The past and the present dealt with simultaneously |
> | Loops | Concentrated time, and the relationship of perceived image to time |
>
> I would like also to mention another aspect of my work because a great many of my discoveries about the time-space dimension of film came about as a result of attempts to solve the problems of filming "expressional" dance. I soon discovered that the only kind of film capable of projecting the feeling and ecstasy of dance was not a film that recorded and reproduced a dance composed for the stage, but was a "cine-dance".
>
> This is dance-film in which a totally new choreography, based on the special attributes and limitations of film, is used to create a form of dance that exists _only_ on film.

Figure 1.7 Narration of 'Plans', page 2. Shirley Clarke collection, U.S. Mss 145 AN, Box 12, Folder 6, Wisconsin Center for Film and Theater Research

Judith Malina, Julian Beck and The Living Theatre were central to then emergent forms of theatre in New York in the 50s and 60s, and beyond. They were a major part of the project of disrupting form in live theatre. Judith Malina describes the necessity of finding a theatrical language for the kinds of things they wanted to work with in the documentary *Signals through the Flames* (1983).[19] Clarke would have felt affinity this kind of disruption of form. As will be discussed in Chapter 3, formal disruption of long-standing

> Shirley Clarke
>
> PLANS (page 3)
>
> Cine-dance is an art form in the process of emerging. It is full of contradictions that occur by having to deal simultaneously with both abstraction and reality, and is engaged in a war between dance and cinema which seems to end in death for both. Yet I believe in the ultimate success of this new form, and all of my films, whether they used actual dance, or the dance of natural gesture, or the dance of the inanimate (created by camera movement and editing), have always danced. In other words, the flowing line and the kinetic response are my constant concerns.
>
> Now to get to my specific plan: At this precise point in my work, after having attained a greater understanding of film techniques and concepts in my dance, documentary and experimental short films, I am ready to go further - to draw together all my resources and channel them into a longer film with a dramatic story line.
>
> My new film (working title "Celebration") will probe the inner life of an adolescent girl - caught at one moment in her life, a positive moment when she must divorce herself from her parents and, on her own, deal directly with a situation. The setting will be a New York City cocktail party that is taking place in a garden while upstairs the daughter is doing her homework. As the party progresses the crisis in the girl's life grows, and as night falls and the party ends, a moment of realistic horror allows her to take the first decisive step of self-recognition.
>
> The story will be told in dimensional time, not sequential time, past, present and future being brought into the film at the instant they

Figure 1.8 Narration of 'Plans', page 3. Shirley Clarke collection, U.S. Mss 145 AN, Box 12, Folder 6, Wisconsin Center for Film and Theater Research

traditions in dance was axiomatic to the modern dance world in which Clarke moved. However, like the iron-willed women of modern dance who dogmatically defined their own right and wrong codes for dancing, Malina and Beck were establishing aesthetic rules, too. These are rules of image theatre, which use an expressionist, associative logic in a live context, to create a theatre

> Shirley Clarke
>
> PLANS (page 4)
>
> are right for the girl's emotional development, not necessarily as they realistically occur in time. This method of revealing the sequences of events should arouse in the audience a sense of discovery and identification similar to what I shall experience as I make the film. In fact, the audience as it watches the film will feel a heightened level of perception and understanding as each new layer is disclosed and explored.
>
> I intend to film actuality - a real cocktail party, and I will also reenact reality through improvisation with the girl and recreate, with her, dramatic narrative passages recalled from my own past and her present life.
>
> What may seem to be making for a confusion of story lines and styles will on the contrary, if I am successful, result in a work of richer texture, fuller understanding and greater fluidity. Once we break away from the restrictions of conventional perspectives of time and space there are new lands to explore, new opportunities for emotional and dramatic expression in film which, if used well, will allow reality and abstraction to exist comfortably and profitably with each other. Remember also the camera's ability to select the telling image and to control at will the point of view. Views from miles away, images in microscopic detail, the many possible variations of examining character and environment, are the very raw materials of film. Yes, film is an art existing in time - where the image is merely the beginning, and the end an orchestration.

Figure 1.9 Narration of 'Plans', page 4. Shirley Clarke collection, U.S. Mss 145 AN, Box 12, Folder 6, Wisconsin Center for Film and Theater Research

of protest. In spite of making a film of *The Connection* (more on this in Chapter 5), Clarke does not get strongly associated with the historiography of The Living Theatre or any of the 'avant-garde' forms of performance-making surrounding her, perhaps because she again moves away from some of these forms of abstraction when she makes *The Cool World* (1963).

                                                    Shirley Clarke

PLANS   (page 5)

    It is for this reason that I intend to make strong use of cine-dance, to take advantage of the enormous kinetic response to movement that both film and dance evoke, so that though we never leave the girl's bedroom or the cocktail party the audience will feel that it has been physically transported through a world in motion.

    I propose to write, direct, photograph, and edit this film with aid as necessary from my fellow film-makers. It will be shot in 35mm black and white, sound, for general release, about 20 minutes long and it will take about one year to make. Up to this time I have written the script outline, devised plans for the location shooting, cast the film, shot several tests sequences, purchased 2000 feet of film. I have at my disposal a 35-mm motion picture camera and a sound recorder.

    Any aid I receive will be used toward making this film, yet I must say in all honesty that one way or another I am committed to complete this picture. It is certainly the logical next step that I must take in my life as a film-maker. Moreover, in terms of subject matter it expresses something close to my heart. I believe that though the imminence of death and destruction is with us, so is the passion for life, and that every positive human act, small as it may be, preserves the world for life for yet a little while.

# # # #

Figure 1.10 Narration of 'Plans', page 5. Shirley Clarke collection, U.S. Mss 145 AN, Box 12, Folder 6, Wisconsin Center for Film and Theater Research

The Cool World is rich with improvisational performances which Clarke directs with an assurance she probably would have developed through her dance training and contact with the likes of The Living Theatre. But *The Cool World's* forms of protest are not white, not sexual, not abstract expressionist. In some ways the form and subject matter of *The Cool World* signals Clarke reacting, once again, to the unwritten dictums of the cultural influencers that are dominating her context. As Paul Monaco notes, in the volume of cinema history called *The Sixties*, 'the representation of sexuality is the focal point of identity politics in the American avant-garde cinema of the 1960s'.[20] This was also a considerable focus of theatre; however, Clarke's work is far more readily associated with politics of race than sexuality.

The Cool World was produced by Fredrick Wiseman, who was at the time a lawyer who wanted to get involved in film. *The Cool World* was his first effort, and the letters between them in the Wisconsin Center for Film and Theater Research archives reveal an antagonistic relationship that Clarke found frustrating, controlling and patronising.[21] I don't know how Wiseman experienced it, but as at time of writing, nearly sixty years later, he is still sufficiently embittered to withhold permission for the film to be distributed – it is not included in the otherwise exhaustive Milestone Collection of Clarke's film work.

By the time they worked together, Clarke had made many films, but *The Cool World* was only her second feature. On the short films she was director/producer/editor and used to running the show herself. On her first feature, *The Connection* (1961), she struggled with a unionised male crew and getting them to do what she wanted. She also persisted through, and won, a two-year censorship battle over the use of the word 'shit' as slang for heroin, and a brief shot of a porn magazine centrefold. This shot is so brief and inconsequential to the narrative, that questions did come up at the time as to why she didn't just drop the shot and get the film out in the world. Clarke's stubbornness and conviction is on display in her handling of this battle. Had she been a man, she likely would have been described as strong rather than stubborn, and certainly her achievement in changing censorship standards would have been lionised rather than forgotten.

On *The Cool World*, Clarke had a much better relationship with her crew. They were her collaborators and she and they worked closely with the community, facilitated by Carl Lee and especially Madeleine Anderson, who was the First Assistant Director. But Clarke and Wiseman had an acrimonious falling out at some point in the process. There were a few things involved, including some kind of disaffection between Wiseman and Carl Lee (who was also Clarke's romantic partner at the time) and, of course, money.

My knowledge of the Wiseman/Clarke stoush comes from correspondence in Clarke's archives in Wisconsin, and conversations with Dennis Doros of Milestone Films. Doros tried valiantly to get the rights from Wiseman when he and Amy Heller re-released all of Clarke's other film work in 2012. Doros also did huge amounts of research on Clarke, is friends with Clarke's daughter Wendy and others in her family, and knows more about the dark secrets of Clarke's 'bad behaviour' than he cares to say or I care to know. What is of interest to me is whether the 'temper' for which Shirley Clarke was known would have just been considered a sign of genius in a man. There are certainly many examples of her male film director contemporaries behaving badly at the time and being celebrated rather than criticised. As feminist film scholar Rebecca Sheehan notes about some of Clarke's male contemporaries in Hollywood, their: 'excesses were ... viewed as a manifestation of and fuel for their genius and helped to build their legends'.[22] Many of these men became commercially successful and historicised as auteurs, while Clarke enjoyed neither privilege, in spite of being at the centre of movements or projects where her colleagues got their starts.

Clarke is associated with the New America Cinema Movement (aka the New American Cinema Group), which expands the thinking of film experimentalists to a broader range of social and political issues. Here, her sometimes testy relationship with Jonas Mekas is central. Clarke is the only woman signatory to the manifesto of this movement, and although many filmmakers are mentioned by name within it, she is not. There is no authorship attributed to the document, but it is believed to have been originally written by Mekas.

As a movement, The New American Cinema Group is righteously opposed to anything commercial. Their manifesto, published in 1962, concludes with: 'We don't want false, polished, slick films – we prefer them rough, unpolished, but alive; we don't want rosy films – we want them the color of blood.'[23]

Figure 1.11 Shirley Clarke, Wendy Clarke, Jonas Mekas and others at a twelve-hour marathon of reading of a Lionel Zippens book, circa 1965, photographer unknown. Shirley Clarke collection, M91-052, Box 26, Folder 17, Wisconsin Center for Film and Theater Research

Filmmakers of the New American Cinema Group are, as Annette Michelson writes: 'committed to an aesthetic of autonomy that by no means violates or excludes their critical view of the society in which they manage, as they can, to work'.[24]

The New American Cinema Group manifesto specifically mentions that they will form a cooperative for distribution. This becomes the Film-makers Cooperative, which was founded by Clarke, Jonas Mekas, his brother Adolfus Mekas, Lionel Rogosin and Robert Downey Sr. The co-op distributed Clarke's films and through the co-op Clarke is also known to have supported John Cassavetes and Lionel Rogosin with gear, contacts and advice.

However, even within a movement devoted to opposition, Clarke finds things to oppose. Her best-known film, *Portrait of Jason* (1967), is profoundly oppositional to methods of observational cinema as practised by Wiseman and her former collaborators, Pennebaker and Leacock.[v] It is also oppositional to montage filmmaking and its aesthetic concerns with creation of time through cutting, and it narratively opposes the 'woes of white men' stories that pervade the work of others in the movement.

Portrait of Jason is possibly as complicated in the twenty-first-century context as it would have been at the time. In the film, Clarke has given voice to a figure who would have been beyond marginalised in the white, heterosexual, male-controlled, modernist circles of the 1960s. But 'giving voice' is not an uncomplicated act. The 2015 film, *Jason and Shirley*, directed by Stephen Winter is an excoriating historical reimagining of the making of *Portrait of Jason*. Its inaccuracies are excused in the context of the significance of its larger point: giving voice to a marginalised person is still controlling that voice, and could be understood as virtue-signalling, or worse, exploitation of someone else's story for personal gain. That Clarke leveraged every affordance of her own marginalised (though considerably less so than Jason's) cultural position and collaborated closely with Jason Holliday and Carl Lee in the filmmaking process seems to be ignored in this satire. Amy Heller of Milestone Films, having exhaustively researched and curated Clarke's work was moved to write that *Jason and Shirley*: 'cynically appropriates and parodies the identities of real

---

[v] Unlike Clarke and Wiseman, Clarke and Pennebaker stayed friends though. Dennis Doros and Clarke's video art collaborator Andrew Gurian have both reported to me instances when Pennebaker warmly acknowledged Clarke's influence in presentations and conversations.

people, stereotyping and humiliating them and doing disservice to their memory ... numerous factual errors and falsehoods have betrayed everyone who was involved in making *Portrait of Jason*'.²⁵ The satire was nonetheless generally critically lauded and received as a revelation, an exciting picture of the times and processes by which *Portrait of Jason* was made. My own view, as will be discussed in Chapter 5, is that the documentary evidence embedded in the film itself suggests additional complex power relations which are not Winter's immediate subject, particularly the major significance of Carl Lee in authorship and power in the filmmaking process.

Things were not simpler for *Portrait of Jason* in 1967. With the film, Clarke moved far outside of cultural conventions of her moment to contend with a subject her contemporaries would not have touched. As Clarke's daughter Wendy says, 'It was the first time a black gay hustler had ever been seen by most human beings'.²⁶

Clarke's formal approach – shooting the whole film in one long, drug and alcohol-fuelled night, exposes some fault lines of emergent documentary-making ideology, which cannot have ingratiated her with the community of documentary makers. Writing about *Portrait of Jason* for the BFI Screen Guide to *The New American Cinema,* Jason Woods refers to Clarke as a 'former experimental film maker', noting that she 'challenged practices of the American cinéma vérité movement' with this film.²⁷ Clarke knew she was doing this. She said so in, for example, a quote I will return to in Chapter 5: 'Most of my films are messages to other film makers about things they are doing that I question.'²⁸

Clarke had also been through a lot personally by the time she got to *Portrait of Jason* – the break-up of her marriage, probably some addictions nourished by her drug-dealing paramour Carl Lee, hospitalisation/time in rehab for what would likely be called now bipolar syndrome,ⱽⁱ censorship battles, fights with producers

---

ᵛⁱ '"As I saw it," Dundy added, "Carl satisfied her need to rebel against bourgeois morality as she had done as a young communist in the thirties and a postwar anti-nuke marcher. I think his outlaw activities must have excited

over money, being sidelined in the editing of the documentary about Robert Frost which later won an Academy Award and, as strongly comes through in her later writing and interviews, frustration with the barriers she faced as a woman. She spoke about this with some distance and wry humour, but her weariness with the issue is a symptom of its prevalence. She compared her career trajectory to the one Stanley Kubrick enjoyed saying: 'i [*sic*] wondered if his success story would have been mine. had i [*sic*] been a guy. ho hum.'[29]

Kubrick is an apt analogy. He changes stylistic modes in every film and is admired for doing so. It interests me that Shirley Clarke does the same and is all but forgotten. The changing of forms and formal approaches gets her excommunicated, or at least marginalised, in various scenes she could, and should, have been associated with – dancefilm, cinema-verité, drama, protest and observational documentary. Would this have been the case if she had been a man? All evidence of her contemporaries suggest it would not. However, without minimising these gender-based inequities and the damage they did to Clarke's opportunities and subsequent legacy, the formal restlessness is also worth noting as a choice. It is a creative choice that frustrates her 'belonging' to any particular group and challenges the myth-making of film movements to reconsider the roles of marginalised communities and inter-art form protest that Clarke embodied.

---

her'... At one point, Clarke decided to tell her mother about the mixed-race relationship, but then abruptly changed her mind. "Absolutely there was a tension surrounding her relationship with Carl," her daughter Wendy Clarke said. "She never told her parents, so it was a secret." These tensions may have contributed to a mental breakdown – though drug use may also have been a factor – and Clarke checked into a rehab facility for six months. After being discharged, she asked her sister to use her connections to get her a place in the Chelsea Hotel, a hotbed of bohemian activity. Dundy told hotel owner and manager Stanley Bard that Clarke was special and should be looked after, and he later moved her into the hotel's penthouse".' Elaine Dundy and Wendy Clarke as quoted in McLeod, K. (2018). *The Downtown Pop Underground*. Abrams Press, pp. 104–5.

Before turning to in-depth looks at Clarke's creative choices in the films she directed and edited, a few thoughts about Clarke's feminism, the ways it manifested, and the ways it did not.

Clarke did not, during her period of actively making films, ever describe herself as a feminist as far as I know. For one thing, she considered her concerns as a woman less important than the race problems she saw around her.[30]

However, the very fact of directing and editing films was certainly an implicitly feminist act, and Clarke's access to the means of production was, for a woman, both unusual and empowering. Clarke was fascinated by, and knowledgeable about, filmmaking gear. Her archives contain many documents in which she makes notes about lenses, film stocks, lighting conditions and other things associated with the tools of cinematography, which was then, and is to this day, an intransigently male-dominated domain. As Lauren Rabinovitz notes in her book about Clarke, Maya Deren and Joyce Wieland: 'The independent filmmaker individually or within a small group controlled the production process using inexpensive technology in what has become known as an artisanal mode of production.'[31] Control is the salient word, and had Clarke not had control through technical mastery of her shooting and editing processes, she likely would not have been able to make films at all.

Clarke was not unreservedly enamored with independent filmmaking though, she would have liked to have made a properly funded Hollywood movie,[32] and this could be another reason why she would not have been vocal in the 60s about her thoughts on women's equality. As Rebecca Sheehan notes,

> Although the success and visibility of women film industry professionals was borne in large part on the back of feminist agitation, any perceived alignment with feminism – whether talking about experiences of sexism or arguing for affirmative action – was effectively a kiss of death for their Hollywood careers.[33]

It would also have pretty effectively been a 'kiss of death' in the white, male, New American Cinema context, and the public/media imaginary of it. Rabinovitz reminds us that

Clarke delighted the popular press because she represented to them the eccentric Beat girl. Descriptions portray her as a diminutive, pixielike woman, whose sleek dancer's body dramatically contrasted her intensity and spoken strings of profanities; she embodied the cool, hip attitude associated with the Beat generation of the early 1960s.[34]

Writing about Clarke, Deren and Wieland, Rabinovitz describes the cultural conundrum of this kind of positioning:

> Whether the women knowingly or unknowingly manipulated such poses is not the issue. They may have individually [known] that they were successful publicity ploys, or they may have wanted to protect the privacy of their identities, but their respective myths fit the fashionable myths of femininity of their times, rendering the women culturally acceptable stereotypes within dominant ideology. Whereas these images helped to draw popular attention to artists and their causes as points of resistance they also contradictorily popularised the idea that such women artists were still feminine.[35]

So, Clarke and other women aspiring to or making films at the time 'tended to distance themselves from the women's movement, deny experiences of sexism, and promote their film-making capacities rather than their identities as women'.[36] Later in her life and career, as the Beat girl persona wears off in the early 1970s, Clarke gets more direct about the ways she navigated the antagonistic landscapes for women in film and the arts. In a 1972 article, Maryse Holder describes Clarke as 'an electric, irritable, woman with a tough, almost street, wit, somewhat defensive, who will later bring down the house by saying that the way she made it was by being a "nasty rotten bitch"'.[37]

Bringing down the house with pre-emptive and self-deprecating wit was one of Clarke's strategies throughout her lifetime. In a 1985 interview with Robert Seidenberg, called 'Shirley Clarke's American Odyssey', she says:

> I don't know what happened, but at some point in my life something clicked and I became very funny ... I was this

serious, little, strange girl, sincere and very Marxist and very cause oriented. I was born on the same day as Groucho Marx and Mahatma Gandhi, and I did notice the humour in that, but I didn't mention it much. And suddenly I realised I had gotten Gandhi's sense of humour and Marx's spiritual qualities, and then I got very funny.[38]

In the later 1970s when working as a professor of film at UCLA, Clarke's humour is still evident, though it is doing battle with her frustration at Hollywood systems which exclude her, and her exhaustion with the fruitless quest to get a film funded. Scribbled on the back of a curriculum document, probably made during an endless faculty meeting at UCLA is my favourite note in all of Clarke's archives. It is where I would like to begin my hybrid fiction/documentary/dancefilm about her life. Clarke writes:

'I would like to commit a crime. That might give me a reason to live. My life is so boring, so predictable nothing at 50 is new any more
This would bring a little excitement to my life – I'd be doing something new + reality based. (not petty crimes like dime store + Vietnam Peace Dem)
But a big Heist
Like the Tiffany theft in NY on day Khrushchev drew all NYC police to protest his visit to the USA
I want to commit a crime...'[39]

More about Clarke as a person in various contexts will be embedded in following chapters, as is congruent with the distributed cognition perspective I am taking on her creative practice. However, in summing up some facts of Clarke's biography, I would say:

Shirley Clarke (1919–1997), made films that were critically lauded, screened at top-tier international film festivals such as Cannes and Venice, nominated for two Academy Awards and won one. Clarke's 'oeuvre is defined by its testing of the edges of form'.[40] Her radical hybrids of documentary and drama are made with people, cultures and rhythms that were invisible to 1960s white-washed Hollywood. However, while the work of male contemporaries in the independent film movements she actively catalysed – for example, John Cassavetes and Jonas Mekas – has been theorised extensively, hers has not. Manohla Dargis notes in *The New York Times*:

> Her work was enormously important, of course, though it has been undervalued and underrepresented, including in histories of the avant-garde and independent film. If she had been a man or hadn't trained her cameras so intently at Black Americans, she would have likely received more attention while she was alive. But then she wouldn't have been Shirley Clarke, pioneer, radical, visionary.[41]

Notes

1 As quoted in the Whitney Museum of American Art, The New American Filmmakers series catalogue (1987), 5–17 December (Wisconsin Center for Film and Theater Research, Box 23, Folder 10).
2 Dundy, E. (2012). *Life Itself! An Autobiography*. Little, Brown Book Group, p. 11.
3 Dundy, *Life Itself!*, p. 242.
4 Ibid., p. 4.
5 Ibid., p. 4.
6 Ibid., p. 11.
7 As quoted in Whitney Museum New American Filmmakers series catalogue.
8 Wendy Clarke, as quoted in: https://madmuseum.org/series/eye-director-shirley-and-wendy-clarke. Accessed 09 June 2023.
9 Ibid.
10 As quoted in Haryse, M. (1972), 'Counter Vulture, in New York City'. *Off Our Backs*, 17–18 (Wisconsin Center for Film and Theater Research, Box 12, Folder 1).
11 Krueger, J. (2014). 'Affordances and the Musically Extended Mind'. *Frontiers in Psychology*, 4(Jan), 1–13. https://doi.org/10.3389/fpsyg.2013.01003, p. 1.
12 Nagrin, D. (1994). *Dance and the Specific Image*. University of Pittsburgh Press, p. 10.
13 Shirley Clarke, 'Plans' section from application for funding from the Guggenheim Foundation, circa 1960 (Wisconsin Center for Film and Theater Research Box 12, Folder 6).
14 McLeod, K. (2018). *The Downtown Pop Underground*. Abrams Press, p. 23.

15 See Burch, N., and Labarthe, A., et al. (1970). *Rome is Burning (Portrait of Shirley Clarke)*. https://www.youtube.com/watch?v=6etkUKAGCpI.
16 Shirley Clarke, as quoted in the interview transcript: 'My life is one long electrical cord (with me crawling around on the floor trying to make a connection)'. Interviewer unknown, circa 1975 (Wisconsin Center for Film and Theater Research Shirley Clarke collection, Box 12, Folder 2).
17 Ibid.
18 Dundy, *Life Itself*, p. 238.
19 Rochlin, S. (1983). *Signals Through the Flames: A Living Theater Documentary*. Mystic Fire Films. https://archive.org/details/SignalsThroughTheFlamesALivingTheaterDocumentary.
20 Monaco, P. (2003). *The Sixties*. University of California Press, p. 248.
21 See, for example, the letter to Wiseman from Clarke dated 23 August 1970 (Wisconsin Center for Film and Theater Research, Box P, Folder 5).
22 Sheehan, R. (2020). '"One Woman's Failure Affects Every Woman's Chances": Stereotyping Impossible Women Directors in 1970s Hollywood'. *Women's History Review*, 30(3). https://doi.org/10.1080/09612025.2020.1770404, p. 2.
23 As reproduced in 'The First Statement of the New American Cinema Group: September 30, 1962', by Mike Everleth, 30 September 2007. *Underground Film Journal, Underground Film News* https://www.undergroundfilmjournal.com/the-first-statement-of-the-new-american-cinema-group-september-30-1962/, accessed 01 April 2023.
24 Michelson, A. (1967). 'Film and the Radical Aspiration'. In G. Battcock (Ed.), *The New American Cinema: A Critical Anthology* (pp. 83–101). E. P. Dutton and Company, p. 96.
25 Heller, A. 'The Cruelty and Irresponsibility of Satire'. https://blogs.sydneysbuzz.com/jason-and-shirley-the-cruelty-and-irresponsibility-of-satire-9037ffc84459; accessed 20 July 2023.
26 Wendy Clarke, as quoted in McLeod, K. (2018). *The Downtown Pop Underground*. Abrams Press, p. 105.
27 Woods, J. (2009). *100 American Independent Films (BFI Screen Guides Series)*. Palgrave MacMillan, p. 176.
28 Shirley Clarke, as quoted in Rice, S. (1972) 'Shirley Clarke: Image and Images'. *Women in Film* 3 (1972): 20–2; p. 22. An interview by Susan Rice which I accessed as a typescript in Wisconsin Center for Film and Theater Research, Box 12, Folder 2, p. 3.
29 Clarke, 'My life is one long electrical cord'.
30 See Burch and Labarthe, *Rome is Burning*.
31 Rabinovitz, L. (2003). *Points of Resistance: Women, Power and Politics in the New York Avant-garde Cinema, 1943–71*. University of Illinois Press, p. 7.
32 For more on this see *Rome is Burning (Portrait of Shirley Clarke)*, the 1970 documentary directed by Noël Burch and Andre la Barthe: in which she

says, at 27 minutes in, that she would like to broaden her audience and reach beyond people who already agree with her. https://vimeo.com/20737456.
33 Sheehan, '"One Woman's Failure Affects Every Woman's Chances"', p. 2. https://doi.org/10.1080/09612025.2020.1770404.
34 Rabinovitz, *Points of Resistance*, p. 9.
35 Ibid., p. 9.
36 Sheehan, '"One Woman's Failure Affects Every Woman's Chances"', p. 2.
37 Holder, 'Counter Vulture, in New York City', p. 17.
38 As quoted in Seidenberg, R. (1985) 'Shirley Clarke's American Odyssey'. *Film*, p. 98.
39 Clarke, Shirley (1978). Handwritten notes on back of Department of Theatre Arts class schedule, Spring 1978. (Wisconsin Center for Film and Theater Research Box 16, Folder 2.)
40 Gustafson, I. (2011). 'Putting Things to the Test: Reconsidering *Portrait of Jason*'. *Camera Obscura*, 26(2), 1–7, p. 3. https://doi.org/10.1215/02705346-1301521.
41 Dargis, M. (2013). 'One Man, Saved From Invisibility'. *The New York Times*, January 30. https://www.nytimes.com/2013/04/14/movies/shirley-clarkes-portrait-of-jason-back-in-circulation.html, accessed 20 July 2023.

2

Distributed Cognition and Creative Practice

Figure 2.1 Shirley Clarke thinking in motion. Date unknown (circa 1950s–60s), photo by Gideon Bachman. Shirley Clarke collection, M91-052, Box 25, Folder 6, Wisconsin Center for Film and Theater Research

This chapter introduces the distributed cognition and creative practice framework I am using to think through the films directed and edited by Shirley Clarke. My aim in introducing this framework is to find a way to write about Clarke as a visionary creator while also disrupting some underlying misapprehensions about film authorship and auteurs.

The misapprehensions that concern me are those which mistake visionary leadership with sole authorship. The idea of a sole author in film is 'an outmoded romantic notion'[1] and, as many have noted,[2] misrecognises the work of multiple experts in manifesting a creative work. More importantly, it also confuses, obfuscates and mystifies creative process in a way that has been damaging for film culture, and, potentially, culture more broadly.

However, discarding the idea of 'auteur' completely is problematic for two reasons:

The first is that there is substantial evidence that the leadership of *particular* individuals can and does generate unique and valuable[3] bodies of work with recognisable qualities across multiple outputs. New theoretical frameworks must account for this even as they also recognise and value collaboration.

The second is that women, LGBTQIA+ people and people of colour are at last beginning to gain recognition and opportunities for creative leadership. Dismantling the framework that recognises and values the distinctiveness of the individual's voice and vision completely would be a cultural shift that denies recognition just as it is within reach of groups of people whose achievements have been marginalised and whose opportunities have been curtailed.

Thus, we have a feminist conundrum: women working in film from the end of the nineteenth century to the present have been obscured, even deliberately effaced, by auteur theories. But complete denial of the impact and significance of individual visionaries would effectively deny women the chance of achieving the status male directors have enjoyed for decades. Is there a third way?

That is what I am aiming for. A creative practice and distributed cognition approach to the dynamics of directors that offers a way of understanding what they do and how they do it, and at the same time understands that the crucial work of a great film director is to lead complex configurations of different experts whose efforts must coordinate, and also achieve excellence individually, in order to successfully realise ideas.

Coming up with such a framework requires thinking through cognition – the ways we think, feel, perceive, assess, interpret and, among other things, come up with ideas and enact them. Understanding cognition as distributed is a way of breaking down the idea that these actions of mind are solely located inside individual brains and recognising the layered entanglements of bodies, tools and worlds involved in creation of cultural objects, particularly films.

So, this distributed cognition and creative practice framework sets out to articulate a way of understanding mind and creativity that can recognise individuals and position them as visionary creative leaders, but also lift the veil on how they work through and with their contexts, tools and collaborators. Further, it offers a way to see how this entanglement, rather than diminishing their value, adds to it. A great director, I shall argue, is a mental nexus with some unique abilities to synthesise multiple inputs, understandings and actions in creative, valuable ways.

This creative practice and distributed cognition approach is not contra other frameworks of authorship that work on understanding collaborative creativity in the generation of a work. In fact, it builds on arguments proposed by Gaut (1997), Bacharach and Tollefsen (2010), Livingston (2011) and others. My additions to frameworks that theorise collaborative authorship are threefold.

First, I bring to the discussion a well-recognised level of experience and achievement in the practices of filmmaking. This experience repeatedly confirms for me – each time I direct a new film – that the generation of a film is the work of multiple experts thinking together, each bringing distinctive creative cognitions. Further, that the work of directing and editing is in significant measure the work of coordinating these multiple forms of expertise into a coherent and compelling production. The distributed cognition framework provides a way of articulately specifying how this is so, and I elaborate further on the creative practice framework below, and throughout the book.[i]

---

[i] One of the issues that vexes philosophers trying to explain creative collaboration in film as an instance of multiple authorship is where to draw the line between someone who is actually a part of the process of ideating, and someone who is working on the film but is not making a contribution to authorship. The two things I would say about this problem are: first, that given the precarity and complexity of filmmaking processes the line is always going to be blurry or soft-edged. The fact that blurriness fits poorly into cultural systems of recognition and accreditation does not justify trying to harden or fix the line. If anything, it is a signal that we should perhaps reconsider the utility of those ways of thinking about working together. The second, more practical, incursion I offer from experience is this distinction: if a crew member needs to read the script or talk to the director in order to do their job, they are making a contribution to the vision. The mechanics of this, briefly, are that crews are generally divided into departments and only the heads of department (HoDs), and occasionally their deputies, talk to the director about what they are doing or need to read the script to do their jobs. As a director, I talk to performers/social actors, the producer, director of photography, production designer, first assistant director, visual effects designer, make-up artist, costume designer, editor, sound designer, mixer, and composer. These people are not interchangeable with other practitioners in their fields. They bring specific experience, taste, and perspective. Also, I cannot do the work they do. I rely on their creativity to manifest the vision, and since the vision does not, as poet Richard James Allen reminds us, 'spring fully formed from the head', their work is a particular and unique contribution to the film. These HoDs respond to direction with their own expertise and insight including their skills in directing the people in their departments. They turn an amorphous contingent aspiration (aka a vision) into an authored work. Everyone else on the crew talks to the head of their department, not to the director of the film. So, from my point of view as the film's director struggling to manifest a vision, they are somewhat interchangeable with other people equally skilled in, for example, handling lights or building sets or getting along well with people and getting things done. It is, of course, a slippery slope, since crews are manifesting the vision of their HoDs, and their HoDs are manifesting the director's, but it is not 'turtles all the way down'. If they have not read the script or talked to me, they have not been directed by me, and are not, therefore, directly implicated in my directorial authorship of the film, though they may be implicated in authorship of their particular HoD's responsive creative contribution.

Second, I am refining the general notion of distributed thinking by offering specific propositions about kinds of distributed cognition that are being activated by people involved in filmmaking, particularly the director and editor. Here I combine my knowledge of the structures of creative practice in filmmaking with understandings of specific forms of cognitive expertise as articulated by cognitive philosophers such as John Sutton, Hanne De Jaegher and Ezequiel Di Paolo, Lambros Malafouris and others. More on the specific forms of distributed cognition theories I apply to Clarke's work below.

Finally, and perhaps most importantly, I am using the distributed cognition framework to repair the mind–body split that can occur in the discussion of authorship. These discussions focus on the originating or controlling 'idea' as the source of an authorship claim, and in so doing split the work of hands from the work of minds. By understanding the work of minds to be distributed across bodies, tools and contexts, distributed cognition allows us to see the work of multiple experts in the filmmaking process as the work of ideation.

Thus distributed cognition also addresses a longstanding, though generally unspoken, cultural issue with the word 'collaboration'. The word labour as embedded in the word collaboration (col-labor-ation) is often understood to be 'only or merely'[4] the work of hands, not the work of minds. The distributed cognition framework supports reclaiming and recuperating the cultural idea of labour from being the work of a lower or less valuable cohort[5] to recognition of the coordination of skills and 'cooperation of practices'.[6] The distributed cognition approach offers the opportunity to notice the 'labor' in collaboration as intrinsic to ideation and realisation of a creative work. It affords recognition of the expert creative and intellectual activity taking place through and with bodies, tools, social interactions and cultural contexts. I thus use the distributed cognition framework to support a more nuanced understanding and recognition of labour as integral to authorship.

Subsequent chapters will unpack this proposition and apply it to Shirley Clarke's directing and editing as a way of understanding her unique creative practices and their outcomes. By laying out this framework and then applying it to Clarke, I aim to illuminate Clarke's unique embodied, embedded and enactive film directing and editing; and also, potentially, to offer a useful approach to understanding film directing and other kinds of leadership in creative collaborations.

The creative practice and distributed cognition framework synthesises multiple inputs, but, for the purposes of this investigation, the two central ones are: theoretical proposals positioning cognition as work that occurs beyond individual skull and skin; and practised professional knowledge of filmmaking and modern dance.

Cognition is not (necessarily) a bad word

Before going further, it is important to clarify that within this framework, the word 'cognition' is used, following Sutton and Bicknell:

> in its broadest senses, not restricted to reasoning or to information-processing, but to include the full diversity of embodied mental life: imagining, grieving, remembering, sensing, noticing, dreaming, wondering, listening, problem-solving, strategizing, pattern-detecting, and indeed designing, balancing, or creating...[7]

In this chapter, I will unpack this broadest sense of the word cognition and introduce some ways of understanding these diverse forms of mental life as being embodied, embedded and enactive. In subsequent chapters, I will then use these to illuminate the ways that Shirley Clarke's distributed cognition can be seen in works she directed and edited, and, at the same time, the ways those works shed light on filmmaking practice as an exemplary instance of distributed cognition.

Within this creative practice and distributed cognition framework, I will move fluidly between three levels of concern.

At the broadest level, I am asking how creative ideas are generated within distributed cognitive systems. This philosophical enquiry underpins the meso-level, more specific question, and the primary concern of this book, which is: how does consideration of Clarke's particular distributed cognitive networks illuminate the works she directed and edited? To address this, the very specific, micro-level discussion of films and videos, narratives, scenes, moments and even individual edits will tackle questions like: how can we see the embodied aesthetics and compositional principles of 1940s and 50s modern dance imprinted in Clarke's film and video narrative choices? Or, how can we see authorial presence in the shot-to-shot editing patterns Clarke's embedded 'editing thinking'[8] created? I use these kinds of questions to find material evidence of Clarke's creative practice in the films themselves, and illuminate the broader concerns and achievements of her oeuvre within her cultural context and the film movements in which she operated.

Filmmaking as an example of distributed cognising

Filmmaking is a distributed cognitive process – embodied, embedded and enactive. A film is not a natural or even fully predictable outcome of creative interactions. It bears the prints of process and people, cultures and contexts. Put colloquially, this means that 'how you make is what you make'.[ii] Less

---

[ii] An expression Richard James Allen and I coined as a shorthand for talking about working processes in dance and video early in our collaboration with each other and these art forms. What we were noticing was at a macro level of the ways that form was tacitly imposed by funding bodies, theatrical producers and curators when commissioning a work that would fit inside the guidelines of their programmes, but also the micro level of the moment-to-moment generation of passages or structures and the ways that technology, training and experience all shaped outcome by shaping approach.

colloquially: 'how an actual entity becomes constitutes what that actual entity is'.[9] This book about Shirley Clarke and her body of work therefore will consider not just the finished films, but the processes of making them, including the bodies, tools and contexts involved, as part of the method of analysing and interpreting the films.

Before taking up this work, a brief consideration of why this is not a common method of doing film studies. Why does film analysis tend to focus on the film object and its reception and not include the processes by which it was made? There are potentially a few reasons for this – some questionable, others sound.

One of the most questionable may be a pre-*Ways of Seeing*[10] notion of an artwork as having intrinsic meaning that can be universally understood: that meaning is not negotiated but fixed. If this were the case, then knowledge of how a work is made and the contexts and creative modes of its makers would be irrelevant to interpretation. The ties of this notion of fixed meaning to protection and upholding of mono-cultural attitudes and structures have long since been exposed. Therefore (as probably goes without saying by now) in this discussion, analysis, valuation and interpretation of created works will be understood to be situated and relational. I will declare my frames of reference, and endeavour to sustain consciousness, in my viewing and writing, of the ways my perspectives are informed by my own cultural positions, training and opportunities.

Another reason why the complexities of creative practices and their shaping of works may be underexamined in film analysis is that early and ongoing authorship theories of film resist consideration of bodies, processes, tools and contexts as relevant to analysis of finished films. These theories tend to seek a single individual to whom generation of a style and coherent body of work can be reliably attributed – for praise or blame.[11] This conception of authorship has some value in that bodies of work can, in the right circumstances (circumstances which for decades were generally available only to white men), be seen to have a common signature of a generative visionary. However, this account of Clarke aims for a novel understanding of the sources and functions of individual signatures in film directing. It will propose that the directing of multiplicity and diversity, through jazz-inflected, structured improvisation methods, is an aspect of Clarke's signature as a filmmaker. The name 'Shirley Clarke', this book will argue, stands not just for an individual brain, but for a dynamic creative weaving of practices and concerns resulting in a particular body of film works.[iii]

This discussion of Shirley Clarke and the works she directed and edited therefore walks a fine line with regard to 'auteurism'. It will not, at this delicate moment in the emergence of recognition of women as leading filmmakers, simply walk away from the notion of an auteur. On the other hand, it also will not simply position Clarke as an auteur within a model of sole author, or the male-defined understanding of genius,[12] thus recapitulating egregious conceptions of 'artist' that have excluded so many.

The novel solution I propose to this conundrum is to consider Shirley Clarke through the lens of distributed cognition. This framework will be unpacked in more detail below: however one of its key strengths as a strategy for the authorship conundrum is that it offers a different way to conceive of an 'individual'. The proposal is that an individual, including an individual artist who directs a coherent body of work, is, as Richard Heersmink notes when summarising a large body of work on the subject, 'not a merely neurological and biological phenomenon, but ... a relational, extended, and distributed entity'.[13] This understanding of an individual as 'distributed' can, I propose, allow us to see the body of work Clarke directed and edited as having a unique signature, but also account for the multiple creative inputs into that signature that extend beyond her particular skull and skin. It allows me to understand 'her' as what philosopher Kathleen Wallace would call a 'cumulative network',[14] and to consider some

---

[iii] My thanks to Dr Iqbal Barkat for discussions and insights on philosophical (particularly Deleuzian) perspectives supporting this idea.

of the multiple strands and entanglements of Clarke-as-network as generative, through her unique experience, skills and ideas, of the films she made. It will allow for consideration of these multiple skills, agents and perspectives as synthesised through and with Clarke's own body without subtracting from her demonstrable creative agency as a director and editor. With that aim in mind, I turn now to a brief precis of some principles of embodied, embedded and enactive cognition, before unpacking some key ideas about creative practice skills as forms of knowledge, and then activating these principles in subsequent analytic chapters.

What is distributed cognition and why use it for film philosophy?

Distributed cognition is a collection of proposals/research programmes investigating the proposition that the work of mind is not exclusively taking place inside individual brains. As Sutton and Bicknell note:

> On this perspective, mental life is embodied rather than restricted to the brain alone, embedded in rich material and sociotechnical settings, enacted in histories of flexible engagement with the environment, and sometimes extended across non-biological or cultural resources outside the body which may become integrated into hybrid cognitive systems.[15]

Different strands within the distributed cognition framework focus on different aspects of cognition and its emergence through bodies, tools, contexts and interactions. All of these, however, start by rejecting what Shapiro and Spaulding call 'the computational commitments of cognitive science', instead 'emphasizing the significance of an agent's physical body in cognitive abilities'.[16]

So, I begin this discussion of distributed cognition with discussion of embodied cognition or what Mabel Todd, kinesiologist, called 'the thinking body'.[17]

Embodied cognition

Shapiro and Spaulding (2021) position embodied cognition as foundational to ideas about distributed cognition. All other forms of distributed cognition – embedded cognising with tools and environments, enactive cognising with actions and interactions, and the very premise of extended cognition being beyond the brain and entangled with the world, rest on the foundational claim that 'we think with our bodies, not just with our brains'.[18]

For a creative practitioner, especially a dancer, this premise is axiomatic. Like any skilled practice – from surgery to cricket batting to film editing[19] – dancing in the context of professional practice is thinking. It demonstrably requires coordination of action over extended periods of time, multiple forms of entrainment with other bodies, sounds and spaces, and communicating, imagining, sensing, predicting, judging and remembering with time, space, tools, structures and physiologies – one's own and others.

Like dance, filmmaking requires all these capacities for embodied cognising. Kirsh notes that 'the by-now classic position of embodied cognition is that the more actions you can perform the more affordances you register (e.g., if you can juggle you can see an object as affording juggling)'.[20] My argument around embodied cognition and Shirley Clarke is that the actions and ideas she absorbed into her body through her dance training directly shape the 'affordances' she can 'register'[21] in filmmaking tools, crews and cultures. She thinks through and with filmmaking gear, people and worlds with a dancer's deeply embodied training. The concepts about community, creativity, energy, form and rhythm prevailing in the dance culture in which her embodied cognising was shaped inform the ways she approaches filmmaking. The traces of this embodied cognising show up in all the filmed works she directed and edited. I argue that her specific dance-driven embodied cognitions, which I describe in more detail in Chapter 3, underpin the specific ways her thinking through directing and editing is distributed in her filmmaking.

Embedded cognition

I have (2006-23) theorised film editing as a form of choreography in multiple contexts and from various perspectives. The crux of this theorising is that skilled film editing is a form of embodied and embedded thinking. Like creation of choreography, it relies upon, among other things, kinaesthetic intelligence to shape the movement visible and audible in the uncut material into significant form.[22] However, unlike choreographers, who generally work with dancers and movement in the world, editors shape the movement of a film through their developed expertise with editing tools and processes. Their kinaesthetic 'thinking' is *embedded* in tools and practices of film editing.

> Embedded cognition assumes that cognitive tasks – dividing a number into fractions, navigating a large ship, retrieving the correct book from a shelf – require some quantity of cognitive effort. The cognitive 'load' that a task requires can be reduced when the agent embeds herself within an appropriately designed physical or social environment.[23]

In film editing what this means is that the cognitive load of designing a film's final form is shared between the editor, the editing tools, the filmed material and the collaborative context. Just as a juggler sees objects as affording juggling, the editor sees movement in the filmed rushes as affording composition into phrases or sequences that convey ideas and valence.[24] They use the affordances of their gear to sort, see, rewind, fast forward, pause, play, stop, splice, join and so on. In other words, they use the gear to make decisions – to *think*. The gear, in fact, in many ways, becomes 'transparent' to them. Heersmink draws on the work of De Preester and Tsakris to describe this process:

> Tools can be experienced as transparent extensions of our sensory and motor system. Transparency comes in degrees and full transparency often takes a relatively long period of training. When transparency is achieved, the tool withdraws from

conscious attention and is experienced as part of the body (De Preester and Tsakiris, 2009).[25]

Achieving this level of fluency with editing tools is done in editing processes, over time, so that the patterns of actions required to navigate the room, operate the gear, and splice together shots do not require much conscious attention to execute. Relieved of these aspects of cognitive load, editors like Shirley Clarke can tune their full array of cognitive capacities to the phrases of filmed movement they are crafting. The resulting edits, and films, are, as I have argued elsewhere, not evidence of the editors' thoughts. The edits are the thoughts.[26]

There is, in the process of generating these thoughts, what Kirsh describes as a 'coordination of internal and external processes'.[27] These editing thoughts arise, as I have argued elsewhere, through watching, sorting, remembering, selecting and composing the actual material.[28] The upshot is that the coordination of internal and external arises through the specific rhythmic propensities of the editor, interacting with the possibilities for form that are suggested by the uncut material, through the affordances of the editing gear.

My interest in Clarke's embedded editing cognition is twofold. One thing I will argue, as I mentioned in Chapter 1 and will develop further in Chapter 4, is that her capacities to think fluently with editing gear gave her an access to power and agency in the filmmaking world that she would not otherwise have had as a woman. Many of the exclusionary, unreflective, or unconscious biases that kept women out of film had to do with expertise with machines being culturally understood as a male domain.[29] That Clarke could run the editing room, operate the gear and think with the tools, meant that she could operate more independently to see her films through to completion, and thereby realise her ideas.

Realisation of ideas is the other, perhaps more important, aspect of my interest in Clarke's editing ability. There is limited comprehension in film theory of the significance of editors' decision-making in the shaping of a final film, and when that significance is acknowledged, it is often attributed, incorrectly, to directors with phrases like 'Nolan edits'[30] when, of course, Nolan doesn't actually edit. But Shirley Clarke did; and her editing is, I will argue, a continuation, indeed a key site of manifestation, of her directorial voice.

Enactive cognition

Manifesting a directorial voice or vision will also be discussed in this book as an instance of enactive cognition. The underlying principle of enactive cognition is that thoughts do not 'spring fully-striped / from the head like tigers'.[31] Rather they are formed through and with action.[32]

The key principles of enactive cognition for the purposes of this book are 'autonomy' which affirms that cognisers are 'internally self-constructive in such a way as to regulate actively their interactions with their environments' and, 'sense-making' which is, as described by cognitive philosophers Thompson and Stapleton, the 'interactional and relational side of autonomy ... Sense-making is behaviour or conduct in relation to environmental significance and valence, which the organism itself enacts or brings forth on the basis of its autonomy'.[33]

Enactive and 'participatory sense-making',[34] is, I propose, core to film directing, and one of the most significant oversights of theories of 'director-as-author'. The decisions that are made about the actual material form of a film are made by a director through and with the expertise, advice and action of others. These collaborators are *directed* by the director, and this action of directing should not be underestimated for its shaping influence on the final form. However, it should also not be understood as something that is accomplished through one brain controlling the minds, bodies, tools and decisions of others.

The director gives direction, not instruction.[35] It is through the director's giving and the collaborator's receiving, responding, interrogating, offering, deflecting, diverting, accepting, blocking, counter-offering, coordinating, embodying, embedding, prototyping, testing and developing that the amorphous, unarticulated and elusive sense known as a director's 'vision' becomes a film.

Enactive cognition is not the term usually used for this understanding that an idea, particularly an idea for an artwork, comes into being through actions with materials in the world. However, the understanding that a creative vision only actually exists through the process of 'becoming' is central to philosophising about arts practice from the perspective of a number of disciplines, including cognitive philosophy,[36] ethnographic anthropology,[37] studio and design thinking,[38] and philosophies of creativity.[39] As Malafouris describes this form of enaction: 'human cognitive becoming is largely handmade: it depends on and emerges from the mindful handling of the world'.[40] Further, in this view, as in those mentioned above (though differently expressed in those fields) 'creative *thinging* is not denoting human action on the environment but action *with* and *through* it'.[41]

A filmmaking process is an environment designed for this sort of creative 'thinging'.[42] It is designed to embed the affordances necessary for making a particular thing – a film. But the design of a particular film production process is not fixed. It is itself enactive: by which I mean responsive to the constraints and affordances of culture, money, personality, convention, rebellion against convention, and more. A filmmaking process is what Kirsh might call an 'enactive landscape'.[43] It is 'the set of possibilities that can in principle be brought into being when an agent interacts with an underlying environment while engaged in a task or pursuing a goal'.[44] For Clarke, as for all filmmakers, this set of possibilities is particular. It includes the particular cultural context, with its overlapping and sometimes contradictory norms, perspectives and attitudes; a particular set of tools; and, importantly, the particular people through and with whom a creative idea is generated.

In this study of Shirley Clarke, I will be especially concerned with enactive cognition in the social sphere. This form of enaction, which De Jaegher and Di Paolo call 'participatory sense-making',[45] involves creating the social world through participating in it – playing a part in its rhythms of call and response, bringing individual propensities and desires into coordination. As they note, participatory sense-making is: 'coordination of intentional activity in interaction, whereby individual sense-making processes are affected and new domains of social sense-making can be generated that were not available to each individual on her own'.[46] The new domain a filmmaking process creates is, I propose, the film itself. Only very particular kinds of films can be made solely by one person filling every function, and these were certainly not the kinds of films that Clarke directed and edited. She worked with collaborators and tools at every stage of the process. Clarke's film directing is, through this process, a clear case of 'how meaning is generated and transformed in the interplay between the unfolding interaction process and the individuals engaged in it'.[47] We can see and hear enactive cognising in the films, in the choices of films to make, in the choices of methods, collaborators and, above all, themes and perspective. Where Clarke stands on questions of community, race and belonging, is her enactive cognising imprinted in the films. And this enaction is ongoing, by which I mean she is, through the films, creating sensory motor experiences and exchanges which continue to convey, express and position us in her perspective. She does this, with the community of collaborators, in the process of making the films.

A final note on the use of the enactive cognition/participatory sense-making frameworks to discuss Clarke's directing. There can be little doubt that as fresh and creative as the films Clarke directed and edited still are, there are also flaws both in the oeuvre and person. That is a given, I think, in the discussion of any body of work, any filmmaker, any person. Just as the works and the person are of their moment, they are subject to re-evaluation in any moment. A particularity of this twenty-first-century moment that Clarke was not contending with was the Black Lives Matter movements and the broad cultural rise of consciousness about egregious theft, misrepresentation or appropriation of cultural property, including stories, that has been perpetrated on Black and First Nations people. Thus, in writing this book the questions arise: was Clarke an extractionist filmmaker? Did she take, for profit or personal glory, things to which she was not entitled from the Black communities with whom she worked? My contention will be that she did not. That in fact, working within the constraints of her culture, and often in clear counter-action to those constraints, Clarke was an ally on questions of racial justice. The idea of participatory sense-making will be used to demonstrate that she was working with actors and crews in ways that recognise and respect their agency in the creation of their characters, images and stories. My hope is that the distributed cognition and creative practice framework I am developing can let us see that in Clarke's work with Black men particularly, she and they were thinking with and through each other.

Through the following chapters on Clarke and her creative processes, I will be working within the distributed cognition frameworks. These, as cognitive philosopher Michael Wheeler writes, clear the way to understanding that 'the path of creation

Figure 2.2 Shirley Clarke thinking with place and collaborators (and cigarettes!) on the set of *The Connection*, circa 1960. Shirley Clarke collection, PH 7162, *The Connection*, Box 107, Folder 4, Wisconsin Center for Film and Theater Research

is ... constituted by dynamic arrays of body-involving and environment-involving processing loops. In other words, the creative mind is embodied, embedded and extended'.[48] Wheeler's articulation that 'creativity routinely has an entangled, inside-and-outside logic'[49] is a core premise of this book, which will use the distributed cognition framework to illuminate the ways that Shirley Clarke directs and edits works that are uniquely and creatively identifiable as authored not solely by what is inside Shirley Clarke but through and with her creative entanglements with the world.

Creative practice knowledge

Having articulated the cognitive framework I will use to write about Shirley Clarke, I return now to creative practice, why it is hard to include in film analysis and how I will address that difficulty by writing from my own embodied knowledge.

Like Shirley Clarke, I am a dancer turned editor turned director. This is not to say I have some special connection to or inheritance from Clarke.[iv] What I claim is merely some relevant first-hand knowledge of the principles, affordances and pressures of disciplinary practices in which Clarke worked.

Of course, I did not know at the time that I was dancing in the 'The Downtown Pop Underground'[50] of New York City, that I was

---

[iv] One problem of inserting auto-ethnographic methodologies is over-claiming or inventing some special relationship. So, to be clear, I do *not* claim that I am like Clarke or do what she does. My modes of filmmaking are *not* the same as hers. Not even really like hers. Also, I've never met her as far as I know, and while I am indebted to her artistically, as so many of us are, I am not claiming special insights have been communicated from her to me. Rather I am arguing that the strong embodied familiarity with the trainings and practices that underlie Clarke's distinctive modes gives me familiarity with the structures of thinking that those embodied, embedded and enactive contexts afford. I use this familiarity to support my analysis of working processes and the ways they shape outcomes.

also an undercover spy for later film theorising. However, what I propose now is to use this long-practised professional knowledge of filmmaking and modern dance to make a leap that I have been warming up for, for the past two decades. The leap is across the divide between embodied knowledge – things that it feels like you just know – to articulated knowledge.

In my warm-up for this leap, I have focussed on understanding the physical, kinaesthetic processes of creativity as mental work. Hence the distributed cognition framework, which allows me to understand the work of hands as the work of mind and to say something beyond 'it feels right' about what we do. The leap I aim to take is to move beyond describing creativity as just 'intuitive'[51] to articulating some of the principles embedded in training, affordances of embodied skills, and the pressures encountered in execution of forms of expertise that may be preverbal, or so deeply absorbed into embodied knowledge as to feel innate. These principles, affordances and pressures of practice have a significant role in shaping aesthetics and outcomes. They matter to understanding authorship and reception.

From my years of dancing I know, for example, that principles of training and performing modern dance include unspoken capacities for entrainment. Skilled dancers develop ability to entrain to multiple rhythms, to coordinate, cooperate and create physically with diverse people and sensibilities. Audiences and critics see these skills operating in one way in one dance company, and in another way in another dance company. Because, like Clarke, I have transferred these skills from dance across to film, I also see them functioning, or dys-functioning, in filmmakers as they operate in complex configurations on set. Putting this knowledge together with close analysis of a given film and Clarke's own writings on process shows the marks these crew co-ordinations make on films that arise from different cultures and configurations of making.

Another transferable dancer's skill might be called mind-reading, though it is really gesture reading and mood reading. Dancers learn to sense what people are trying to say because the people we are working with are not always skilled at verbally articulating their ideas. Clarke was known for flying into rages when she could not make herself understood. She probably learned this from her 'rage-aholic'[52] father, but she would have picked it up in dance studios, too. I know I had chairs thrown in my direction in my dancing days when I could not interpret fleetly enough. You learn to jump, duck and 'mind read'.

It isn't just that choreographers aren't verbally articulate though. Dance ideas, like film ideas are not really anything until they are gestures and movements shaped into form. So, the same 'mind-reading' skill is part of a high-functioning film crew. Though people will more often say that they share a 'shorthand' than that they are mind-reading, what they mean is similar – the quick and responsive reading of gesture and mood to help someone to realise their ideas. Understanding a dancer's way of sensing and physically articulating ideas helps me to see how Clarke worked with actors, dancers, cinematographers and movement in her directing and editing.

Most importantly, as a dancer/creative dance maker you learn to shape movement into significant form. To do expressive things with time, effort, shape and space.[53] Filmmakers are doing this too. They use different words but reach for the same objective: making meaning with moving images. Reading films directed and edited by Shirley Clarke as movement phrases will be productive to recognising their expressive forms.

Theories of editing proposed in this book also build on first-hand experience of working as a film editor, which generates an understanding of the decisions editors make and how these shape films. Editors are generally silent about these decision-making processes. Thus, understanding of the influence of editing decisions on story, form and audience experience is limited in film theory. From the perspective of someone who has not edited a film this may be because a film, once edited, is, or appears to be, in a sense 'naturalised'. It is difficult to imagine what other ways it could have been, and there is rarely cause to do so because it is being judged on its form as presented. However, what this form masks is a painstaking process in which thousands of decisions are made by editors. Through first-hand knowledge of multiple professional editing situations, I will write about this decision-making process as an individualised creative propensity, visible in the final film – especially the films edited and directed by Shirley Clarke.

Finally, always necessarily missing from any official history or document is a record of the fleet on-the-ground decisions, the deeply social processes and the lucky catches and near misses of filmmaking. The omission of these vital, unspoken and coordinated creative moments is part of what leads to an understanding of the director's thinking as bound by skin and skull. I have directed some films, and this has taught me how deeply social a process directing is. This experience supports my claim that directing is participatory sense-making. It gives me a way of seeing the sense-making that Clarke is doing through and with her communities of practice, and to see where this is visible in the stories, shots and gestures that make the films into the films they are.

Conclusion

The development of this distributed cognition and creative practice framework aims to contend with auteurism by repairing some of the damage it has done. The framework is being designed to reveal the multiple agencies involved in creative filmmaking practice, while at the same time not diminishing the significance of particular individuals.

Art historian Griselda Pollock asks: 'How can we make the cultural work of women an effective presence in cultural discourse which changes both the order of discourse and the hierarchy of gender in one and the same deconstructive move?'[54]

I'm proposing that using a creative practice and distributed cognition framework for film analysis may be able to shift the 'cultural discourse'[55] by changing the terms of authorship. In so doing it can also pull apart some of the hierarchy of gender in film by repositioning the work of women that has been overlooked.

Applying a creative practice and distributed cognition framework to study of the films directed and edited by Shirley Clarke proposes that Clarke is an author in the artistic sense: her decisions about projects and style demonstrate a unity of intention over time, arising from her specific skill, perspective and fascinations.[56] At the same time, applying this framework to Clarke's processes and productions is a strategy to deepen understanding of the creativity she embodied by also understanding the ways it is embedded in her tools and enacted in her culture and communities.

One offshoot of this strategy will be an understanding that the creative process is multi-faceted, and many forces and people are agents within it. However, this is not a subtractive proposition. It does not take away from Clarke's autonomy or iconoclasm. It adds to them by attempting to explain how they are made up of a unique synthesis/entanglement of her individuality and her context.

The premise of this book is that that is what filmmaking is: embodied, embedded, and enactive cognising. It is led by individual agents in the leadership position of director, and it produces, through the entanglement of dozens of 'cumulatively networked'[57] individual selves, films.

Clarke is undeniably unique, as her productions clearly evidence. No other individual has the specific combination she has, or capacity to synthesise in the ways that she did. So, an auteur, distributed.

Proceeding from that premise, I now turn to looking at Shirley Clarke as a particular leader (director/editor/instigator/organiser) in a range of complex, but nonetheless particular distributed systems of her own experience, her training, tools, techniques, social and cultural context.

Notes

1 Polan, D. (2001). 'Auteur Desire'. *Screening the Past*, 11, 1–9. http://www.screeningthepast.com/2014/12/auteur-desire/.
2 See: Pearlman, K., and Sutton, J. (2022). 'Reframing the Director: Distributed Creativity in Filmmaking Practice'. In M. Hjort and T. Nannicelli (Eds.), *A Companion to Motion Pictures and Public Value*. Wiley, pp. 86–105. Shambu, G. (2021). 'Indigenous Cinema and the Limits of Auteurism'.

Criterion Collection, 1–11. Livingston, P. (2011). 'On Authorship and Collaboration'. *Journal of Aesthetics and Art Criticism*, 69(2), 221–5. https://doi.org/10.1111/j.1540-6245.2011.01463.x. Bacharach, S., and Tollefsen, D. (2010). 'We Did It: From Mere Contributors to Coauthors'. *Journal of Aesthetics and Art Criticism*, 68(1), 23–32. Gaut, B. (1997). 'Film Authorship and Collaboration'. In *Film Theory and Philosophy* (pp. 149–72). Kael, P. (1963). 'Circles and Squares'. *Film Quarterly*, 16(3), 12–26 – and so on.

3 For elaboration of the definition of creativity generating something unique and valuable see: Boden, M. (2004). *The Creative Mind: Myths and Mechanisms* (2nd edn). Routledge.

4 See Pearlman, K., MacKay, J., and Sutton, J. (2018). 'Creative Editing: Svilova and Vertov's Distributed Cognition'. *Apparatus. Film, Media and Digital Cultures of Central and Eastern Europe*, 0(6). http://www.apparatusjournal.net/index.php/apparatus/article/view/122/306.

5 See Williams, R. (1981) *Keywords, a Vocabulary of Culture and Society*. Fontana/Croom-Helm, p. 147.

6 'Cooperation of practices' is an idea being developed by Dr Kersti Grunditz-Brennan through her work as a collaborator with skills in multiple filmmaking disciplines, particularly editing and directing and her development of curricula for training film students in multiple university and cultural contexts.

7 Sutton, J., and Bicknell, K. (2022). 'Introduction: The Situated Intelligence of Collaborative Skills'. In K. Bicknell and J. Sutton (Eds.), *Collaborative Embodied Performance* (pp. 1–18). Bloomsbury, p. 4. https://doi.org/10.5040/9781350197725.ch-00i.

8 See Pearlman, K. (2016). 'Editing Thinking and Onscreen Drafting'. In K. Pearlman, *Cutting Rhythms: Intuitive Film Editing* (pp. 231–47).

9 Whitehead, A. N. ([1929] 1978). *Process and Reality*. New York: Free Press, p. 23. As quoted in Malafouris, L. (2021). *Making Hands and Tools: Steps to a Process Archaeology of Mind*. https://doi.org/10.1080/00438243.2021.1993992, p. 38.

10 Berger, J., Dibb, M., Blomberg, S., Fox, C., and Hollis, R. (1972). *Ways of Seeing*. Penguin.

11 See, for example: Astruc, A. (1948). 'The Birth of a New Avant-garde: La Camera-Stylo'. In S. Mackenzie (Ed.), *Film Manifestos and Global Cinema Cultures: A Critical Anthology* (pp. 603–7). University of California Press. Also Sarris, A. (1963). 'The Auteur Theory and *The Perils of Pauline*'. *Film Quarterly*, 16(4), 26–33. https://doi.org/10.2307/3185951.

12 See Battersby, C. (1989). *Gender and Genius*. The Women's Press.

13 Heersmink, R. (2020). 'Extended Mind and Artifactual Autobiographical Memory'. *Mind and Language*, 37(4). https://doi.org/10.1111/mila.12353, p. 2.

14 Wallace, K. (2019). 'A Theory of the Relational Self: The Cumulative Network Model'. *Humana.Mente Journal of Philosophical Studies*, 36, 189–220.
15 Sutton and Bicknell, Introduction: The Situated Intelligence of Collaborative Skills', p. 5.
16 Shapiro, L., and Spaulding, S. (2021). 'Embodied Cognition'. In *The Stanford Encyclopedia of Philosophy*. http://plato.stanford.edu/entries/embodied-cognition/.
17 Todd, M. E. (1937). *The Thinking Body: A Study of the Balancing Forces of Dynamic Man*. P. B. Hoeber, Incorporated. https://books.google.com.au/books?id=sOEHAQAAMAAJ.
18 Kirsh, D. (2013). 'Embodied Cognition and the Magical Future of Interaction Design'. *ACM Transactions on Computer–Human Interaction*, 20(1), 124–66. https://doi.org/10.12849/40202013.0709.0008, p. 124.
19 See: Sutton, J. (2007). 'Batting, Habit and Memory: The Embodied Mind and the Nature of Skill'. *Sport in Society*, 10(5), 763–86. https://doi.org/10.1080/17430430701442462. Also Sutton and Bicknell, *Collaborative Embodied Performance*, p. 4.
20 Kirsh, 'Embodied Cognition and the Magical Future of Interaction Design', p. 127.
21 Ibid., p. 127.
22 See Pearlman, K. (2016). *Cutting Rhythms: Intuitive Film Editing*. New York; London: Focal Press. https://www.routledge.com/Cutting-Rhythms-Intuitive-Film-Editing/Pearlman/p/book/9781138856516.
23 Shapiro and Spaulding, 'Embodied Cognition'.
24 See Pearlman, K. (2018). 'Documentary Editing and Distributed Cognition'. In C. Brylla and M. Kramer (Eds.), *A Cognitive Approach to Documentary Film*. Palgrave/MacMillan, pp. 303–19. Pearlman, K., and Heftberger, A. (2018). 'Recognising Women's Work as Creative Work'. In *Apparatus. Film, Media and Digital Cultures of Central and Eastern Europe* (Issue 6). [s.n.]. http://www.apparatusjournal.net/index.php/apparatus/article/view/124/276. Pearlman, K., and Gaines, J. (2019). 'After the Facts – These Edits are my Thoughts'. *[In]Transition*, 6(4), 1–7. http://mediacommons.org/intransition/after-facts.
25 Heersmink, 'Extended Mind and Artifactual Autobiographical Memory', p. 4.
26 For more on the distinction between something being a record of thinking and something being the actual thought, see Clark on Richard Feynman, in: Clark, A. (2008). *Supersizing the Mind*. Oxford University Press. https://doi.org/10.1093/acprof:oso/9780195333213.001.0001 see also: Pearlman and Gaines, 'After the Facts'.
27 Kirsh, 'Embodied Cognition and the Magical Future of Interaction Design', p. 159.
28 Pearlman, 'Documentary Editing and Distributed Cognition'.

29 For discussion of class and gender-based separation of skills see: Williams, R. (1959). 'Culture and Society'. *Essays in Criticism*, IX(4), 432–37. https://doi.org/10.1093/eic/IX.4.432. For discussion of the inaccessibility of core creative tools and contexts to women artists see: Parker, R., and Pollock, G. (1981). *Old Mistresses: Women, Art, and Ideology*. Routledge and Kegan Paul.
30 Brody, R. (2023). '*Oppenheimer* is Ultimately a History Channel Movie with Fancy Editing'. *The New Yorker*, 27 July.
31 Allen, R. J. (1995). 'Tigers'. In *The Air Dolphin Brigade*. Paper Bark Press and Shoestring Press, in association with Tasdance, p. 40.
32 See, among other works by Evan Thompson and collaborators on enactive cognition: Thompson, E., and Stapleton, M. (2009). 'Making Sense of Sense-making: Reflections on Enactive and Extended Mind Theories'. *Topoi*, 28(1), 23–30. https://doi.org/10.1007/s11245-008-9043-2.
33 Ibid., pp. 24–5.
34 See: De Jaegher, H., and Di Paolo, E. (2007). 'Participatory Sense-making: An Enactive Approach to Social Cognition'. *Phenomenology and the Cognitive Sciences*, 6, 485–507. https://doi.org/10.1007/s11097-007-9076-9.
35 See: Pearlman and Sutton, 'Reframing the Director'.
36 See for example: Malinin, L. H. (2019). 'How Radical is Embodied Creativity? Implications of 4E Approaches for Creativity Research and Teaching'. *Frontiers in Psychology*, 10, 1–12. https://doi.org/doi: 10.3389/fpsyg.2019.02372.
37 See, for example: Ingold, T. (2010). 'Anthropology Comes to Life'. *General Anthropology*, 17(1), 1–4. https://doi.org/10.1111/j.1939-3466.2010.00001.x. Also Pink, S., and Leder Mackley, K. (2014). 'Re-enactment Methodologies for Everyday Life Research: Art Therapy Insights for Video Ethnography'. *Visual Studies*, 29(2), 146–54. https://doi.org/10.1080/1472586X.2014.887266.
38 See Brown, T. (2008). 'Design Thinking'. *Harvard Business Review*, 86(6), 84–92, 141. http://www.ncbi.nlm.nih.gov/pubmed/18605031. Hetland, L, Winner, E., Veenema, S., and Sheridan, K. M. (2007). *Studio Thinking: The Real Benefits of Visual Arts Education*. Teachers College Press.
39 See Carter, p. (2004). 'Preliminary Matters'. In *Material Thinking, The Theory and Practice of Creative Research*. Melbourne University Press. Also Csikszentmihalyi, M. (2014). 'Society, Culture, and Person: A Systems View of Creativity'. In M. Csikszentmihalyi (Ed.), *The Systems Model of Creativity: The Collected Works of Mihaly Csikszentmihalyi* (pp. 47–61). Springer Netherlands. https://doi.org/10.1007/978-94-017-9085-7_4.
40 Malafouris, L. (2021). 'Making Hands and Tools: Steps to a Process Archaeology of Mind'. *World Archaeology* 53(1), 38–55. https://doi.org/10.1080/00438243.2021.1993992, p. 45

41 Ibid., p. 44. Emphasis in original.
42 Ibid., p. 44.
43 Kirsh, 'Embodied Cognition and the Magical Future of Interaction Design', p. 138.
44 Ibid., p. 138.
45 See De Jaegher and Di Paolo, 'Participatory Sense-making'.
46 Ibid., p. 497.
47 Ibid., p. 485
48 Wheeler, M. (2018). 'Talking About More than Heads: The Embodied, Embedded, and Extended Creative Mind'. In B. Gaut and M. Keiran (Eds.), *Creativity and Philosophy*, pp. 230–50. https://www.routledge.com/Creativity-and-Philosophy/Gaut-Kieran/p/book/9781138827684, p. 247.
49 Ibid., p. 231.
50 McLeod, K. (2018). *The Downtown Pop Underground*. Abrams Press.
51 Brennan, K. G., and Pearlman, K. (2023). 'Creating Character in Editing'. *Media Practice and Education* 24(3), 235–52. https://doi.org/10.1080/25741136.2023.2172655, p. 235.
52 See: Dundy, E. (2012). *Life Itself! An Autobiography*. Little, Brown Book Group, p. 11.
53 See: Bartenieff, I., with Lewis, D. (1980). *Body Movement: Coping with the Environment*. New York: Gordon and Breach Science Publishers.
54 Pollock, G. (2013). *Differencing the Canon: Feminism and the Writing of Art's Histories*. Taylor & Francis, p. 24.
55 Ibid., p. 24
56 See: Pearlman, K. (2010). 'Beyond Bonnets'. *Lumina, the Australian Journal of Screen Arts and Business*, 3, 129–39.
57 See: Wallace, K. (2019). 'A Theory of the Relational Self: The Cumulative Network Model'. *Humana.Mente: Journal of Philosophical Studies*, 36, 189–220.

3

Dancing Cognitions

> I've realized that all my films are dance films. Every film of mine is dance. Every one. It's clear in the way I use the camera, my editing, my sense of rhythm. I learned so much from being a dancer. I could not have been as good a film-maker had I not danced.
>
> Shirley Clarke[1]

Figure 3.1 Shirley Clarke in full flight, circa 1950. Shirley Clarke collection, M91-052, Box 25, Folder 5, Wisconsin Center for Film and Theater Research

Shirley Clarke's first film was a dancefilm. Since then, almost nothing ever written about her fails to mention that she was a dancer before she was a filmmaker. In this chapter I will consider the ways that American mid-century modern dance culture, aesthetics and techniques impact on her creative processes and cinematic ideas. Much of the chapter is devoted to discussion of the first film Clarke directed and edited, *Dance in the Sun* (1953). I look at the ways it engages strategies of movement phrasing through editing, and the tensions it navigates between making art films and mainstream narratives that will stay with Clarke throughout her career. However, I begin with an extended discussion of some of the dance context in which Clarke lived and worked. My aim is to illuminate how the kinds of intelligence and ways of thinking that the years of dance would have imprinted on Clarke manifest in the films she directed and edited. This is not a new claim about Clarke, it is an idea she frequently expresses herself.[2] What I hope to add with this chapter is some insight into the specific aspects of the imprint of dance on her thinking – *how* the

> time and space in film turns out to be relevant to almost every concept I have about film: how I choose the subject, as a way of looking at film, and as a way of understanding and looking and working with it ... There is no doubt in my mind that the way I film *The Connection* (1961), *The Cool World* (1963) and even *Portrait of Jason* (1967) came from these concerns.[3]

My discussion of the ways dance-thinking manifests in Clarke's creative oeuvre builds on the key premise of embodied cognition theories that: 'Movements are at the centre of mental activity: a sense-making agent's movements – which include utterances – are the tools of her cognition'.[4] A trained professional dancer such as Clarke deploys 'a sense-making agent's movements'[5] that are arguably both more expert and more particular in their physical forms than that of a person without the imprint of years of instruction in formal ways of thinking with limbs and lungs. My aim here is to identify some of these imprints and reflect on how they inform Clarke's directing and editing.

Professional dancers generally share some level of training in reading, writing, arithmetic and social behaviour modes with their western, educated, non-dancer communities, so there is substantive overlap in a dancer's embodied cognition and that of other humans of roughly comparable cultures. However, I propose that dancers also share specific and distinctive ways of conceptualising action in time and space with each other.[6] Dance training and execution of choreography demonstrably require coordination of action over extended periods of time, multiple forms of entrainment with other bodies, sounds and spaces, and communicating, imagining, sensing, predicting, judging and remembering with physical rather than verbal gesture. If cognition is embodied, and if a group of dancers shares deeply

Figure 3.2 Shirley Clarke with cinematographer Peter Buckley directing *Bullfight* (1955). Credit: Halcyon Pictures. WCFTR Name photograph file, PH 7163, Box 52, Folder 1, Wisconsin Center for Film and Theater Research

ingrained patterns of being bodies in the world, then, I argue, they share ways of cognising that bind them to each other and create their specific ways of perceiving, being and creating. Clarke's immersion in mid-century modern dance training and aesthetics shaped her early creative filmmaking, and this choreographic, kinaesthetic, embodied and rhythmically distinctive creativity is sustained throughout her filmmaking life. The first question of this chapter therefore is: what are the social ethics and creative aesthetics of modern dance that shape Clarke's dancing cognition?

Dance thinking

Born in 1919 and coming of age in New York City in the 1930s and 40s, Shirley Clarke's decision to distinguish herself from the rest of her high school class by becoming a dancer would have put her in the thick of the emergence of modern dance as an art form in the USA. Doris Humphrey, one of Clarke's key modern dance influences, notes in her widely read (and still in print) 1959 book *The Art of Making Dances* that this period is modern dance's 'awakening'.[7] Humphrey is talking about American and European modern dance forms coming into being through introductions of the perspectives and ideas of specific artists such as Isadora Duncan and Ruth St Denis, but also in response to modernism, jazz, World War I, the Russian Revolution, rapid industrialisation and more. She describes modern dance as conceptually distinct to ballet, writing: 'this is not to say that ballet form was bad, only that it was limited and suffered from arrested development – a permanent sixteen, like Sleeping Beauty herself'.[8] Sleeping Beauty, in her long-term repose, is necessarily passive. By contrast, modern dance culture encouraged 'individuality and independent thinking'.[9]

Students, Humphrey writes, should 'learn principles of movement and be encouraged to expand or embroider on these in their own way'.[10]

The process of first mastering principles of movement form and then moving beyond them to 'expand and embroider' lays the groundwork for a creative tension that Clarke embraces and embodies throughout her working life.

One side of the tension is striving for achievement in form. Formal rigour and capacity to execute received principles in a skilled, full-bodied way are valued in Clarke's modern dance context, and she trained rigorously. She went on to work professionally as a dancer, and in the collegial community of dance with its cooperative/competitive, collegial/dictatorial tensions and affordances. In the roughly twenty years from when she committed to being a dancer in the 1930s to when she started making films in the 1950s, she would necessarily have absorbed and embodied the ethics and aesthetics of this modern dance milieu. This absorption, or formation of identity as a dancer, is axiomatic to dance training and it also coincides with what psychologists call peak periods of cognitive development – the period of life in late teens and early twenties where ethical and aesthetic allegiances are formed. Clarke's dance thinking – her embodied cognising – is therefore shaped, in part, by respect for and work towards achievement in form.

However, another key imprint from her dancing days is somewhat oppositional to the capacity to execute received principles, and that is how to 'expand or embroider'[11] on form. In modern dance this is not just a skill, it is a kind of permission to be individually expressive, even an imperative for development of identity. As Clarke's collaborator in dance companies and dancefilms Daniel Nagrin notes, 'If you were a modern dancer in those days [circa 1936] ... you possessed real dignity only if you were "creative".'[12] Like many dancers who go on to work as creative instigators,[i] Clarke excelled in the expansion and embroidery rather than the execution of form.

---

[i] For example, Merce Cunningham, Bob Fosse and Twyla Tharp, whose biographies all report their struggles against the imperative to acquiesce to the formal imprints of their mentors.

One of her contemporaries, Stuart Hodes, reports being in a dance composition class with Clarke and watching her make a dance from her fingers walking.[13] In comparison to the leaping and arcing that would have been going on all around her as the other members of the class worked to express themselves with their whole bodies and simultaneously to show off their mastery of form, Clarke's two-finger composition demonstrates a commitment to standing out by challenging form. It also, not coincidentally, illustrates her sense of humour and emergent understanding that dance could be fodder for camera frames that are not always wide shots.

In this precis I am building of a modern dancers' cognitive profile, it is important to remember that these capacities – to respect and execute form, and to expand form to create a personal signature or identity – do not originate or manifest verbally or in writing. They are physical, embodied. They are cognitive capacities for thinking rhythmically, spatially and in phrases of movement. Thinking in these ways, particularly rhythmically, is germane to generative creativity in modern dance. As Nagrin describes it: 'one of the critical elements that defines our individuality is our rhythm',[14] and 'Everything is shaped by rhythm, and I think of rhythm as central to the creative act'.[15]

Clarke's intrinsic body rhythms partly define her individuality. Clarke was small and not especially loose-limbed, so her body would have gravitated towards generation of up tempo, even buoyant rhythms rather than languid, lyrical ones. This kind of rhythmic propensity is seen repeatedly in her editing choices, particularly in films where rhythms are foregrounded such as *Skyscraper* (1959), *In Paris Parks* (1954), *Bridges-Go-Round* (1958) and *Brussels Loops* (1957). This way that she – her body, her physiology – *does* movement is visible in the ways that she shapes movement.[16]

Clarke's creative rhythms are also indelibly imprinted with diverse rhythms of jazz music. Clarke's peak period of cognitive development is not only spent in modern dance studios training and performing, it is spent in jazz clubs, dancing. About dancing to music in clubs Nagrin writes:

> The dance floor is the birthplace of much of what we dancers do. On it, we can encounter some parts of what we really are, unexpected truths, joy, and a profound reservoir of what makes us dance. Many dancers make a habit of this experience. Too many do not.[17]

Both Nagrin and Clarke did make a habit of dancing in jazz clubs and, as is evident in her collaborations with jazz composers on film scores and stories, Clarke transferred this 'reservoir'[18] as a source of ideas from dance to film.

Other aspects of jazz are also salient to Clarke's aesthetic and approach, including the balance of structure and improvisation, contrapuntal use of rhythms and the distributed cognitive community that is formed by a group of jazz musicians working together. More on this in Chapter 5, where I look at the ways the casts and crews Clarke directed function like skilled jazz improvisers.[19]

Another very significant aspect of the culture of mid-century modern dance that leaves a strong imprint on Clarke is the capacity to collaborate ethically with a diverse community of practitioners.

Doris Humphrey offers the idea of heterogeneity as central to modern dance creative practice. She claims that '[T]he first mark of a potential choreographer is a knowledge of or at least a great curiosity about the body – not just his own but the heterogenous mixture of bodies which people his environment'.[20] So, unlike ballet which emphasises homogeneity of bodies, modern dance creators' ethics and aesthetics seem to be intent on working with distinctive cultures and perspectives. In the relentlessly racist, homophobic and sexist culture of the USA in the 1940s and 50s, modern dance communities are, by comparison to commerce, law or even other forms of art such as the visual arts, radically diverse in welcoming people of different ethnicities and sexual orientation. Further, these cultural enclaves are often led by strong women: for example Martha Graham, Doris Humphrey, Anna Sokolow and others. Looking back at these studios it is difficult to see how strong this engagement with diversity would have been in context – we see it now as limited and affording little space for leadership by people other than white people, often with intergenerational wealth to support them. However, one thing that can be said about the heterogeneity that did exist is that it was not self-consciously performative. There was no cultural imperative to demonstrate diversity as a value, and the participation of diverse practitioners arose from a level of acceptance that was not demonstrated in culture more broadly or mandated by cultural policies. In context, and particularly given Clarke's immersion in jazz music and clubs, and her consistent advocacy for civil rights, the ethics and aesthetics of diversity were imprinted and, as will be discussed when analysing films she directed and edited, sustained throughout her creative life.

This time in modern dance may also have trained Clarke in collaborative practices that respect individuals while at the same time focussing on communities. This is one of the dictums of dance artistry that Humphrey lays out, saying

> (I)n composing for other dancers ... (a choreographer) ... must have a high regard for their individuality, remember that they are not like himself, and bring all his intelligence to bear on the problem of understanding them, physically, emotionally and psychologically'.[21]

Respect for individuality and capacity to perceive and work with distinct rhythms and forms of physical, emotional and psychological lives are skills acquired through practise. Clarke starts her creative life practising them, and though these dance-informed ways of thinking and working manifest differently in different phases of her creative life, I argue that they can be seen in all of her work.

In this section, I have laid out some ideas about what a dancer knows. As journalist Lisa Robinson summarises in an interview with Clarke, 'Dance laid the groundwork for film, and her studies with Martha Graham, Hanya Holm, Doris Humphrey and others – studies that stressed originality, personal expression, rhythm and movement – became integral to her philosophies of life and art'.[22] These studies encompass knowing how to respect, conform to and excel in form; how to distinguish oneself creatively by expanding or disrupting form; how to utilise rhythm as a central tenet of creativity, including the rhythms of one's own body and those of their embedded culture; and how to respect individuals and create in ways that sustain that individuality while at the same time weaving a dynamic community.

In Chapters 4 and 5 I will consider how these capacities manifest in Clarke's editing and directing in the 1960s and beyond, but first I turn now to consider how they manifest in her dancefilm and documentary collaborations of the 1950s. All of the films to be discussed in this chapter can be found on the *Project Shirley: The Magic Box* DVDs researched, collected and released by Milestone and now available through Kino-Lorber.[23]

I begin with the first film Clarke directed and edited, the one on which she established that credit – directed and edited by – which

Figure 3.3 Collage of production stills from *Bullfight* (1955) and *Dance in the Sun* (1953). Shirley Clarke collection, U.S. Mss 145 AN, Box 12, Folder 1, Wisconsin Center for Film and Theater Research

she claimed (except when impeded in doing so) throughout her working life.

Dance in the Sun

Dance in the Sun, the first film directed and edited by Shirley Clarke, and the winner of the New York Film Society Best Dance Film of 1953, instigates the innovations and transformations across media, form and ideas that characterise Clarke's oeuvre as a filmmaker. As Clarke herself notes: 'All the kinds of things I discovered about the choreography of editing and the choreography of space/time came from making that very first film'.[24] The questions of this section are: what did she learn? And how does what she already knew, from the years of dancing, make its way from dance into her creativity with film?

In *Dance in the Sun* a man (Daniel Nagrin) begins his dancing day in the studio, consulting with a rehearsal pianist (Sylvia Marshall). As he begins to dance, an imaginative cinematic leap is made, from the studio to the beach, to dance in the actual sunlight.

To illuminate what Clarke 'discovered' from 'making that very first film'[25] I will focus on two aspects of it.

The first is the conventions of cinema and dance that are hybridised in the imaginative cinematic leap from studio to beach. I am interested in how this hybridisation signals both the sources of Clarke's unique signature and some of the cultural blocks to recognition of that signature. The film analysis question here is: what moves the man from the studio to the beach? Is this transformation of place caused by the force of his movement, or the power of his imagination? This is not just a question of narrative, but of the conventions and affordances of cinematic form, craft and sensibility versus those of modern dance.

The second part of my analysis of this film will focus on the rhythmic style of Clarke's construction of this 'imagined geography' (with its antecedents in Maya Deren and in Soviet montage); and the choreographic artistry that is evidenced in the timing and trajectory phrasing of the cuts themselves.

Dance in the Sun: dance becomes dancefilm

There is nothing in the dance choreography of *Dance in the Sun* that could not be performed on a stage, live, as a continuous dance. In fact, Clarke saw it performed live before deciding to film it, and the whole dance was shot first on a beach and then in a rehearsal studio at the YMCA.[26] When it was a theatrical performance, the title, the lighting and perhaps a soundscape would, or could, have been used to suggest that Nagrin was dancing out in the sun, not on a stage. The conventions of modern dance spectatorship would have accepted and supported this suggestion. In an era where modern dance had not entirely eschewed the idea of a dance narrative,[27] dancers were often positioned as characters undergoing some kind of journey, which they express in abstract movement. A performance live onstage of the choreography of *Dance in the Sun* would have been this kind of expressive dance. The wide, bounding movement could have been understood as metaphorically being the freedom and joy associated with expansive space and limitless horizons.[ii] The human body would have implicitly been a vehicle of the narrative content, a vehicle of human-centred desires and conflicts, moving through an experience that, for an audience, is necessarily abstracted. In the audience experience the dancer isn't in the sun, he is expressing the feeling of being in the sun. The sun is implied, his feelings are expressed. The story, if there is one, is being constructed in the viewer's mind through association of the abstracted movement feelings with the literal title, lighting and soundscape.

[ii] These 'limitless horizons', in this period of American post-war confidence, would have been evoked without irony. No concerns about humans being centred in the natural world would have shadowed the sunny confidence of manifest destiny: but that is another story, for another book.

The relationship of narrative and character journey to abstract modern dance was an uneasy one, though, even before it became the explicit target of formal attacks by post-modern and formalist thinking[28] or concerns about the human-centred focus on 'man's' experience of the world began to trouble us. Humphrey notes that dance as a 'language' has 'definite limitations and should not be forced to communicate beyond its range which is ... that part of experience which can be expressed in physical action'.[29] Humphrey implies her own and many audience's frustrations with unexplained narratives when she writes about watching dancers 'agonizing for ten minutes or so for unknown reasons'.[30]

Dance, in other words, is good at physical action, but not so good at narrative. However, as long as it is performed by humans it will evoke some narrative associations for an audience. In mid-century modern dance, the story is not the primary concern. The danced expressiveness is the site of the art. So, the narratives are vague, and the expressive actions that would be explicable inside a character-driven story become unspecific, potentially overwrought, dull, or worse.

Dance in the Sun proposes an innovative solution. It adeptly balances the tradition of expressive modern dance with the affordances that cinematic form offers for creating and conveying character perspective and journey. In her cutting between studio and beach, Clarke explores dance as both an abstract expression of feeling state *and* as a physical monologue of a character's thoughts. By setting up the situation in the studio and then taking us outside to the beach, and back inside to the studio, Clarke makes an important and largely unremarked innovation: she puts the dancer's inside on the outside. She situates the feeling that motivates the dancing into a causal narrative about imagining freedom and sunlight.

The film begins with a work-light on stage. Nagrin walks into frame from where the camera is standing, walking into his own point of view. He shifts the work-light towards the piano, pulls sheet music from his briefcase, hands it to the pianist with a bit of light banter, does a quick stretch, takes off his shirt. The film's first cut occurs when he ties a sweater round his shoulders. Draping his bare shoulders is an intimate gesture and coming in close is motivated by this intimacy, as well as the easy connection we have to a recognisable gesture. The feeling of draping a sweater cues our kinaesthetic empathy with its familiarity.

But then he hesitates. The film's next cut is here, as he reaches into his briefcase and pulls out a seashell. Ok, it is a bit corny in light of what happens next, but in the context, it is interesting. It demonstrates a concern for keeping an audience grounded in the narrative idea – a concern for which Clarke's contemporary (and rival) Maya Deren would likely have had some disdain.

I see this sequence as important because Clarke will follow it through, leaning her sensibility towards the widely legible rather than the self-consciously arty.[iii]

Clarke notes in various interviews and notebooks held in the Wisconsin Centre for Film and Theatre Research that she would like to have made Hollywood films but could never get the chance. In *Rome is Burning* (1970) a documentary film about Clarke directed by Noël Burch and André Labarthe, she reflects with some self-deprecation on the failure of her works to reach mainstream audiences due to their themes and forms.[31] However, in a 1978 diary I viewed at the Wisconsin Center for Film and Theater Research,[32] Clarke writes a list of twelve things that 'If I were God I would like to HAVE' (emphasis in original); as in, to have done or accomplished, or to have come

---

[iii] She says as much in her interview with Rabinovitz when she describes realizing that she could save *Dance in the Sun* by shooting it in the studio and framing it with a filmic device: 'I can also shoot the dance on stage, shoot the exact same angles, and then cut from the stage to the beach and you will know why he's dancing on a beach. Otherwise, he looks artsy or pretentious leaping around the beach in a stylised dance. But if you see he goes from the stage and I have a little shot at the opening of the film of him taking a shell out of its case and staring at it, a special film connection is made.' (See Rabinovitz (1983), 'Choreography of Cinema', p. 8.)

true as she wishes. The first thing on the list is 'To make a movie musical comedy'.[iv]

Dance in the Sun is not a comedy per se, and not a musical in the sense that no one sings, but it is a narrative that unfolds within a music-driven dance. Even more importantly, it is a narrative that is established through a sequence shot and cut in what might be called 'classical' Hollywood style continuity. The wide-shot Nagrin has walked into cuts to a mid-shot as he looks into his briefcase. This is an 'invisible' edit in continuity style, meaning it is perfectly matched in timing and movement to efface its presence and convince the viewer's perception that it is all one action taking place continuously. From the mid-shot of him looking in the suitcase, the next cut is to a close-up point-of-view shot as he picks up a seashell. From the close-up we go back out to a mid of his expression – how he responds to the shell, then back out to a wide. Wide–mid–close–mid–wide, all 'seamlessly' matched on action. This is textbook classical cutting from someone who has never read the book.[v]

[iv] The other eleven things are: "2) have Wendy happy, successful, and have a baby, 3) Fall in love, 4) have fun most of the time, 5) Do something important for the world – (posterity), 6) live by the ocean or in Santa Fe, 7) start a successful film festival or/and commune, 8) have a penthouse in NYC, 9) make an important film (a classic), 10) keep things neat and clean, 11) learn about who I really am. Who IS Shirley, 12) learn to be honest and not to fear it . . ." Of these twelve things, #2 can be factually confirmed to have occurred. It is this book's contention that #5 and #9 were also achieved. Re #8, having a penthouse in NYC, Clarke did rent a penthouse apartment in NYC at the Chelsea Hotel for many years, where she lived and worked in video mostly. She also lived in Los Angeles for a while, though not very happily, so probably not by the sea. Whether Clarke fell in love, had fun most of the time, kept things neat and clean, learned who she really was or to be honest and not fear it, is, well, hard to say.

[v] According to 'The Downtown Pop Underground' by Kembrew McLeod, Clarke studied film at City College in the 1950s where she and Jonas Mekas were classmates under the tutelage of Dadaist Hans Richter. Given his creative interests, it is unlikely that Richter would have relied on texts on how to do Hollywood style continuity coverage in his teaching.

Still in the wide shot, Nagrin turns away, slips through a couple of symbolic stretches (shorthand for a dancer's warm-up), signals the piano player who starts the music, and the next cut is back into a mid: a faraway look in Nagrin's eyes as he walks towards the camera. Cut to what he sees in his mind's eye: the long horizon with a lone bird circling the beach, and we're off into the imagined geography of the dance.

What Clarke does by starting with a narrative sequence shot and cut in continuity style, is communicate something beyond the range of experience that can be communicated solely with physical action. She asserts that the change of scene from studio to beach is a move into the dancer's imagination, not just an expressive movement. A body on stage cannot do this. But a camera and a cut can. This apparently unremarkable sequence marks that shift. The unremarkableness is important, skilled and, in the context, unusual.

It is important because it sets up Clarke as a narrative filmmaker, unwilling to mystify her audience. She wants us to understand her story and thus uses continuity style to articulate it.

It is highly skilled in its execution, and could indeed have been planned, shot and cut by a competent Hollywood crew. In fact, it was planned by Clarke, working with her husband and two of his friends[vi] and Nagrin, and Clarke had never made a film before. These skills are anything but natural and show a high degree of awareness of cinematic storytelling conventions, as well as a highly sophisticated eye for the cut. More on this sophisticated eye for the cut in a moment. First, a note on why the unremarkableness of the sequence is in fact remarkable in its context.

Abstract expressionist film as modelled by Maya Deren and others would have strongly eschewed this clarity of narrative. In the unwritten rules of an avant-garde or experimental artist's cultural perspective, it would be considered pandering to an audience. This idea that dancefilm as an art should eschew

---

[vi] Camera operators credited on *Dance in the Sun* are: John J. Murphy (lead credit), Bert Clarke and Ted Greenspun.

narrative clarity persists through Clarke's lifetime and beyond.³³ Clarke's long arguments with the avant-garde, which she loves and hates, challenges and is challenged by, begin here, with this short sequence which would have been commonplace in a Hollywood musical, but which was not common practice in 'avant-garde' film.

In truth, there is something a little bit cringe-worthy in the sequence. The man of action encounters the woman of music. She accompanies/plays for him as he strides out for freedom and adventure. These gendered roles and gestures are hallmarks of the modern dance context in which Clarke is embedded. They would have sat easily with her teachers Hanya Holm, Anna Sokolow, even Martha Graham. They were certainly a hallmark of one of the most successful women choreographers of the 1940s and 50s, Agnes de Mille, who was moving fluently, and lucratively, across Broadway, Hollywood and what was then called concert dance. De Mille's choreographic concepts in Broadway shows and Hollywood films (for example, for *Oklahoma!* the Broadway show in 1943 and the film in 1955) no longer resonate with viewers looking for feminist independence of thought or action. Conversely, Deren's films radiate this embodied quest for many, if not most feminist theorists, even as, for me anyway, they continue to raise questions about women trapped behind glass (windows and mirrors) or the positioning of sensual experience as circling the edges of madness.

I propose, however, that Clarke's unremarkable opening sequence, with its classical Hollywood cutting in the context of a modern dance film is asserting a different kind of independence. Clarke's brand of independence is challenging the abstract expressionism of modern dance, which is disrupted by Clarke with this opening sequence.[vii] This continuity style is a direct challenge to the limits of dance and abstraction to work with social ideas, and as Clarke becomes increasingly concerned with social issues,

---

[vii] This kind of narrative clarity and use of conventional techniques is also in some ways antithetical to the New American Cinema manifesto that Clarke and Joans Mekas, among others, authored in 1960.

she will exploit this. Expanding or embroidering forms by cross-pollinating them in this way is highly salient to Clarke's broader oeuvre and artistry. In *Dance in the Sun*, we see Clarke's first hybridisation of the (unwritten) conventions of form, in her use of conventions of mainstream continuity with the idea of cutting together imagined geographies.

Imagined geographies and real bodies

As noted above, Clarke and her collaborators are deliberately, and methodically, situating the dancing in *Dance in the Sun* in two places and using narrative shooting and editing techniques to clarify that we are being transported from the studio to the beach by the force of the character/dancer's imagination. It could be argued that they are thus creating a literal, material manifestation on-screen of what Dee Reynolds calls kinaesthetic imagination.[34] However, Reynolds is not only writing about this kind of depiction. Her thesis, rather, is that great choreographers think in movement. They have kinaesthetic imaginations. I have made use of Reynolds' idea about kinaesthetic imagination in numerous articles about editing to say that editors also think in movement, and will do so again herein, in my discussion of the balance of *A Dance in the Sun*.

I begin with discussion of the 'phrase'. Descriptions of movement phrases, musical phrases and linguistic phrases are common in analysis and critique of dance, music and literature. Conversely, although it is an art of movement, sound and word, 'phrase' is not commonly used to describe segments in the design of film. However, I have introduced 'phrasing' in my arguments about editing as a form of choreography (see *Cutting Rhythms*) and I will focus on the idea of phrasing now, to illuminate the ways that Clarke's dance knowledge underpins her expertise in directing and editing.

Doris Humphrey (on whom I rely because of her proximity to and influence on Clarke's artistic development), writes of the phrase that, as a communicative tool, she thinks it originates in prelinguistic expressive communicative sound. Humphrey describes 'a time-shape in the sounds which had two characteristics: their length was limited by the breath, and they had a rising and falling intensity and speed due to their emotional basis'.[35] Whether this origin story has empirical basis or not is not really of concern. It would have informed Clarke's thinking and approach through the classes and performances she did under Humphrey's tutelage and with Humphrey's contemporaries, who also subscribed to these notions.

In my theorising of rhythm in film editing and editing as a form of choreography I pick up on the idea of a movement phrase as having communicative and compositional significance, and describe what an editor does to compose them:

> The movement through time and energy of all of the filmed images is shaped into phrases of related movements and grouped emphasis points. These phrases are then varied, juxtaposed, interpolated, and shaped within themselves and in relation to each other to make the overall experience of time, energy, and movement in a film that is known as rhythm.[36]

In the analysis of moments from *Dance in the Sun* that follow I will use this framework of the phrase of danced or musical movement and apply it to discussion of the phrase of edited movement (which I call a 'trajectory phrase'[viii]). My aim is to illuminate how Clarke's embodied knowledge of dance becomes, in her first film, an editing skill at which she excels and which she continues to build on throughout her creative work. Clarke's sense of movement phrasing characterises her artistic style/signature as a filmmaker.

[viii] Trajectory phrasing is one of three key tools an editor employs in the shaping of the movement of story, movement of emotion, and movement of image and sound. Trajectory is movement under force. An editor phrases the movement impelled by narrative, emotional, or physical forces into time–space configurations of appropriately significant form. See *Cutting Rhythms: Intuitive Film Editing* (2016), Chapter 3.

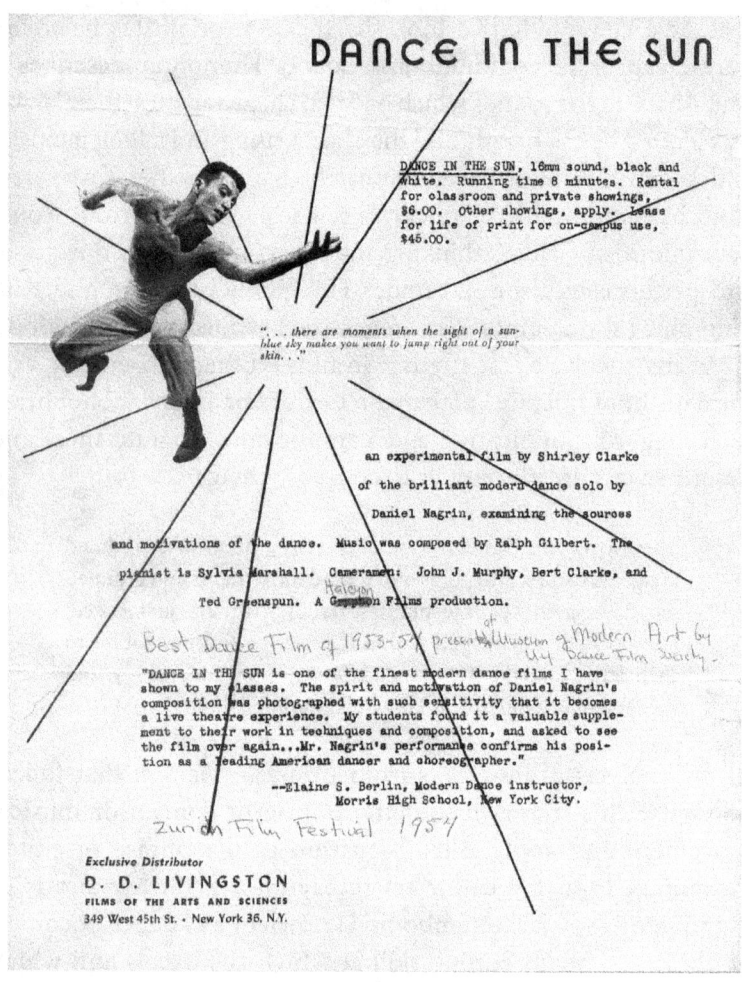

Figure 3.4 Daniel Nagrin in *Dance in the Sun*, promotional flyer annotated by Shirley Clarke with notes on screenings and prizes for the film, circa 1954–5. Shirley Clarke collection, U.S. Mss 145 AN, Box 13, Folder 5, Wisconsin Center for Film and Theater Research

In the composition of the pro-filmic dance, Nagrin has crafted a series of dance phrases that vary and expand over the course of the choreography. Dynamics within these phrases are built from repetition and variations on horizontally sweeping gestures of arms which read as a kind of embracing of the openness and fluidity of space and sometimes as a stylised imitation of waves. These gestures are punctuated with vertical jumps in which he uses his straight body and directed force to pierce the space above him. To these two motifs – the sweeping arms and the vertical jumps, Nagrin adds a series of leaps as the dance reaches the climax of its energy and buoyancy. These leaps divide and delineate kinds of expressive effort in the movement, and they combine the two qualities – the open embrace of space and the piercing through it. The leaps vary the dynamics in the phrases of movement over the structure of the whole, giving it shape overall.

Nagrin has created these movements and their phrasing, and Clarke claims to have learnt everything she knows about making films from the process of shooting and cutting them.[37] Her idea for the film evolves during process. She says that she originally shot the whole thing on the beach and when she got the filmed material back she 'burst into tears. He looked like an ass prancing around'.[38] She was 'horrified'.[39] This is the first thing she learns – that space and the camera collaborate with the dancer to redesign movement phrases. The soft sand and limitless horizon, Clarke found, were not the best collaborators for conveying the dance's ideas. Rather than allowing Nagrin to embrace and pierce the space, they swallowed him and his agency. So, Clarke organised another shoot, this time in the studio, which allowed her to use the architectural confines to reframe Nagrin. The studio floor also gives him back his agency – as he pushes against its resistance he has a palpable antagonist – gravity – against which he takes action.

The next, and probably more important thing that Clarke learned from directing this film is about editing: that it makes and remakes movement phrases and in doing so shapes audience experience of event, emotion, image and sound into an experience of a coherent, rhythmically designed story. Clarke discovered, in making *A Dance in the Sun* that she could use timing, pacing and trajectory phrasing,[40] and her kinaesthetic sensibility, to move this film from being a record of a dance to a creative cinematic composition. In films yet to come, this sensibility will drive her decisions about what narratives to create and how to create them.

Some examples of this in *Dance in the Sun*:

The transition from spatial continuity to imagined geographies of dancefilm is made on the pedestrian gesture of Nagrin dropping his sweater, which slides off of his shoulders on the beach, and lands on the floor of the studio – a seamless and seductive edit taking us at once from the highly plausible (I'd take off my sweater in the sunshine on the beach, wouldn't you?) to the impossible pleasure of moving our actual bodies to where they long to be. In a 24th of a second.

Clarke's artistry of the edit begins at the start of the dance, but her first cut is awkward. As Nagrin lifts his leg in an adagio move, Clarke cuts to complete the gesture on the beach. This is the least effective of her cuts. It disrespects the principle that will be so evident later – that the edit creates or collaborates with the phrasing of the dance. In an adagio leg lift, the arc of movement is too slow, there is no clear originating impulse to propel the cut. An adagio leg lift is too undynamic to support moving the eye *with it*. So instead of creating a feeling of freedom and space to move, this cut and this gesture emphasise labour and its constraints.

Interestingly, this kind of mismatch of the edit with the middle of a sustained movement occurs over and over in Maya Deren's famed and undeniably germinal 1945 composition *A Study in Choreography for Camera*. Whether Clarke has seen this film or not,[ix] she very quickly exceeds its skill in execution.

As Nagrin moves forward, the camera pans with him. He drops down, out of frame and begins a jump series on the beach. A phrase of *side jump–side jump–forward leap* lands him back in the studio and here is the most effective of cuts. It is a visible and material action. It is a leap and a metaphor: he leaps across the spatial divide. The timing and work with directionality is what

---

[ix] Accounts differ on this question, but Rabinovitz, whose information is first-hand writes: 'Although Clarke had not yet seen any of Deren's films, *Dance in the Sun* resembles *A Study in Choreography for the Camera*'. (See: Rabinovitz, L. (2003). *Points of Resistance: Women, Power and Politics in the New York Avant-garde Cinema, 1943–71*. University of Illinois. p. 97.)

makes this cut so compelling: the movement up in the first shot, down in the next is dynamic. The cut lands precisely as his back foot leaves the ground, matching the action of his trajectory in relation to expectations of gravity and trajectory. So, as he leaves the beach he soars across the cut and into the studio space.

In the next sequence, Nagrin takes hold of the sturdy responsive floor once again for a series of running gestures that would not have been problematic to execute on the beach, but which would have lost their sense of directionality when done in a visually limitless expanse of sky. Clarke uses her low angle shot here, to compress Nagrin's emotive longing for limitless space under the roof of the studio, but also to magnify his form's stature. She cuts when he is furthest from the camera, to a high angle shot where he is even further from us, now compressed not just by space but by frame. The static camera creates a contrapuntal dynamic as he surges towards and away from us. Cuts around angles in the studio allow the dance to unfold as designed – we see it displayed in its optimal stage form, but not for very long. Abruptly, the movement quality shifts to a brief, arm-raised, stillness.

A small pulse of the arms here is followed by a cut to the sky again. This cut feels to me like an editor's solution to a coverage problem. The indoor dancing is the most formed, but Clarke has just given us three shots of it, and it is time to go back outside. However, there is no jump for her to use to propel us. The phrase of jumps as an idea has been completed. The pulse of upraised arms cutting to the sky is an ingenious solution. That gesture lacks the necessary propulsion to take us from one place to another on matched movement. Instead, the pulse asks a question about what the dancer is gesturing towards, and where their next onrush of energy might come from. The sky is a reply.

The camera's slow tilt down from the sky to the dune lines could be smoother, but Clarke's editing eye uses its slightly jumpy flaws as the downbeat on her next phrase of movement. In the previous cuts on jumps she has used the dancer's propulsion upward to connect the spaces in a jumping phrase. Now, she uses the little jerk in the move coming down from the sky to motivate a cut that grabs Nagrin mid-air and continues the trajectory downward and into a backward step. This coalesces in the same 'sky-reaching' vertical shape we have just left behind in the studio.

Nagrin squints as he looks out to the sea and drops his arm slowly again. This time the little pulse of his arms before they drop impels a step into a walking phrase. These steps are harder to cut with – they have a deliberate, static quality and the next cut is not to a human move but to the waves' move. This brief shot of water contrasts liquid flow with Nagrin's labour, and the shot that follows contrasts his slight vertical form with the broad ocean he faces. He keeps stepping: one forward, one side, pause, one forward, one side, leg circles outward. Forward, side, pause. Arms thrown upward and he steps back from the sea, arching his sternum to the sky in a gesture that has a distinct limit. He can only arch and splay his arms behind him so far before reaching a place where his spine pushes back, and Clarke uses this push back to propel her next cut. As arms spring upward from the resistance, she cuts so that they complete their arc back in the studio.

It is almost as though you can see her confidence growing with her cutting skills as she realises how cuts make movement phrases and where the points of resistance in the body – not just in the space – can push the dancer and the filmmaker into the next phrase, the next place.

The gesture of arms up, cresting, back, rebounding, is repeated in the studio from the low angle wide shot and two things are revealed by this repeat of angle. One is that Clarke and the team covered this dance in the studio from three camera positions and they are now returning to their first. The other is that Nagrin is giving an interpretation of a wave action with his arms and body. This gesture belongs in the studio from this angle because it is doing what staged modern dance can do – imitating the feeling of something which is not there, to convey that feeling expressively not literally. Nagrin circles and we are experiencing what waves feel like to him. As he repeats his arm cresting gesture Clarke cuts again using the same propulsion point in the gesture, but this time taking us out of the studio and back to the beach.

In the low angle shot of the beach that Clarke cuts to we only see torso, arms and sky; Nagrin is moving away from us, heading, it seems from the tiny slice of ocean visible at the bottom of the frame, out to the sea. Before he gets there Nagrin does a series of tilting gestures – *towards-away, towards-away,* and finally leaps upward. Here Clarke goes with him again. She uses the lift-off to propel the cut back to her trusty low angle shot in the studio.

In the studio, the dancing energy reaches its climax in leaps and tilts and leaping tilts. Back and forth Nagrin bounds – the low angle shot panning slightly with him and adding height to his elevation with its admiring angle.

The next cut uses a different directional motivator. It lands in the middle of a turn that starts facing frame left. The turn spins through the edit and finishes with Nagrin's back to us once more as he jostles with the edge of the sea.

The cutting and the dancing are partners now. Nagrin turns again, back towards us, leaps up, and a mid-air slash of the leg finishes its stretch, still mid-air, back in the studio. If it has not been clear before, it is abundantly clear now that Clarke has understood what she can do with dance, the frame and the cut to create a movement phrase that has its own significant form.

This is what she has learned, and what she will keep 'dancing with' in all the films to come: that the movement's phrase is hers to make. The phrase is what will convince, cajole and pull the eye and with it our emotional engagement with the movement's rise and fall.

Nagrin repeats his dance phrase, Clarke repeats her slashing leap edit and we are back on the beach when finally, the vertical jumps and the cuts come together and make sense of each other.

cut, jump, cut, jump jump, cut, jump, cut, jump jump

This is a phrase made of movement of dancer and movement of edits. The creative cognition that generates it is situated in the dancer, the camera, the cutting tools and the cutter. It is distributed, embodied creativity that unifies intentions and elevates action to significant form.

Now the cuts are faster but not just faster. They are also more staccato and unpredictable. Clarke has held her fire, observing but not contributing to the dance's counterpoint with the music until now. She has learned something else about making films by getting this far, which is about the phrasing of the whole, not just the parts. There is nothing especially original about building a crescendo in this way. However, by waiting to reveal what she can do with editing (not just with dancing), Clarke manifests her embodied understanding of the congruence of physical and emotional narrative phrasing.

The dancing slows, the climactic build was designed into the dance, but the cutting stays quicker than it was at the start – it shudders out of the imagined geographies it has created – beach, studio, beach, studio, beach, until Nagrin reaches for his sweater on the beach, lifts it in the studio and walks into the wings. Then he comes back, shares a wry smile with us and a has a cigarette with the accompanist. It has all been in his mind. Except it hasn't, because it is not film of dance or even about dance, it is dancefilm.

Imagined geographies are not an invention of Clarke's or even of Deren's. In the early 1920s, Soviet montage filmmaker Lev Kuleshov writes about and apparently (in exercises now lost) creates imagined geographies. The most famous of these describes an actor walking left to right in front of the Kremlin and another actor walk right to left in front of the White House. They meet and shake hands, apparently connecting the two edifices as though they are a mere five steps from each other.[41]

As I have written elsewhere, Kuleshov did not invent these techniques, he observed them as they were being developed by filmmakers around the world.[42] However, Kuleshov and his colleagues in the Constructivist Soviet montage movement, did substantial theoretical work around movement and meaning, and Kuleshov's explicitly extends into an interest in dance. He was interested in remaking dance for the screen for very similar reasons to Clarke. Clarke, as Bruce Bebb explains, 'started directing films in 1953 because all of the dance films that she had seen struck her as needlessly bad'.[43] Similarly, Kuleshov was 'vexed by the problem of putting dance on screen',[44] as Ana Olenina observes; in 1920, he lamented that 'the dance that lasted only thirty seconds on stage seemed to drag on forever'.[45] To solve this disjunct between the temporal experience of a live performance and what we call 'screen time', Kuleshov and Clarke both appreciated the distinction between, in Clarke's words, 'a dance film that was a record of an existing dance and one that was choreographed for the camera'.[46] Given this distinction – which is now axiomatic in dance filmmaking – Kuleshov 'urg[ed] film makers to recognise editing as the most powerful tool they have at hand'[47] in the cinematic presentation of dance.

Drama, documentary, dance, all of the above

One question that plagues screendance theory is whether a dancefilm is indeed a distinct form or is it simply a fiction involving a lot of dancing; or a documentary of a lot of dancing. The better approach to definition, I propose, lies not in determining where it fits within established categories, but in slipping under the boundary ropes of the categories themselves and bringing process and intentions to bear on analysis.

Dance in the Sun provides a clear instance of slipping under the boundary ropes of drama and documentary. It is clear from the careful design of the frames and coverage that the events which take place in front of the camera were not spontaneous instances of actuality but were planned. The events' durations are truncated in a way that is congruent with fictional screen storytelling, especially in the story set up at the beginning. Here, the representation of a warm-up and consultation about the day's work, actions which could, in actuality, take anywhere from ten minutes to an hour or two, is compressed into under a minute. The actions are symbolically sketched and concisely executed. In the dancing that follows, Nagrin may or may not be *actually* imagining that he is on a beach while dancing. However, even if he were, the force of his imaginings would not, within the laws of gravity and physics that we generally live by, be able to transport him to the beach. So it is fiction.

On the other hand, those actions that take place in the beginning of the film – consulting and warming up – are certainly actions that take place in actuality in a dance studio. Further, truncating them in this way is common practice in documentary and factual films. Having made and participated in a number of these myself, I can reliably report that actions like these are frequently repeated a couple of times from a couple of angles during the shooting process so that the editor can cut easily. In this case what may start as actuality evolves into a planned performance of the actual.

The dance choreography/performance is also factual. It is a pro-filmic fact that Nagrin, an actual dancer, performed the dance in the studio and on the beach. At the beginning, when they talk, the dancer, Daniel, and the pianist, Sylvia, use each other's real names. At the end when they smoke, they smoke because they are smokers.

Even the cutting between the studio and the beach is a montage practice with plenty of precedents in filmed actuality. Consider, for example, *Man with a Movie Camera* (Vertov et al., 1929), which suggests the connection of gesture across the whole of the Soviet Union is an actuality that exists whether we have the capacity to see it or not. Or the temporal ellipses of documentaries about the cause and effect of actions and work; as in, for example, *When We were Kings* (Gast et al., 1996) where sequences of preparing to fight are cut together with sequences of fighting. So it is a documentary.

In addition to the problem of pro-filmic inventions v. pro-filmic actuality, of which *Dance in the Sun* is sort of both, is a question I have discussed elsewhere, of 'who is the dancer'?[48] Is the dancer a person trained to represent a character as an actor does? Not really. There may be a character embedded in the dance's structure, but the dancer's dancing belongs always to that dancer. So, is the dancer themselves a documentary subject? Not really. The dancer is not the subject of the film, and we learn little about who they are beyond how they dance. So not a fictional character, and not a documentary subject. This slippage of position of the performer is one of the things which makes dancefilm a unique form. The film's narration is movement of dance in a cinematic frame, not movement of character in a diegesis or movement of a person in the world.

At this point the ropes binding the rules of the two forms, drama and documentary, dissolve. This is another thing that Clarke learned to do while making this first dancefilm – to ignore or dissolve the formal boundaries. Certainly this hybridity is a hallmark of much of her later work where she slips between, for example, an image of someone imagining to an image of what they imagine in *Bullfight*, or casting an actor who was probably also a real drug dealer as the drug dealer in *The Connection;* or documenting Harlem as the *not* fictional place in which a fictional character plays out his dramas.

Given that the distinction between drama and documentary seems to have been of most interest to Clarke in its transgression, the question of dancefilm form, and whether there are clearly marked boundaries or simply distinctive emphasis in their construction, arises.

In 2006 Douglas Rosenberg, Katrina McPherson, Richard James Allen, Ellen Bromberg, many other artists/scholars and I met at the first Screendance Conference of the American Dance Festival and grappled with the thorny question of 'what is screendance?' at length. One outcome of this conversation was a Venn diagram that mapped intentions and techniques of various kinds of screendance.

This diagram maps and names three approaches and sets of concerns, and notes that these may, and frequently do, overlap. Characteristically, Clarke moves fluently across the boundaries of these approaches. Looking at how and when she does this illuminates Clarke's strategic approach to filmmaking. Her hybrid approach to film form is not only a hallmark of her decades as a documentary/drama film director and editor, it is also a way of galvanising her dance cognitions and responding to the

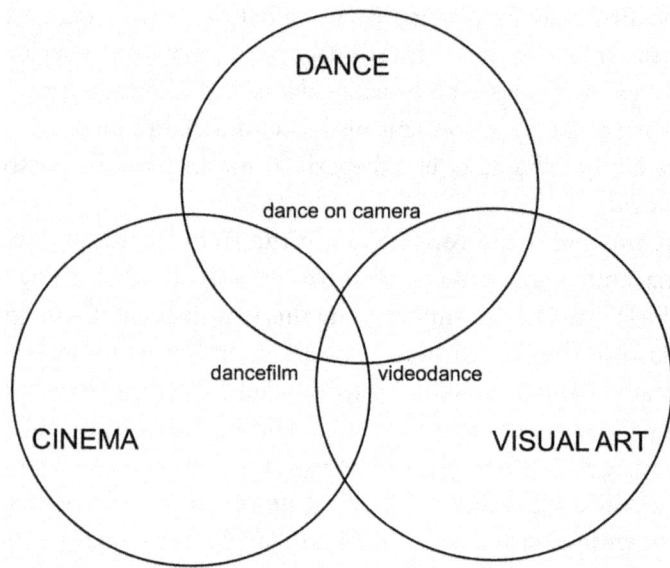

Figure 3.5 Diagram of three overlapping 'genres' of screendance: dancefilm, dance on camera, and videodance

affordances of the technology and cultures in which she was embedded as they shift and change around her.

Videodance

Videodance is defined in this diagram as prioritising abstracted aspects of form which may certainly include the forms of the body in motion, dancing, but which will not necessarily do so. *Videodance* makers tend to be versed in the theoretical concerns of visual art or performance art rather than film drama or documentary film. In the practice of this approach to screendance, the plasticity of the visual media is a consideration that may take equal or greater precedence over the dancing. Pattern and shaping of visual form, rather than narrative or planned choreography, guide construction.

In the 1970s and 80s, Clarke leant her aesthetic and technical interests into the affordances of videodance in works such as

Savage/Love (1981) and *Tongues* (1982). Here, as Rabinovitz writes, she

> processes the taped images through a variety of special effects that slow down, repeat, distort the image and insert similar images within the frame. Clarke heightens the expressive abstract qualities of the actor's performance, and in so doing, she transforms the material into rhythmic video dances.[49]

Similarly, the plasticity of video image and the concerns and patterns of visual art can be seen as her priority in her *24 Frames per Second* (1977) and *Four Journeys into Mystic Time* (1979). In these productions, time and space are often disrupted by manipulations of the surface form of the video itself. That said, these two videodance works also overlap with compositional strategies of dance on camera.

Dance on camera

The Venn diagram of definitions proposes that dance on camera refers to a filmed work that prioritises the danced performance. It gives primacy to the framing and editing of the dancing as a display of skill or expression of emotion. It is structured according to the needs of conveying the dancing and choreography to its optimal effect.

Four Journeys into Mystic Time (1979), a series of films that Clarke directed but did not edit with choreographer (and UCLA dance professor) Marion Scott, is not just videodance, it is also dance on camera. In these four videos there are many lighting effects, image-blur effects and chroma key effects, but they start when the dances start and end when they end. They keep all figures full frame for the duration, and the edits do not remake the choreography temporally or spatially.

The credits on these videodances go some way towards explaining this highly uncharacteristic set of films in Clarke's oeuvre. In one, *One-Two-Three*, the one most characteristic of

Clarke for its humour and character-driven ideas, she gets 'a film by' credit, but even in this one she does not get an editing credit. Without Clarke's editing, or her follow-through on the form and structure into editing, the films bear little resemblance to the rest of her outputs. Clarke's diaries in this period where she was teaching at UCLA reveal mostly frustration and even some despair, and to my eye, *Four Journeys into Mystic Time* looks like Clarke phoning in her artistry. That she abandons her lifelong commitment to editing the images she directs may or may not mean that she wasn't committed to making these videos. But it certainly means that they lack the creative techniques that would lift them from being technologically manipulated records of dances to being creative film works characteristic of Clarke.

As noted, Clarke, like Kuleshov, basically eschews the dance-on-camera approach. Nonetheless, this approach is visible within *Dance in the Sun*, particularly through the wide shots that convey the dancer's whole body in space. The material that is danced inside the narrative frame is also basically structured according to the logic of the choreographed dance. However, the invented geographies, the choreographic edits and the capacity to convey inner thoughts in material form all shift this work into the overlapping area between dance on camera and dancefilm, an area that Clarke expands and plays with in all the other films she directs and edits in the 1950s.

Dancefilm

Dance in the Sun, In Paris Parks, Bullfight, A Moment in Love (1956), *Bridges-Go-Round, Brussels Loops* and *Skyscraper* are all closest to the category of dancefilm in this diagram of screendance forms. They are driven by the concerns of montage in their design and execution. They involve characters, narratives and the shooting logics of cinema. Later, in the 1960s, when Clarke directs and edits most of her long-form works, her skilled use of these cinematic techniques is always fuelled by her choreographic sensibility and embodied kinaesthetic intelligence.

Coming straight after *Dance in the Sun*, *In Paris Parks* is a great example of Clarke using what is to hand to make a film that is imbued with a choreographic sensibility. Shirley, Bert and Wendy Clarke were in Paris, where Shirley Clarke had intended to make a film with Etienne Decroux. But Decroux didn't show up, so Clarke turned her gaze instead to movement happening in the park where Wendy was playing every day. Clarke says that '*In Paris Parks* simply establishes the fact that you can make a dancefilm without using dancers'.[50] I think it establishes more than that.

In Paris Parks establishes that movement trajectories from non-dance sources can be shaped into affective phrases – phrases that convey feeling through their timing and dynamics. And it establishes that these phrases can convey feelings of community, power relations and patterns of sociality in the world. These are formal and thematic concerns that reappear throughout Clarke's creative oeuvre. Even when she directs and edits a film with only one character, for example *Portrait of Jason* (1967), these thematic concerns dominate. *Portrait of Jason* isn't just about an individual, it is about that individual's community, power relations and patterns of sociality.

Five years after *In Paris Parks*, when Clarke puts together footage that was originally shot by documentary filmmakers Willard van Dyke, Irving Jacoby, Wheaton Galentine and D. A. Pennebaker to create *Skyscraper*, she essentially takes over directing the film by designing its story, characters and phrases of movement.

Skyscraper is a film about people working together, and is a film 'by' five people, working together. Clarke's name comes first, though. The credits are not alphabetical. She is 'first author' because of her creation of the rhythms, which are the real subject of the film. These rhythms are cheerful, optimistic, the rhythms of cooperation. Because they are constructed in editing, and unfold rhythmically with invented narration performed by actors, *Skyscraper* is fictional. However, it is also factual. It documents the construction of a real skyscraper (666 Sixth Avenue) by actual workers.

The invented voice-over is written from the perspective of the construction workers as they supposedly watch the montage that Clarke has cut from images of them working. In a passage early in the film, they, and we, see a huge mechanical shovel and its operator. One of the fictional commentators complains about how they were feeling the day the footage was shot. The other says: '*they invite us to see a movie about ourselves and right away you start complaining*'. These interlocutors into the film's world are not unlike Bob Hope and Bing Crosby. One is relentlessly upbeat, the other prone to dry commentary. His toothache is what he remembers of that day, but, he says, '*The shovel looks good*'. These characters frame the montage. But they are a fantasy version of workers. They perform a patter that is close to the way musical comedy characters of the 1950s were written: upbeat even when complaining.

Skyscraper exemplifies, throughout, the kinds of cutting that Clarke's collaborator Andrew Gurian calls 'Shirley-ish'.[51] At roughly fourteen and a half minutes in, for example, bystanders on the street look up. But before we follow their gaze, a truck cuts horizontally across the frame. Clarke is phrasing both the vertical and the horizontal moves. The look up sends our point of view back up the length of the skyscraper under construction, and the truck driving across drives us into the start of a rhythmic song. Singer Gene Mumford croons: '*It takes a lotta men, a lotta time to build that scraper high*'.[52] Shots that follow create a counterpoint between aspiration and effort that are entangled with each other rhythmically.

In another example, there is a montage of explosions. The detonator plunges. Its downward thrust propels the explosion that makes a pile of rock tumble. The rock, in turn, is the bass drum that kicks off a sax melody. These and many other sequences in *Skyscraper* consolidate Clarke's key ideas that montages of movement can create feelings and stories, and that these rhythms express the dynamics of community relations.

In *Skyscraper* we have uncynical Americana, uncynical celebration of work, uncynical making of a musical. *Brussels Loops*, as will be discussed in Chapter 4, is similarly optimistic in its rhythmic creation of community. However, in all these films there are passages or shots that reveal undercurrents of other concerns.

These films are mostly the best possible version of the 1950s, created through montages that circumvent strife and create largely harmonious images of community, work and play. In the 1960s optimism gives way to more explicit concerns with justice and race (see Chapter 5). Nonetheless, even as it shifts from optimism to anger, Clarke's perspective on these issues continues to be conveyed with movement phrasing choreographically shaped in editing.

Conclusion

To recap: Clarke's first film frames its danced expressionism and 'avant-garde' aspects with skilled Hollywood continuity cutting styles. This positions her, in the 1950s, as a dancefilm maker as opposed to a recorder of dance on camera. The mix of the aesthetics of dance and of narrative fiction in *Dance in the Sun* also demonstrates an interest in hybridising approaches of the avant-garde and the mainstream. As this continues throughout her career, the emphasis shifts more towards narrative and, later, back towards dance. This tension between the art film and the mainstream is a tension she will continue to navigate throughout her life, while always sustaining her deep embodied commitment to modern dance. Clarke's dancing cognitions shape choices of material and approaches to it even when the films ostensibly have nothing to do with dance. She draws on embodied knowledge of movement phrasing, rhythm and her commitment to valuation of the individual voices of a heterogenous community, to 'extend and embroider'[53] received forms with her own creative ideas and perspectives.

Notes

1 Shirley Clarke, as quoted in Clark, V. A. (1977). 'Interview: Shirley Clarke, July 15, 1977, Hollywood'. Typescript with accompanying cover letter of 8 December 1985, expressing intention to publish the interview in *The Legend of Maya Deren, A Documentary Biography* (Wisconsin Center for Film and Theater Research, Box 22, Folder 51); p. 13.

2   See for example Rabinovitz, L. (1983). 'Choreography of Cinema: An Interview with Shirley Clarke'. *Afterimage*, December, 8–11. https://www.vasulka.org/archive/4-30c/AfterImageDec83(300).pdf; see also the interview transcript: 'My life is one long electrical cord (with me crawling around on the floor trying to make a connection)'. Interviewer unknown, circa 1975 (Wisconsin Center for Film and Theater Research Shirley Clarke Collection, Box 12, Folder 2).
3   Clarke, as quoted in Rabinovitz, 'Choreography of Cinema', p. 8.
4   De Jaegher, H., and Di Paolo, E. (2007). 'Participatory Sense-making: An Enactive Approach to Social Cognition'. *Phenomenology and the Cognitive Sciences*, 6, 485–507, p. 489. https://doi.org/10.1007/s11097-007-9076-9.
5   Ibid., p. 489.
6   For elaboration of this idea by cognitive scientists, see, for example: Kirsh, D. (2013). 'Embodied Cognition and the Magical Future of Interaction Design'. *ACM Transactions on Computer–Human Interaction*, 20(1), 124–66. https://doi.org/10.12849/40202013.0709.0008. Stevens, C., and McKechnie, S. (2005). 'Thinking in Action: Thought Made Visible in Contemporary Dance'. *Cognitive Processing*, 6(4), 243–52. https://doi.org/10.1007/s10339-005-0014-x. Cross, E. S., Kirsh, L., Ticini, L. F., and Schütz-Bosbach, S. (2011). 'The Impact of Aesthetic Evaluation and Physical Ability on Dance Perception'. *Frontiers in Human Neuroscience*, 5, 102. https://doi.org/10.3389/fnhum.2011.00102.
7   Humphrey, D. (1959 [1984]). *The Art of Making Dances*. Rinehart, p. 15.
8   Ibid., p. 15.
9   Ibid., p. 18.
10 Ibid., p. 19.
11 Ibid., p. 19.
12 Nagrin, D. (1994). *Dance and the Specific Image*. University of Pittsburgh Press, p. 3.
13 See Hodes, S. (2021). *Onstage with Martha Graham*. University Press of Florida. pp. 80–1.
14 Nagrin, *Dance and the Specific Image*, p. 7.
15 Ibid., p. 7.
16 For extended discussion of the ways that editors' body rhythms shape editors' choices, see Pearlman, K. (2016). *Cutting Rhythms: Intuitive Film Editing* (2nd edn). Focal Press. https://www.routledge.com/Cutting-Rhythms-Intuitive-Film-Editing/Pearlman/p/book/9781138856516.
17 Nagrin, *Dance and the Specific Image*, p. 10.
18 Ibid., p. 10.
19 For discussion of musicians collaborative cognising, see Geeves, A., Mcilwain, D. J., and Sutton, J., (2014). 'The Performative Pleasure of Imprecision:

A Diachronic Study of Entrainment in Music Performance'. *Frontiers*, 8 (October), 1–15. https://doi.org/10.3389/fnhum.2014.00863. See also Millard, K. (2014). *Screenwriting in a Digital Era* (Palgrave Macmillan) for insight into the ways that screenwriting and film production processes are analogous to the structured improvisations of jazz ensembles.
20 Humphrey, *The Art of Making Dances*, p. 20.
21 Ibid., p. 21. For noting: Humphrey publishes these ideas, but they are common to the modern dance community in which she works. Humphrey is observing them in action around her and offering them as creative strategies, not simply prescribing them to novices.
22 Robinson, L. (1992), 'Ellipsing Time and Space'. *Daily Californian*, p. 12. https://cinefiles.bampfa.berkeley.edu/catalog/9662
23 See https://milestonefilms.com/collections/shirley-clarke for useful notes from Milestone directors Dennis Doros and Amy Heller about the collection, and for links to buy the DVDs or stream the films. *Dance in the Sun* is available on the Milestone *Project Shirley: The Magic Box* collection. It also has been posted by the Daniel Nagrin Foundation, here: https://www.youtube.com/watch?v=vSnfrPLr0zA.
24 Clarke, as quoted in Rabinovitz, 'Choreography of Cinema', p. 8.
25 Ibid., p. 8.
26 See, among other sources, Winner, K. (1988). 'A Filmmaker's Love Affair with Video'. *Chelsea Clinton News*, 28 April, p. 10.
27 For discussion of design of danced narratives by mid-century modern dance choreographers, see Cohen, S. J. (1977). *The Modern Dance: Seven Statements of Belief*. Wesleyan University Press.
28 For discussion of reactions against narrative dance, see Banes, S. (2011). *Terpsichore in Sneakers: Post-Modern Dance*. Wesleyan University Press.
29 Humphrey, *The Art of Making Dances*, p. 34.
30 Ibid., p. 39.
31 See Burch, N., and Labarthe, A. (1970). *Rome is Burning (Portrait of Shirley Clarke)*. https://www.youtube.com/watch?v=6etkUKAGCpI&ab_channel=joucy
32 Clarke, S. (circa 1978). Diary entry. Wisconsin Center for Film and Theater Research, Box 12, Folder 5.
33 For more on the uneasy relationship between narrative and screendance, see Rosenberg, D. (2012). *Screendance: Inscribing the Ephemeral Image*. Oxford University Press.
34 See Reynolds, D. (2007). *Rhythmic Subjects, Uses of Energy in the Dances of Mary Wigman, Martha Graham, and Merce Cunningham*. Dance Books.
35 Humphrey, *The Art of Making Dances*, p. 66.
36 Pearlman, *Cutting Rhythms*, p. 47
37 See Rabinovitz, 'Choreography of Cinema', p. 8.

38 As quoted in Winner (1988), 'A Filmmaker's Love Affair with Video', p. 10.
39 Shirley Clarke, as quoted in Robinson, 'Ellipsing Time and Space'.
40 Pearlman, *Cutting Rhythms*, Chapters 2 and 3.
41 See Tsivian, Y., Khokhlova, E., Thompson, K., Kuleshov, L., and Khokhlova, A. (1996). 'The Rediscovery of a Kuleshov Experiment: A Dossier'. *Film History*, 8(3), 357–67. http://www.jstor.org/stable/3815314.
42 See Pearlman, K., and Gaines, J. (2019). 'After the Facts – These Edits are my Thoughts'. [*In*] *Transition*, 6(4), 1–7. http://mediacommons.org/intransition/after-facts.
43 Bebb, B. (1982). 'The Many Media of Shirley Clarke'. *Journal of the University Film and Video Association* 34(2), 3–8; p. 3.
44 Olenina, A. (2016). 'Moto-Bio-Cine-Event: Constructions of Expressive Movement in Soviet Avant-garde Film'. In *The Oxford Handbook of Screendance Studies* (pp. 79–104), p. 87.
45 Ibid., p. 87.
46 Berg, G. (1967). 'Interview with Shirley Clarke'. *Film Culture*, 44, p. 53. https://cinefiles.bampfa.berkeley.edu/catalog/9652
47 Olenina, 'Moto-Bio-Cine-Event', p. 87.
48 See Pearlman, K. (2010). 'If a Dancing Figure Falls in the Forest and Nobody Sees Her …'. *Participations*, 7(2). https://www.participations.org/07-02-04-pearlman.pdf.
49 Rabinovitz, 'Choreography of Cinema', p. 8.
50 Clarke, as quoted in Rabinovitz, 'Choreography of Cinema', p. 8.
51 Gurian, A., in email correspondence with Wendy Clarke, 13 February 2021.
52 Music by Teo Marceo, Words by John White. See: https://www.imdb.com/title/tt0053282/ for full credits.
53 Humphrey, *The Art of Making Dances*, p. 20.

4

Editing Thinking

'Editing – really creative part – most satisfying'
(Shirley Clarke, circa 1958[1])

'The reason film can be called an art is due to the fact that it can be edited'
(Shirley Clarke, circa 1960[2])

'I developed into a good director by becoming an excellent film editor'
(Shirley Clarke, 1975)[3]

'if you know film, you know how important editing is'
(Shirley Clarke, circa 1975)[4]

'Film is a director's/*editor's* medium'
(Shirley Clarke, 1982)[5]

'Editing is the essence of film'
(Shirley Clarke, 1983)[6]

'film is made during editing'
(Shirley Clarke, circa 1983)[7]

'I never allow anyone to ever, ever edit. To me that's what filmmaking is.'
(Shirley Clarke 1988[8])

As this long list of epigraphs suggests, editing is not just central to Shirley Clarke's practice, it is her understanding of what filmmaking is. The film industry truism that 'films are made in the edit suite', is, to Clarke, axiomatic. Clarke understands editing to be part of directing, possibly even the most important part. In thinking of editing this way she follows her influential predecessors in the Soviet montage era, for example Esfir Shub who writes: 'A person who cannot edit should not make films at all'.[9] This approach was not the standard industry practice in mid-century America. The Taylorist "factory" model of filmmaking in Hollywood separates each 'job' so that it can be done more efficiently, and Hollywood directors rarely edit their own work as a result. Training of filmmakers tends to follow this model in the USA and Europe, where directors and editors are trained separately and the functions of the two roles are usually embodied by two different people.

Clarke, however, considered film to be 'a director's/*editor's* medium'.[10] She said:

> Most great directors also control the editing. A lot of them do it. I do both. I have people helping me, but I would never let anybody do the editing because that's really when I take all the wonderful pieces I have and create what I'm doing.[11]

What Clarke describes here is editing as part of authorship. Below I provide some key ideas about how this works before turning to close descriptions of passages in films that Clarke directed and edited. By finding language for the rhythms and phrases of Clarke's editing work, I aim to illuminate what is uniquely authorial in Clarke's editing, what her 1970s collaborator Andrew Gurian calls 'Shirley-ish'[12] about her cuts, that can not only be seen as a signature style but as a formal strategy for conveying meaning and perspective.

My look at Clarke's cuts also considers them as exemplary case studies for understanding editing as embodied and embedded cognising. By looking this closely at the edits, the ways that the movement in one shot is phrased in a rhythmic relationship to the movement in the next to create ideas and affects, I am pointing to the generation of cinematic ideas through and with the material and machinery of editing.

My argument about Clarke's authorial editing is that in the edit suite the movement in the filmed shots becomes the raw material for a choreographic process of composing movement into 'significant form'.[13] This form is neither natural nor necessarily entirely predictable when the film is being shot. It is, however, what makes a film coherent and comprehensible: an immediate, resonant, embodied experience of narratives, ideas or patterns. As I have written elsewhere: 'A film's significance is not just "this happened and then that happened." A film's impact is in the *way* that this, then that, happened, including how fast or slow or bumpily or smoothly or forcefully or limply'.[14] These rhythms are constructed in editing.

The choreographic process of editing involves responding to the filmed material and generating ideas with it. In other words, it does not occur before editing, or outside of the hands-on process.[15] It is thinking that is embedded in process and tools. Shirley Clarke's dance thinking, as described in the previous chapter, becomes editing thinking in the suite, and her edits are her thoughts.

That she is able to 'think' these thoughts into and through film form in a context when few women had the opportunity to make films, arises at least in part from her ability to fluently embed her cognitive actions in the editing gear. As the reels move on the moviola; and the uncut material moves across her screen; and her hands move across the controls; and her body moves responsively, in a little shift of weight, or nod, or a lean in or away; she constructs the rhythms, spaces and stories of the films she is directing.

I pause briefly here to fill out the picture of how this editing thinking functions in creative process, and the significance of rhythms in understanding stories and their subtexts, before returning to specific passages that illuminate the ideas and significations generated by Clarke's cuts.

Figure 4.1 Shirley Clarke in the edit suite. Photos by Peter Buckley, 1958. Shirley Clarke collection, M91-052, Box 26, Folder 7, Wisconsin Center for Film and Theater Research

Editing as part of authorship

It is not unusual to hear good editing described as 'invisible'. The American Cinema Editors organisation, for example, celebrates mastery of the 'Invisible Art' (americancinemaeditors.org). However, unless the film itself is invisible, the editing is not actually invisible.[16] We may not see edits, but what we see is the flow of movement (moving pictures, a movie). This flow of movement of events, movement of emotions, movement of image and sound has been designed, shaped and ultimately determined by the editor.[17] It is a flow designed from fragments that could be composed into many possible rhythms and thus many variations on the nuances of subtext and affect. Editors shape these flows through a process of making decisions about which shot to use, where, and for how long, which is a deceptively simply description of the complex responsive and generative work of inflecting actions and relations between people, objects and spaces with nuanced temporal unfolding and trajectory phrasing.

Editors often describe this decision-making process with variations on the word intuitive,[18] which is a catch-all word for knowledge and ability that has been acquired through implicit learning and experience.[19] Indeed, Clarke uses the word intuitive and sometimes even instinctive, to describe how she makes decisions. Intuitive is not incorrect.[20] However, refining this generalised word by identifying the implicit knowledge and capacity for expert judgement that Clarke (and all expert editors) activate in editing processes is helpful to understanding how editors are authors, and why Clarke resisted relinquishing her own authorial presence in the editing process.

One key aspect of what editors call intuition is sensory/aesthetic expertise that is a developed form of embodied simulation[21] or what dance theory would call 'kinaesthetic empathy'.[22] It is a heightened capacity to feel with and think through movement. Editors compose movement's dynamics into forms or phrases expressive of textual and subtextual actions, pressures, responses, moods and feelings. Which is a complex way of saying editors expertly see and sense what movement means, or could mean, when timed and juxtaposed with other movement.

Clarke excels in this form of expertise. Her dance training and her immersion in jazz music build on her intrinsic proclivities, or movement feeling. They heighten her sensitivity to actions and reactions, intentions and significations conveyed in movement. Clarke perceives, or kinaesthetically empathises with, expressive possibility in movement in a specific, modern dance and jazz-inflected way. Letting someone else edit the material she has directed would, in a sense, be relinquishing some of this direct, embodied access to the material. It would curtail the ways that she could feel with it, and thus alter the possibilities she imagines for it. This may be why she finds it strange that directors let other people edit their films. To her, this is a disruption of a key connection to the material. Clarke's connection to the material is a common experience amongst editors. As I note about the construction of rhythm by editors in other contexts:

> Some part of what they see or hear in the material's movement will provoke an empathetic response, and that part will be selected and juxtaposed with another part that also has a qualitative affect. Putting two shots together, each of which inherently has rhythm, makes a third rhythm, which is not the same, or even just the sum of the first two ... So, the edit begins to have a rhythm of its own. At this point, editors cannot simply recognize a 'right' rhythm. Their own internal rhythms must come into play to shape rhythm through an editing process. As editors begin to do more than neurologically imitate existing rhythms, we draw on rhythms known to us through what Arnold Modell might call 'corporeal imagination' (2003), *as well as* latent rhythms in the film material, to create the finished film's rhythm.[23]

Clarke's unique editing signature arises when her particular embodied responses to the movement she sees and hears spark what neurologist Arnold Modell called 'corporeal imagination',[24] but which dance theorist Dee Reynolds might call her 'kinaesthetic imagination'.[25]

I borrow the phrase 'kinaesthetic imagination' from Reynolds to describe the thinking involved in making decisions that shape movement in editing. Reynolds is describing the ways that choreographers use their own bodies in concert with those of dancers to invent expressive movement phrases and choreograph dances. I have adopted Reynolds' idea to describe the ways that editors use their own bodies in concert with the movement imprinted on the uncut film's material, to invent expressive movement phrases.

Movement phrases are 'compositions of movement into perceptible and intentionally formed rhythmically expressive sequences'.[26] We see and hear these kinds of intentionally formed phrases of movement all the time. So frequently, in fact, that they are often mistaken for natural or inevitable compositions of the material.

For example: conversations between people. To construct a conversation's feeling and narrative idea from disparate takes, shot sizes and performances, the editor chooses a shot with the kind of feeling and dynamics to be conveyed by one speaker and then juxtaposes it, with close attention to the precise timing of the rise and fall of energy and emotion, to a shot of the other speaker. Each piece of movement with its particular accents and intentions builds on the last, and the next, to form a dynamic phrase of actions and reactions. These dynamics carry the material's affective power. They are not simply conveyed by putting the text in the order that it was written or the actions in the order they occurred in actuality. The editor is a composer of dynamics, a choreographer of the dynamic trajectory of movement that creates meaning.

Over the course of the 1950s and 60s, the work that Clarke is editing moves gradually from being abstract/expressive dance, where the movement phrasing is responsive to the movement of dancers; to poetic forms of documentary where phrases are composed from movement of pedestrians or objects; to narrative films where the movement of characters in relation to each other, their environments and their narrative challenges conveys the ideas.

Having looked closely at the phrasing of dance in the previous chapter, I turn now to look at the editing of abstract movement in *Bridges-Go-Round* (1958); the creative documentary montage in *Brussels Loops* (1958); and the opening scene of *The Cool World* (1963), in which Clarke creates an image of a dynamic community through a hybrid of continuity and thematic montage. What interests me here is Clarke's particular way of thinking with the material. What she sees and designs as phrases of movement that create rhythmically heightened impressions of ordinary gestures.

She thinks with her hands and tools and the filmed material, to create a world in unique, 'Shirley-ish' motion. She does this in film editing, not staged dance, in part because, as she says: 'The medium of film became much more intriguing and exciting than just dance in terms of action and passivity. Dance for me started to be too limited. There were too many other things that danced.'[27]

Bridges-Go-Round

My first case study is one of the best-known films directed and edited by Clarke, *Bridges-Go-Round* (1958). Originally shot as potential material for one of the *Brussels Loops*, the composition of steel girders and spans that Clarke generated in editing was not included the Loops exhibitions at the 1958 World's Fair, possibly because the material was too abstract/non-figurative. The abstraction was embraced in the art film circuits, though, and *Bridges-Go-Round*,[28] is now often used as an exemplar of abstract/ expressionist movements in film and of women's work within those movements. It is also used as a teaching tool for demonstrating the power of music to influence visual perception: because two different, complete, scores were composed, synchronised and produced for *Bridges-Go-Round*, one by Teo Macera and one by Louis and Bebe Barron. Both scores are included, one after the other, in the currently distributed version of the final film.

Bridges-Go-Round continues Shirley Clarke's work of making dancefilm without dancers – something well established in *In Paris Parks* (1954), but here continued into non-human realms. Clarke has, by the time of making *Bridges-Go-Round* written and spoken a lot already about this 'new kind of dance' that makes use of the 'fabulous technical devices of film and takes full advantage of the limitless dimensions of time and space offered by the film medium. This kind of dance is made for film and can exist only on film.'[29]

Writing some time after making *Bullfight* (1955), her third dancefilm, Clarke lists many things still to be explored in dance filmmaking, including lenses, shots sizes, colour ('not representationally but for emotional and kinetic affect'), uses of space, backgrounds, props and sets, 'cutting and editing on various levels of co-existing reality and fantasy'; and, especially salient for discussion of *Bridges-Go-Round*, 'the use of sound track, as I feel sure it should be used, to make you <u>see</u> better' (emphasis in original).[30]

As noted, the version of *Bridges-Go-Round* that is on the Milestone collection *Project Shirley: The Magic Box* presents the whole film twice, once with each score composed for it. However, since both the scores made for *Bridges-Go-Round* responded to the visual edit, and were composed after the completion of the edit, it is useful to look first at a moment in the composition without music, to see what Clarke was seeing and how she was composing the visuals.

Taking an early sequence starting just after the titles at 27 seconds:

One strong stone vertical tower of the Brooklyn Bridge dominates the image. The tower towers. It presses towards us as the camera zooms in. The semi-opaque overlay of sparkly water softens its menace but increases its mystery. A second tower fades in, nearly meeting its twin in a softened collision. The towers start the visual melody of verticals that will be composed rhythmically, in a range of contrasts and congruences with the horizontals of the girders and the roadways, and the diagonals of the arches and suspension cables. If the towers had a sound in this visual jazz band, they would perhaps be the trumpet's long, high, sustained notes.

Diffuse patches of wavering light rain diagonally down on the towers in a semi-opaque overlay of a shot of the water's sparkling surface. Sparkles of light on water augment the verticals. Give the towers a sense that they are set in viscous space. Space that has body, is fluid, and will persist in movement, impervious to the immobile stone. The first tower's press towards us is through the Z-axis of the image (depth), an axis that will be used sparingly in the composition. Much more dominant are Y-axis verticals, X-axis horizontals. These are the lead instruments. They are shaded or punctuated by diagonals which, like snares or bells, accent them.

But this is just how I see it. I watch the pattern with the music off and see phrases of movement that 'plays' the horizontals as voices in counterpoint to the vertical's melodic line. The bridge spans (which are still) are made into movement through the camera's glide or lift across them. The shots pick up each other's notes and carry the energy in a different direction.

When watching in silence, we see movement in shots as Clarke saw it in the edit suite. We can only see the parts of the shots that she picked out and included, not the full arc of movement available in the shot or what she excluded. However, seeing her composition in silence is nonetheless an experience of movement as she would have seen it when sensing the possibilities latent in those more extended pieces of material. She would have watched the whole shot and marked, with a grease pencil, selected segments as possible montage pieces to be used in the creation of a rhythmic phrase of movement.

The way that Clarke lines up the verticals so that they relay my attention from one shot to the next; the horizontals so that they drive me to the punctuation points the verticals make; the diagonals so that they interrupt the forward momentum, but gently, gliding or curving my eye across the image's planes; are all visible when seeing the composition unadorned by the movement of sound. Clarke seems to be almost hearing the visual movement and composing it geometrically, like music.

She is making phrases of repetition and punctuation that will develop, like a jazz improvisation, on themes and variations in collisions and connections of vertical, horizontal and diagonal lines of movement.

The verticals, horizontals and diagonals are gestures in time and space. Their movement is derived from movement of the camera, movement of the eye around the frame, and movement from shot to shot. None of these kinds of movement is in the bridge itself, but Clarke is making the bridge 'dance' with her editing.

Once Clarke has selected segments of shots and composed them into sequences, it is possible to 'hear' the movement of her composition in many ways. By ratifying two very different scores for the same film, Clarke embraced the fact that different composers see and 'sound' these rhythms differently, and in so doing create a different movement of the viewer's attention.

The presence of two scores makes *Bridges-Go-Round* excellent fodder for discussion of the relationship of images and music. The two scores each cause the viewer to see the film differently, to 'see better'.[31] My interpretation of what Clarke means, in this case, by 'see better' is that sound–image juxtapositions create a stronger or more immediate impression of patterns, dynamics and rhythms in the visuals. When seeing sound and image synchronised, we become entrained to the visual and aural rhythms combined. The synchronised score and visual movement complement each other and co-create each other's significance.

Comprehensible abstract rhythms and patterns are generally more directly apprehensible to people in music than they are in movement, and so music can perceptually shape images in a way that images cannot perceptually shape music. This is what becomes evident when viewing *Bridges-Go-Round* twice, once with each of its scores. The music directs the eyes differently in each case, and Clarke seems to enjoy the playful possibilities that the different sound/images juxtapositions offer. *Bridges-Go-Round*, with its two scores, seems to be an instruction to the audience about how we could get better at seeing and hearing the conjunction of image and sound.

Brussels Loops

Brussels Loops, is a series of films first screened in the American Pavilion of the Brussels World's Fair in 1958, where they were projected on walls in continuous loops that visitors experienced from a moving platform at the centre of a vast hall. The impression would have been one of the United States in motion, and no

Figure 4.2 Shirley Clarke editing with splicer and Moviola, circa 1966. Shirley Clarke collection, M91-052, Box 25, Folder 9, Wisconsin Center for Film and Theater Research

visitor ever had exactly the same experience as anyone else. Clarke was one of the filmmakers, working alongside D. A. Pennebaker, Richard Leacock and Willard van Dyke. She directed some of the 'Loops' and edited others. She did not edit all of them, but she did edit all the ones she directed, and her signature style is particularly visible in this moment in the *Loops*.[32]

We see a pair of men's polished leather shoes of the lace-up 1950s style. The shot tilts up to show a handshake between two white men – firm, certain and square. The momentum of the pumping hands propels a cut to another young white man. He lifts his hand to his hat and springs to his feet, as though the cut between the shots is the downbeat at the start of a tune. Which, of course, it is. But it's a visual tune, one played by Clarke's hands as she joins the frames and spins the moviola. The young man leans into the visual music he is there to make by reaching out to shake the hand of an acquaintance who strides into view. Sunlight warms the easy-going, well-dressed white folk and the friendly connection of white hands, dark suits, white faces, dark hats.

In the embodied and embedded editing process, Clarke might have hummed along with the movement she was seeing and shaping.[33] Her mental, or possibly even vocalised, song would have been something like: *tilt-up stand-up*, a rhythm of rising inflections. Or she might have bobbed her head ever so lightly with the *up-down up-down* of the handshakes. But I think that what really makes the cut 'Shirley-ish'[34] is that it is contrapuntal, composed of two rhythms. What she made – what we see – is a phrase that goes like this: *tilt-up, pump-up-down-up-down-up-down / hat-tip, stand-up, pump-up DOWN*.

The hat-tip is also the first note of the new measure – the shot that resolves the handshake rhythm with a firm *DOWN* also starts the melodic line of hat-tipping. In the shot right after the *white hands-dark suits-white faces-dark hats*, the hat motif is carried on. An older man stands up, tipping his hat downwards and off his head to greet a woman. He and the woman lean in to converse, and another cut brings us to a scene of two white ladies doing the same. They carry on a pleasant conversation for a word or two before Clarke cuts yet again, returning to her original motion motif. As two (new) white men shake hands, the tall trees behind them underscore the vertical *up-down* of their hands, their suits and smiles.

Clarke has set up this rhythm for a purpose, as the next shot reveals. She is not just making a pleasant tune of congenial handshakes and head nods, she is creating a pattern into which she now seamlessly introduces a Black man. I think that Clarke's point, made with the continuation of the easy-going rhythms that unfurl across the screen and now include people of different shades of skin and ethnic background, is that integration could be easy and accepting. It does not need to be remarkable, unusual, or disruptive. 'There it is', she seems to say with the edit, 'integration can be an easy rhythm'.

In the context of the racially segregated, violent and oppressive USA of the 1950s this kind of statement was profoundly aspirational.

120 Shirley Clarke: Thinking Through Movement

It would likely pass by unremarked in the cultural context of filmmaking of the 2020s. However, clearly the change of attitudes that Clarke was modelling with her creative rhythmic phrasings have not yet actually become the norms she hoped and worked for.

Clarke is not introducing a Black man into the rhythms to say, naively, that all is well with race in America. She knows it is not, and racial oppression and inequality are central preoccupations throughout her life. Rather, what she is doing by weaving this element into the rhythms she is constructing, is offering a rhythmic proposal to the world. This is how it could be, she says, rhythmically. These dynamics *could* be normalised. They can be created in film as flows of integrated movement, and modelled here, to be created in life.

Clarke's optimism is not normalised, however, and it would not be an exaggeration to say her edited construction of racial

Figure 4.3 Shirley Clarke on the street in Harlem during the shoot of *The Cool World*. Photo by Leroy McLucas, circa 1963. WCFTR film title photograph file, PH 7162, *The Cool World*, Box 108, Folder 32, Wisconsin Center for Film and Theater Research

dynamics moves from cheerful to confrontational as she moves from the 1950s to the 1960s. In five years, her optimistic editing, and the possibilities for warm and welcoming racial integration that she cuts together for the 1958 World's Fair, becomes more enraged, active and creative in making its points about race in America. I turn now to the opening of *The Cool World* (1963) for a look at how this happens.

The Cool World (Opening)

The final case study for articulating how Clarke's editing shapes cinematic movement to generate ideas is *The Cool World*, a radical and insufficiently recognised film directed and edited by Shirley Clarke. My analysis looks closely at the opening of the film to identify how its movement phrases, as shaped in editing, convey or create experiences of community, space and subtext – experiences that cannot be created on paper or even in shots until the shots are edited.[35]

My analysis also notices that editing is the process of authoring these movement sequences that comprise what has been called the 'cinematic expressive movement'.[36] These phrases don't exist when the film is directed, although the director has actively conducted the movement of camera and performers' embodied actions that imprint their individual rhythms on the film strip. However, the significance of the movement that has been inscribed, by multiple agents, is at least partially dormant until finally choreographed in editing.

Through the close description of a scene from *The Cool World* that follows, I am aiming to describe not the cuts she makes, but the world. Clarke's mature signature as a director, her authorial style, is visible through her edited patterns of movement, her juxtapositions and associations, and her spatial and temporal compositions. Editing, in other words, *is* the generation of her film style.

The Cool World was Shirley Clarke's second feature film. It is often called a hybrid, because its startling look at the actual streets of Harlem in 1963 is mixed with a fictional storyline in a method similar to that of the Italian Neorealists Clarke admired. This film was also Frederick Wiseman's first foray into filmmaking. As is evident from multiple documents held in the Clarke's archives (in the Wisconsin Center for Film and Theatre Research) Wiseman, a lawyer turned producer, and Clarke did not have an especially smooth process or trusting relationship. Since his company owns the rights to the film, Wiseman has let his animosity be known by tightly controlling screenings and blocking offers of wider distribution for almost five decades since *The Cool World*'s original release and few years of distribution. I watched it on a 16mm print at the New York Public Library, but the excerpt I analyse below is available in a somewhat degraded and French subtitled version on YouTube.[37]

Nb. Unless otherwise specified, everyone in this sequence is Black. Only the cops are white.

>CUT
>
>*'And you wanna know the truth about the white man?'*[i]

The film opens on a man's face. He's yelling at us. Accusing. Berating. Calling us out.

>*'The white man is the devil. The Black man is the original man.'*

Framed in isolation, an angry, vehement, righteous Black face against a blown-out white of sky or stone. Actor Richard Ward is playing the Street Speaker whose rasping shout sets the record straight.

>*'... he is the maker and the owner of the universe and from him all others come.'*

---

[i] All text in italics in this section is the speech given by the character called 'Street Speaker' in *The Cool World*. The role of *Street Speaker* is played by actor Richard Ward. Unlike some of the other people who are seen in this sequence, *Street Speaker* is not a real person who just happened to be there. His speech is scripted, his presence planned.

A slow pull back. Shoulders, suit and tie. The corner of the building on whose steps he stands. The top of a head just below him nods.

'Brown. Yellow. Red and White.'

Other voices chime affirmations.

'Brothers'

Glaring at the right edge of the frame the Speaker growls and demands of his unseen audience:

'listen to me.'

CUT.

Profile, four listeners, tightly packed in a mid-shot. Black men. A street in Harlem stretches behind them. The stoop in the back looks connected – same stone, same style – to the one the preacher stands on. On the far left of the frame, the likely owner of the nodding head. Still left, but not so far, a man in a white shirt. Arms crossed. Terse nods. Unseen gritted teeth tense the muscles of his posture. Eyes intent on the speaker, who is out of frame but whose voice prevails. Foreground centre, a heavier shape. Dark head, dark suit. He nods. Shifts his weight and reveals another man behind him, same bulk, dark suit. Their nods are synchronised – they hear, believe and respond to the same thing. The man behind them, filling the right edge of the frame, nods in counterpoint, rhythmically syncopating and expanding the wave of agreement. The five of them make a crowd. Assembled around urgent words.

'White is but the absence of colour.'

CUT.

Four other men. Same street in reverse angle? Possibly. Probably. Behind the scenes photos suggest that it is. The colours and the light match. The building's materials are different, but they could be in reality, since this is a reverse shot. The eyelines of the listeners clearly match, and the voice continues. So, the magic trick is set up. We are primed. The eyelines, the frame size, the composition of the crowd, the continuing sound, make the edit itself 'invisible' to us. By which I mean that instead of seeing the cuts, we see the scene compiled by the cuts. We experience it not as a shot of four men followed by a shot of four men, but a gathering of eight. And, crucially, possibly many more men are implied, shifting, listening, nodding. There is no wide shot and the two mid-shots cut together do its work. Clarke is deliberately withholding information about the size of the crowd because she has a larger point to make, which is that any- and everyone in Harlem is affected by this speech. So in two shots she makes us infer a crowd of unknown size, one that feels big and tightly compacted.

Watch closely now.

At the centre of the second shot of listeners, a tall man in a hat turns to look towards the camera.

> '... hence the white man is incomplete ...'
>
> CUT
>
> '... and imperfect.'

A white cop.

The magic trick is done. The hat man's eyeline, the pace of his turn, are completed by a cut to a white cop standing exactly where he looks to. Which, on reflection, we know is impossible. Because that is where the camera is standing. So where is the cop standing?

The editing has just constructed a phrase of movement: Speaker–listeners–listeners–cop. If I were a better writer, I could make that phrase more palpable with syllables and words. But the clunky writing is, in a sense, my point. The editing has constructed a phrase not with words on a page, but with movement.

It is well known that editing constructs spatial continuity. That eyeline matches, and matches on action are the tools of the conjuring trick, the misdirection that makes the disparate elements feel like a single flow. They are what pulls the eye away from the join. What convince us there is, in fact, no join. That it is 'seamless'. We know all this from years of Hollywood films. But what director-editor Shirley Clarke does next with it is unique to her.

The cop doesn't flinch. He shifts his weight to the left and the camera slides off to the right. A tension-creating counter-move. In the crew's parlance that is just a counter-move of the camera. In a peaceful street protest, it is a *counter-move*. It counters the cop by moving off him. It counters his presence by replacing him with a Black man who looks further to the right as the speaker continues.

'A true knowledge of black...'

CUT

'and white...'

Here, in the 'crowd' (three figures in this shot, dominated by a man's face), is the first woman we've seen. She looks up. Adds her gesture to the movement phrase being composed. Think of it as an invisible ball of energy.[38] The man's look left-to-right throws the energy. She 'catches' and transforms it by looking down-to-up. That is the edit's job. Left-to-right-to-down-to-up. The movement phrase is being built. Does his 'throw' to her instigate her catch in real life, the way someone looking over at you might cause you to look up? The edit phrase instils acceptance of that belief before we ever ask ourselves that question. The phrasing of movement across the cut becomes one 'story'. The people listening become one community. Connected by this invisible ball of energy they seem to throw between them. The energy is comprised of gesture, word and frame in crafted juxtaposition. That is the editor's job. To compose the timing, pacing and trajectory phrasing[39] of movement so that the energy of the physical action in one shot appears to cause or 'launch'[40] into another.

Attend then, to where Clarke takes us next. She uses the ampliation of gesture and energy to create a bigger idea. What we see next through the selection, limitation and phrasing of movement across shots is the work of a director composing her idea through her own embodied, choreographic, editing process.

The 'idea' here is that a whole community of people in Harlem, whether present or not, are affected by the speech. They are, and know themselves to be, described by it and connected to it. They and the speaker are in dialogue, amplifying each other. This is a big idea, that a community is connected by this incendiary rhetoric and yet still functioning as a warm and generous community. This big idea is created in a matter of seconds, by movement phrasing.

Having set in motion, through motion, the belief that the listeners and cops are all in the same place at the same time. Clarke continues to sustain the speech throughout the sequence, though the speaker is never seen again.

> 'a true knowledge of black and white...'

> CUT

> 'should be enough to awaken you to the truth...'

Foreground: a listening man. Background an approaching woman. She crosses behind the foreground man and glances up towards the camera. Her glance impels the camera...

> CUT

... to a whip pan blur that lands on two white cops.

> 'the TRUTH about the white devil.'

> CUT

The walking woman bites her lower lip. Continues walking into the foreground. Another glance connects her to...

> CUT

... profile of the two burly white cops. Someone walks in front of them. It feels like her, our walking woman. The pace the same, the direction the same. Only the top of the head is visible. Unlikely as it is to actually be her, it feels just like her. Again, belief is quicker than knowledge. The someone moves past the cop. The cop shifts and starts to look to left of frame, as though to follow, but,

> *'who after a hundred years...'*

> CUT

> *'of so-called freedom...'*

A cop in profile, walking, toward frame left. Half his face excluded, until the shot widens out. Once we've 'bought' that the shots are connected by a single trajectory of movement, it is easy to believe that this cop is one of the same two from the last shot, and that he is escorting a Black man away from the speaker with a controlling hand pressing on his back.

> *'is still persecuting...'*

> CUT

To the sixth shot in twelve seconds. For comparison the first five shots took forty-three seconds. Before this sixth shot, though, there is an opportunity to hit pause, and reflect on what Clarke has accomplished with ten shots in fifty-five seconds, five slow, then five quick. She has constructed a crowd listening to a speech even though we never see all the listeners in the same shot. She has positioned three or four white cops in the 'crowd' of Black people even though we never actually see the cops with the people. She has doused the entire combustible concatenation with the fuel of the speaker's rage, even though the speaker may not be present at all – he hasn't been seen with the people either. And she has revealed a truth about whiteness and Blackness in America. But she is not done with us yet.

In the tenth shot of the film, the man being 'escorted' away from the camera turns. Looks over his shoulder, gestures.

> *'is still persecuting...'*
>
> CUT
>
> *'Beating...'*

another whip pan blur and a man on a park bench reading a paper looks up.

> *'jailing...'*

Is he looking up in response to the gesture or the word 'jailing'? Or both? In fact, on the shooting day he would have heard neither. Even if it wasn't a different day and in a different location, the direction he would have been given, if any, would have simply been 'look up'. The juxtaposition of word and gesture is made later, in editing. The energy sails across the cut to prod his response, timed so that it *feels* like a response. Which, I emphasise, it could not possibly be in actuality. What is interesting here is that we are now moving into actuality. A series of twenty-five shots that could be from any place in Harlem, any members of the community. They are clearly not in the same light, or space, or even necessarily in earshot of the speaker. These twenty-five shots mix plausible listeners with people chatting, smoking, reading, sketching. They mix what seems to clearly be actuality with some things we learn later are fiction. The scripts and notes for shooting *The Cool World* (found in many boxes of the Wisconsin Center for Film and Theater Research Shirley Clarke collection) include notes about all kinds of shots that will be taken in different places on different days, and this sequence could have drawn its montage material from any of these places or days. These shots earn *The Cool World* its status as a hybrid. They take us later to a shot of the film's fictional protagonist, yet to be introduced, who seems to be listening too. Our easy belief in the continuousness of the first ten shots, our rising pulse with the rising anger and pace, segues us into belief in the continuousness, the connectedness, of the next twenty-six.

CUT

'... and killing our brothers.'

A whip pan lands on a face worn with time, a cigarette burning down between his fingers. He looks right at us on the words.

CUT

'God gave the white man the right to rule for s...'

A restless, heavy man turns his head sharply left.

CUT

'six thousand years...'

A white cop, arms folded, mouth set, surveys the scene. Looking right. Centre. Left.

CUT

'and that rule is terminating.'

The white cop's gaze throws to a Black man in mirror image of arms folded, mouth set. Whip pan off left.

CUT

'We should rejoice...'

A Black woman, hands on hips, chats to someone left of frame, she looks straight at us as she turns her head to laugh. Her companion's head juts into frame, throwing the line of movement to...

CUT

'... rejoice together.'

... a gap-tooth man laughs in delight.

> CUT

> *'For the time we are living in ...'*

A man in an embroidered kufi does not share his mirth.

> CUT

> *'is a time for reclaiming our own.'*

A huddled man lights his smoke and opens his posture to throw to ...

> CUT

> *'... our own.'*

... a young woman's open arms, that come together with a clap and a smile.

> CUT

An older woman responds with animated chat.

> CUT

Shoulders of a walking figure carry us across the gaze of another man.

> *'Together, we have suffered ...'*

> CUT

> *'... at the hands of the white devil.'*

This guy's cigarette is unlit. His dark glasses opaque. Still, you feel a challenge in his stare.

CUT

'Together, we have known the slavery.'

The speaker's exasperated exhale on 'slavery' elides with this gaunt smoker's exhale. The smoker glances up.

CUT

A big man, with a long, curved pipe sucks inward, exudes smoke, returns the pipe to his lips.

'Not only of the body...'

CUT

'... but of our very...'

A tall smoker sitting on a stoop turns his head as he takes a drag. Is that glimmer of an eye roll towards the pipe smoker? Towards the words? Towards us?

CUT

'soul.'

An artist's arm and back curved over the sketch he is making of someone's face.

'They have...'

CUT

'taken from us our dignity...'

Framed from slightly above, this woman looks good and mad. Brow furrowed; words spit through tight lips.

'as men and women.'

Her nod coincides. But for the different background, the different light, the implausibility of setting a camera so close to someone intent on a speaker, you'd be sure her nod was aligned with the speaker's actual words, not cut in later in a deft contrapuntal move.

CUT

Tilt down from a heavy grandmother's face to the clasp of her hands.

'They have given us their god...'

CUT

'But they haven't given us their hands.'

Tilt down along a poster of a pretty, white, Jesus, holding a cute white lamb. Then whip pan away to the grim lonely stare of a pot-bellied old man. He pauses. Looks down. Away.

'Friends!'

CUT

Someone says yes, but it is not the vibrant young woman who is as surprised by the camera as we are by the portrait studio she is in.

'Do you hear me?'

She turns her head to look.

CUT

'Then join with me in reclaiming...'

Children squirm and laugh.

CUT

'what is rightfully ours.'

Children look sceptical. One chews a string.

> CUT
>
> *'It's the devil. The white man devil.'*

A sleeping baby. Tilt up from the pram to a smiling young mother.

> *'Hear you...'*
>
> CUT
>
> *'together...'*

Duke, the kid we'll follow from here forward, looking in the direction of the speaker. The voice fades, Dizzy Gillespie's trumpet slips in, and we're off into the film's diegesis, which will bounce deftly between what could not be real and what could not be fiction, seeing, selecting, composing and framing the movement between and through the worlds. By phrasing the gestures in relation to the words and to each other, Clarke crafts a closely connected, semi-fictional community from a loosely connected actual one.

And this is her 'director's idea'.[41] The choreography of the edit is Clarke's textual and subtextual directorial idea – what she wants to convey about Blackness in this moment, about community, about anger and acceptance. About oppression and opposition. About moves and counter-moves. These are all conveyed in this short prologue to our actual story. A montage sequence created, as the best ones are, from an idea nascent in the director and editor's head, hands and 'kinaesthetic imagination'.[42]

Conclusion

Clarke's editing conducts and choreographs the movement imprinted on multiple discrete bits of film into the singular flow the viewer experiences. Her edited movement phrases are a source of affect and understanding for audiences. They gestate her film's style, reveal its subtext and characters, and the significance of interactions. Because there is no intermediary between her body and her editing gear, Clarke has enormous control over meaning, nuance and ultimately reception that editing produces.

Clarke is clear on the significance and power of this as establishing a film's style and the ideas it conveys. She is bemused by industry power-brokers who don't seem to get this. As she says:

> they allow women to be editors, which has always struck me as very strange, because anyone who knows anything about film knows that the very thing a film is going to say can be changed in the editing. The whole way a film is going to go can be given a complete switch by how it is put together. And they will give that responsibility to a woman and yet would not allow her, supposedly, what they would consider the highest responsibility as producer-director.[43]

Clarke knows how much power editing has, even if the Hollywood industry does not.[44] She knows she can use her choreographic sensibility to create phrases of movement and that these will convey her ideas and meanings. She uses her technical, kinaesthetic and conceptual editing expertise to get around the barriers to entry for women in film and to convey her voice and vision. With this in mind, I turn now to a chapter on directing. However, the chapter break is not intended to split these two actions of editing and directing. What I aim to show in the next chapter is how Clarke and her collaborators generate the raw materials Clarke will cut together through an improvisational, enactive process that tessellates seamlessly with the choreographic compositional processes of editing.

Notes

1 Clarke, S. (circa 1958–59). Handwritten notes on 'Analysis of *Bullfight* the story of this specific film' (Wisconsin Center for Film and Theater Research, Box 11, Folder 2).
2 Clarke, S. (circa 1959–60) Handwritten notes for 'Forsdale Lecture' (Wisconsin Center for Film and Theater Research, Box 11, Folder 2).

3 Shirley Clarke, as quoted in Murphy, M. (1975). 'Women in Film'. *Hollywood Reporter*, 3 January.
4 Clarke, as quoted in Murphy (1975), 'Women in Film'.
5 Emphasis in original: Shirley Clarke, as quoted in Bebb, B. (1982). 'The Many Media of Shirley Clarke'. *Journal of the University Film and Video Association* 34(2), 3–8; p. 7.
6 Shirley Clarke, as quoted in Rabinovitz, L. (1983). 'Choreography of Cinema: An Interview with Shirley Clarke'. *Afterimage*, December, 8–11. https://www.vasulka.org/archive/4-30c/AfterImageDec83(300). pdf, p. 8.
7 Clarke, S. (circa 1983). Handwritten notes in ORNETTE notebook (Wisconsin Center for Film and Theater Research, Box 21, Folder 3).
8 Shirley Clarke, as quoted in Winner, K. (1988). 'A Filmmaker's Love Affair with Video'. *Chelsea Clinton News*, 28 April, p. 10.
9 Esfir Shub as quoted in Kostina, A., and Dyshluk, L. (2016). 'Esfir Shub: Selected Writings'. *Feminist Media Histories*, 2(3),11–28, p. 22. https://doi.org/10.1525/fmh.2016.2.3.11.
10 Emphasis in original: Clarke, as quoted in Bebb, 'The Many Media of Shirley Clarke', p. 7.
11 Ibid., pp. 7–8.
12 Correspondence from Andrew Gurian to Wendy Clarke (13 February 2021). For further insights from Gurian on Clarke's methods and working processes see Gurian, A. (2004). 'Thoughts on Shirley Clarke and The TP Videospace Troupe'. *Millennium Film Journal*, Fall (42), 1–13.
13 See Gibson, R. (1999). 'Acting and Breathing'. In Stern, L., and Kouvaros, G. (Eds.), *Falling For You*. Power Publications.
14 Pearlman, K. (2019). *On Rhythm in Film Editing – The Palgrave Handbook of the Philosophy of Film and Motion Pictures* (N. Carroll, L. T. di Summa, and S. Loht, Eds.; pp. 143–63). Springer International Publishing. https://doi.org/10.1007/978-3-030-19601-1_7, p. 159.
15 See Pearlman, K., MacKay, J., and Sutton, J. (2018). 'Creative Editing: Svilova and Vertov's Distributed Cognition'. *Apparatus. Film, Media and Digital Cultures of Central and Eastern Europe*, 0(6). http://www.apparatusjournal.net/index.php/apparatus/article/view/122/306 and Pearlman, K., and Gaines, J. (2019). 'After the Facts – These Edits Are My Thoughts'. *[In]Transition*, 6(4), 1–7. http://mediacommons.org/intransition/after-facts.
16 See Pearlman, K. (2016). *Cutting Rhythms: Intuitive Film Editing*. New York; London: Focal Press. https://www.taylorfrancis.com/books/mono/10.4324/9780080927763/cutting-rhythms-karen-pearlman
17 See Pearlman, *Cutting Rhythms: Intuitive Film Editing*; Pearlman, *On Rhythm in Film Editing*.

18 See, for example, interviews in: Oldham, G. (1992). *First Cut, Conversations with film editors*. University of California Press. McGrath, D. (2001). *Editing and Post-production Screencraft*. Roto-vision. Oldham, G. (2012). *First Cut 2: More Conversations with Film Editors*. University of California Press.
19 See Atkinson, T., and Claxton, Guy. (2000). *The Intuitive Practitioner: On the Value of Not Always Knowing What One is Doing*. Open University Press.
20 See Grunditz-Brennan, K., and Pearlman, K. (2023). 'Creating Character in Editing'. *Media Practice and Education* 24(3), 235–52. https://doi.org/10.1080/25741136.2023.2172655.
21 See Gallese, V., and Guerra, M. (2012). 'Embodying Movies: Embodied Simulation and Film Studies'. *Cinema: Journal of Philosophy and the Moving Image*, 3, 183–210. https://philpapers.org/rec/GALEME-4.
22 See Reynolds, D., and Reason, M., Eds. (2012). *Kinesthetic Empathy in Creative and Cultural Practices*. Intellect Press.
23 Pearlman, *On Rhythm in Film Editing*, p. 146.
24 Modell, *Imagination and the Meaningful Brain*.
25 Reynolds, *Rhythmic Subjects, Uses of Energy*.
26 Pearlman, K. (2009). *Cutting Rhythms, Shaping the Film Edit*. Focal Press (an imprint of Elsevier), p. 30.
27 Shirley Clarke, as quoted in de Hirsch, S. (1968). 'A Conversation – Shirley Clarke and Storm de Hirsch'. *Film Culture*, 44–55. https://cinefiles.bampfa.berkeley.edu/catalog/9681; p. 46.
28 *Bridges-Go-Round* is widely available on YouTube: https://www.youtube.com/watch?v=2gxX74iGRTc.
29 Clarke, S. (undated) 'Notes on dance filmmaking' (Wisconsin Center for Film and Theater Research, Box 14, Folder 16), p. 2.
30 Ibid., p. 3.
31 Clarke, Handwritten notes on 'Analysis of *Bullfight*' (emphasis in original).
32 An earlier version of the discussion of *Brussels Loops* that follows was commissioned by Alix Beeston and Stefan Solomon for their groundbreaking volume, *Incomplete: The Feminist Possibilities of the Unfinished Film*. See: Pearlman, K. (2023). 'One Long Electrical Cord: Dance, Editing, and the Creative Unfinished'. In A. Beeston and S. Solomon (Eds.), *Incomplete: The Feminist Possibilities of the Unfinished Film* (pp. 211–25). University of California Press, p. 215
33 See Pearlman, *Cutting Rhythms: Intuitive Film Editing*, Chapter 6, for a discussion of 'singing the rhythm'.
34 Gurian, A., in email correspondence with Wendy Clarke, 13 February 2021.
35 A version of the discussion of *The Cool World* was first crafted for the 2021 special issue of *Textual Practice*, edited by Paul Sheehan and James Alexander Mackenzie. See: Pearlman, K. (2021). 'Editing, Directing and

The Cool World: Filmmaking as a Choreographic Art'. *Textual Practice*, 35(10), 1587–605. https://www.tandfonline.com/doi/full/10.1080/0950236X.2021.1965291. Reprinted by permission of the publisher (Taylor & Francis Ltd, http://www.tandfonline.com).

36 Scherer, T., Greifenstein, S., and Kappelhoff, H. (2014). 'Expressive Movements in Audio-Visual Media: Modulating Enactive Experience'. In C. Müller, A. Cienki, E. Fricke, S. H. Ladewig, D. McNeill and S. Tellendorf (Eds.), *Handbücher zur Sprach- und Kommunikationswissenschaft / Handbooks of Linguistics and Communication Science (HSK)* 38/2 (pp. 2081–92). De Gruyter. https://doi.org/10.1515/9783110302028.2081

37 Available here: https://www.youtube.com/watch?v=5WwfGUlH7i0.

38 See Pearlman, *Cutting Rhythms: Intuitive Film Editing*, Chapter 7, for discussion of 'throwing the energy'.

39 See Pearlman, *Cutting Rhythms: Intuitive Film Editing*, Chapter 3, for discussion of timing, pacing and trajectory phrasing.

40 For more on this idea of the movement in one shot appearing to cause the movement of the next, see Carroll, N. (1996). 'Causation, the Ampliation of Movement in Avant-Garde Film'. In *Theorizing the Moving Image*:Cambridge University Press.

41 Dancyger, K. (2006). *The Director's Idea: The Path to Great Directing*. Routledge.

42 Reynolds, *Rhythmic Subjects, Uses of Energy*.

43 Clarke, as quoted in de Hirsch, 'A Conversation – Shirley Clarke', p. 48.

44 For more on this question, see: Friedrich, S. (2018). *Edited By – Women Film Editors*. Princeton University. https://womenfilmeditors.princeton.edu/. Pearlman, K., and Heftberger, A. (2018). 'Recognising Women's Work as Creative Work'. In *Apparatus. Film, Media and Digital Cultures of Central and Eastern Europe* (Issue 6). [s.n.]. http://www.apparatusjournal.net/index.php/apparatus/article/view/124/276. Kaganovsky, L. (2018). 'Film Editing as Women's Work: Ėsfir' Shub, Elizaveta Svilova, and the Culture of Soviet Montage'. In *Apparatus Film, Media and Digital Cultures of Central and Eastern Europe*, 6, 1–20. https://doi.org/http://dx.doi.org/10.17892/app.2018.0006.114. Hatch, K. (2013). 'Cutting Women: Margaret Booth and Hollywood's Pioneering Female Film Editors when an Editor was a Cutter'. In J. Gaines, R. Vatsal, and M. Dall'Asta (Eds.), *Women Film Pioneers Project*. Center for Digital Research and Scholarship, Columbia University. https://wfpp.columbia.edu/essay/cutting-women/. Gaines, J., and Vatsal, R. (2011). 'How Women Worked in the US Silent Film Industry'. In J. Gaines, R. Vatsal, and M. Dall'Asta (Eds.), *Women Film Pioneers Project*. Center for Digital Research and Scholarship, Columbia University. https://wfpp.columbia.edu/essay/how-women-worked-in-the-us-silent-film-industry/.

5

Directing Enaction

Philosopher Evan Thompson writes that 'living is sense-making in precarious conditions'.¹ This chapter will propose that filmmaking is too.

In Chapter 2, I wrote about Clarke's perspective on questions of community, race and belonging being imprinted in the films she directed through a process of enactive cognising.[i] In this chapter I unpack that idea.

One reason for writing about Clarke's directing as enactive cognising is to develop another way of looking at the problem of whether Clarke was an extractionist filmmaker, taking advantage of the people, communities and cultures that are central to the feature films she directed and edited. Thinking of directing as enactive cognising offers an opportunity to see how Clarke is thinking *with* people, communities and cultures. This, I propose, allows us to see the films as the thoughts of everyone working on them, rather than merely an extraction of value, like mining, that then gets crafted into the will or voice of one person.

Before I start this complex dance around sensitivities and certainties, a caveat: while all film directing is enactive cognising, not everyone treats their collaborators well, fairly, or with intentions that can be recognised as good across all cultures and

---

[i] Enactive cognition is defined more fully in Chapter 2 as thinking, perceiving, assessing, creating and so on, through and with action in the world, not before it, and not solely in the brain.

times. Clarke is, of course, not always ideal herself – she was known for her rages, and it is certainly possible that some of her collaborators may have grievances about her.

Further, there are times where Clarke's enculturated perspective allows ideas or statements that I now find pernicious to slip into the work. For example, she is unreflective about using words like 'queer' as a denigrating term (as in a monologue in *The Connection* about a character named Leach (Warren Finnerty), and even (in the same monologue), denigrating women and minimising their agency in social interactions. The characterisation of the young woman 'Luane' (Yolanda Rodriguez) in *The Cool World* is painfully acquiescent to cultural ideas about women as property and willing collaborators in sexual violence perpetrated on them. While these things could perhaps be excused by her cultural context and the accepted norms of thinking about difference within it, they nonetheless are hard to take in a contemporary viewing.

However, it is worth noting that, contra common parlance of mid-century America, Clarke never makes racist comments or includes racist dialogue. On this issue she was not just outside of the norms of her times, but actively working on dismantling those norms.

Since Clarke's stated social justice concerns were with problems of race more than sexuality or gender, I will also focus on her creative attention to working with Black people and making films with them. I will look at the films themselves to see if their forms – the images, sounds and rhythms imprinted in and embodied by them – can reveal Clarke working through and with her collaborators in a way that imprints and affords their voices rather than extracting or exploiting them.

My interest in directing as enactive cognising is not simply in positioning the work ethically, however. I also aim to use this idea to strategically disrupt understandings of how film style is generated.

I will use the films Clarke directed and edited in the 1960s as case studies to demonstrate how a visual style is *directed* towards a common goal and, as a result, takes on a stylistic form identifiable with one person. By framing directing in this way, I aim to demonstrate that the style itself is generated through a distributed process and ultimately bears the fingerprints of many.

As part of this same strategy, I never refer to the films as 'Clarke's films' or even films 'by Clarke'. Rather, I describe them as directed and edited by Clarke, or films that she directed and edited. This is not intended to minimise the value of directors (or editors). Rather it is a clarification through which we can see what a director does and how that work of giving direction is a form of authorship through action and interaction with others in the world. Films are not, in other words, 'by' one person, even if that one person's style can clearly be identified in films they direct. Style is what directors *direct* and what they, *with* their collaborators subsequently make.[2]

In this chapter I will look at directing process and notice Clarke's particular approach to the enactive work of directing as a source of style and way of manifesting ideas on-screen.

The underlying question of writing about creative process, improvisation and enactive cognising in a book devoted to the artistry of an individual director is this: how does that individuality make itself known in films made through a process of responding to others? So, these two questions – can her enactive approach help us to address concerns about extractive filmmaking; and can we see how a singular artistic voice can arise from within a distributed cognitive process – are discussed in this chapter through the three feature-length films Clarke directed and edited in the 1960s: *The Connection* (1961), *The Cool World* (1963) and *Portrait of Jason* (1967).

The Academy Award winning *Robert Frost: A Lover's Quarrel with the World* (1963) gets short shrift from me mainly because it was a frustrated production for Clarke. Briefly, Clarke was invited by President John F. Kennedy and then-Secretary of the Interior Stewart Udall to direct the documentary. She did largely direct the shoot. However, due to clashes that are not entirely clear, Clarke extracted herself, or was extracted, or both, before editing was complete and did not edit the film. She comments in various places that she does not feel a sense of ownership over the film because she did not edit it. In the interview transcript 'My life is one long electrical cord', Clarke has one word for this film: 'Nonsense'.³

The idea that not editing means not having a sense of ownership is important to my argument about Clarke altogether, but specifically in this chapter about her work with improvisation and how she turns it into film style. As she says:

> Part of why I place so much in the editing is that it's at that point somehow I'm discovering the film. That I really don't know that well when I start off and have an idea in mind – that I don't know that well even during the shooting of it exactly what I'm up to. And that when I look at the material later and start to live with it, I discover what its possible values or problems are. And then partly pride, partly I'm not going to be done in – pushes me, drives me, into the editing binge where I will go sometimes eighteen, twenty hours a day, sometime for weeks and weeks on end, and not even notice it because while I'm doing it, I am so wrapped up in this thing, in the solving of problems.⁴

My point, and Clarke's, is that discovering the film happens in process. The director holds a vision but a vision is an amorphous thing, a mental state about which little is known. Manifesting a vision is a process of discovering more and more about what it is as it takes material form through the planned, improvised and responsive processes of working with people and creative problems in the world. I turn now to articulating a few things about this interactive creative process in general, and Shirley Clarke's in particular.

The key argument I'm proposing in this chapter is that making films is an instance of enactive cognising through a process of 'improvisation'⁵ and 'participatory sense-making'.⁶ Further, that the people and places through which this sense-making improvisation takes place make a difference. A big difference. My aim, as ever, is not to minimise Clarke's unique and significant expertise and skills, but to show how her particular, 'autonomous'⁷ perspective, skills and expertise are salient *in context* to producing ideas and film form.

To do this work I start with a quick recap on participatory sense-making as described by philosophers, and improvisation as discussed in studies of dance, screenwriting, filmmaking and jazz music. I then turn to dissecting an extended quote from Clarke about planning and improvisation that illuminates how her cooperative and collaborative sense-making was activated in the process of making films.

Directing: participatory sense-making in action and improvisation

Some of the underlying principles of 'participatory sense-making' are that cognition (which includes, as noted in Chapter 2, the full range of mental activity from perception through emotion to action) is 'an ongoing and situated activity'.[8] It doesn't happen before an interaction, it happens during it, and it doesn't just happen in the head, it is 'embodied action'[9] that happens between us, amongst us and in our shared environment. In this process, human cognisors are 'autonomous'[10] but not 'self-sufficient'.[11] We are profoundly entangled systems that make thinking possible and constrain what it is possible to think.

As cognitive systems, people, including filmmakers, are, as De Jaegher and Di Paolo note: 'not in the business of accessing their world in order to build accurate pictures of it. They actively participate in the generation of meaning in what matters to them; they enact a world.'[12] When De Jaegher and Di Paolo say we are not in the business of accessing our world to 'build accurate pictures of it' they are countering what is known as the representational view of cognition. Representationalism proposes, roughly, that we make mental pictures in our brains of the world, then make decisions based on these representations about how to understand the world and take action in it. By contrast, enactive cognition theories propose that we don't build pictures in our brains and then act on them, we make decisions and develop understanding through action. We are, in other words, actively generating meaning through actions in the world. Generating thoughts, ideas, understandings, insights, feelings and, in this case, films, are cognitive actions that are profoundly entangled with the world exterior to our brains.

Why does this matter to a discussion of filmmaking? There are two reasons.

The first is that asserting that film directing is an instance of enactive cognising is actually a direct challenge to the very common understanding in the film industry that a director's vision comprises a well-formed, a priori mental representation of a film in their heads.[13] Positioning directing as an instance of enactive cognition proposes that film directing is not a case of having a film fully form itself as a mental representation in the brain, it is a matter of creating pictures (and sound and movement) in the world, through and with others.

Collaborators commit to realising a director's vision, but a vision isn't a movie. It might more accurately be called something like a contingent aspiration. Contingent on a myriad of people and conditions. Aspiration as in a hope or a feeling, until materially realised. A vision might have a sketched material form as a storyboard or script or notes. It almost certainly becomes clearer and more fully formed in directors' imaginations as collaborators share visual references, ideas for shots and models of sets or costumes, and as casting and locations are finalised.

Through these processes, and even before them, a vision might have some palpable form for directors as glimpses of tone, moments, words, gesture, framings, juxtapositions, perspectives and so on that occur in their imaginations. However, in the process of materialising these, many unexpected, fortuitous, disruptive, creative or accidental things could happen.

Further, the material manifestations of each fragment of the vision has influence on what the subsequent pieces will be and how they interact. The vision evolves in response to the actualities. Every decision made about sets, shots, performances, time, money, priorities and more is thus a sharpening and focussing of the direction of the production, in that it narrows the focus of everyone working on it towards the same object and cuts off the 'roads not taken'. The director sets the direction, and the crew goes down the road the director points toward, bypassing roads not taken and pathways not pursued, to get to a place that does not fully exist until the end of the journey.

Then, in editing, as pieces of film are juxtaposed, they take on new significances. Story structure and rhythm are revised and created, and, as discussed in Chapter 2, themes and perspectives crystallise. The vision develops fully only as it becomes a film. Directing a film is, on this account, giving direction, focus and purpose to the enactive cognition of multiple collaborators, their embedded skills and embodied sensibilities.[ii] It is leadership in the distributed creativity of 'generation of meaning'.[14]

This proposition is substantiated by Clarke in many things that she says about filmmaking. In the quote I dissect below, Clarke writes of the numerous ways that this occurred in the process of directing *The Connection*, and I link her statements to the distributed cognition and participatory sense-making frameworks. My dissection of her quote demonstrates how her directing process developed more and more towards principles of enactive cognition as she became a more and more sophisticated director. Clarke seems to recognise, and her work to ratify, the notion that the more entangled her ideation is with the world, the more distinctive her films become.

The second reason that understanding filmmaking as an instance of participatory sense-making is that the word 'collaboration' has been an ineffective prophylactic against the

---

[ii] In making these assertions I draw on: my own embodied experience of directing (see www.physicaltv.com.au and karenpearlman.net); analysis of multiple making-of videos where directors can be seen in action making decisions through and with collaborators and tools; and post-film videos where directors explain their processes. An excellent example of a director acknowledging the distribution of ideas through and with collaborators is in this Vanity Fair video of director Emerald Fennell analysing *Saltburn* (Fennell et al. 2024) https://youtu.be/nlVtm5jrgoY?si=PkV2RuXWZm-88r9H.

insemination of film theory with ideas about sole authorship. The enactive cognition frameworks address misapprehensions about the lone genius director by demonstrating that what skilled members of the cast and crew of a film do, and their expert work with bodies, tools and each other, is substantive to ideation.

Recognising skilled embodied action as creative rather than 'just' technical or manual counters what cultural theorist Raymond Williams has described as the pejorative imputations of the word 'labour'. Williams notes that the word 'labour' which sits at the heart of the word 'col-labor-ation' is often used to divide people who work with their hands along 'class lines'. In this division of types of work, the 'operation of the technology itself' creates an opportunity for 'doubt whether such workers were truly part of cultural production'.[15] Indeed, in America, anyone involved in the direct handling of tools on a filmmaking set is referred to as a 'technician', a class that leads to exclusion from authorship claims in both the cultural and the legal domains.

However, the distributed cognition framework counters this by demonstrating that the labour collaborators do in the filmmaking process is not the execution of a fully formed mental representation in a material form, or the following of step-by-step instructions to assemble a pre-authored object that has an already determined form. It is, rather, the co-creation of images, sounds, rhythms and responses. Directors are important. They conceive and direct the enactive manifestation of these ideas through and with bodies, tools and context. Different directors do this differently and it is possible in some cases to see a particular director's 'signature' approach to directing across a body of their work. However, directors' ideas only come fully into being as they become material, articulated through an enactive process, distributed through bodies, tools and context.

This expertise, which is enacted 'on the fly', has been compared to jazz improvisation.

Philosophers and jazz musicians Torrance and Schumann connect enactive cognition and participatory sense-making specifically to jazz improvisation, in a move that is especially salient to thinking about Clarke's directing, given her immersion in jazz music. They write:

> It is perhaps not too far a stretch to say that the continual unfolding of the process of an organism's meaning-making encounter with its environment is like an improvising jazz musician generating musical responses that make sense in the context of her fellow players' (and her own) previous musical 'moves'.[16]

Improvisation and enactive cognition involve thinking on your feet, thinking with the world, and therefore thinking in time, energy, movement and space. The question here is what is special or specific about Clarke's ways of doing this?

I propose that two things make Clarke's enactive directing methods unique. The first is her dance-trained embodied cognition, and the second is the collaborators and concerns with which she works and the context in which she, and they, are embedded.

A brief note follows about 'dancing cognitions' (more on this in Chapter 3) before the rest of the chapter focusses primarily on the collaborators, concerns and contexts of her three feature-length films, starting with analysis of a quote from Clarke on planning, improvising, finding a way and responding in the work of making films.

Re: dancing cognitions, Clarke's dance colleague and collaborator Daniel Nagrin's writing on improvisation in his book *Dance and the Specific Image* (1994) sheds some light on the ways that Clarke's fluency with improvisational technique in dance becomes a skill set in directing drama.

Nagrin critiques dance improvisation methods that focus solely on *abstract* time, space and movement dynamics. He proposes that dance improvisation and composition need something more specific to make them compelling. His approach draws on the training of actors in human action and interaction.[17] This approach to improvisation makes use of dance technique (human action), but also specifies the particulars of a given interaction's context, the power dynamics, shades of intention, or responses to other's actions. These principles are especially well-suited to cinema, which is an art of time, space and movement, but also, in drama and documentary, an art of specific human interactions. When she turns her gaze to drama scripts or documentary characters in the 1960s, Clarke does not abandon her dance-trained sensibilities. She, like Nagrin, incorporates them. Clarke is thinking about, through and with human action and interaction, by thinking through movement in the world. As she says, in a 1967 interview with Gretchen Berg, she is concerned 'at all times, with the choreography of what is happening on the screen'.[18]

Plan, improvise, find a way, respond

Clarke frequently talks about skilled improvisation in her directing processes. She does not use words I use, like participatory sense-making or enactive cognition. She uses more functional words, like 'let it hit me and then respond' that put these concepts into action. She says, for example:

> Right from the beginning a film must have a plan ... Art is always improvised and always planned. It is a conception; and then you must go with it as freely as you can while it is happening – in the shooting, in the acting, in the editing. But you must always have a plan. I believe that an artist must have something to say and therefore he makes every attempt he can to find a way to say it. I don't go through life just letting it hit me, I let it hit me and then respond.[19]

There is a lot in this statement, including:

- the idea of a *'plan'*,[20] a script, or a structure on which to build
- the dialogue between the *'improvisation'*[21] and the plan,
- the understanding that having something to say is not enough, you need to *'find a way'*[22] to say it,
- and the notion that the way to improvise it, and to find it, to enact a vision, is to *'respond'*.[23]

To focus on these things one at a time:

1. Plan

In her book *Screenwriting in a Digital Era*, Kathryn Millard makes the case that filmmaking is a form of improvisation. However, 'Far from requiring no preparation, improvisation most often occurs within a loosely prepared structure'.[24] For Clarke, particularly vis-à-vis the creation of film style, the script is not a rule book, it is a 'prepared structure'.[25]

Millard refers to social psychologists who use jazz ensembles as an example of 'an organisational prototype'.[26] Saying that they 'propose that minimal structures bring projects alive. Minimal structures provide enough of a framework to give everyone a sense of a shared project'.[27] Over the course of the 1960s, Clarke's structures become more and more minimal, and some would argue that her films become more and more 'alive'. In planning *The Connection*, she worked with a pre-existing, eponymous, produced play and its cast on what, as compared to *Portrait of Jason* seven years later, is a highly detailed, prepared structure. However, Clarke says of the scripting process with playwright Jack Gelber that they:

> proceeded to work on the screenplay for months. We sat at the kitchen table in my little house on E. 87th St., and we would write down screen directions like 'pan slowly up to eyes then pull back.' I mean, endless camera directions, all of which were being paced out in a room all of 10 feet. But when we got on the set, it was not possible to make a single shot the way it was written. That was wonderful for me because I had to improvise and react emotionally to the actors and what was happening. It saved me because I found a style that was real . . .[28]

Note that they do 'pace out'[29] the camera directions. They get on their feet and imagine the *mise en scène* together, in time and space. But then the actual time and space of the set and the actors on the shoot day overthrow all of their planning. Clarke feels liberated by this. It gives her a chance to make sense of the world *with* the actors, the design, the crew and the camera. To create *with* them what happens temporally, spatially and kinetically in their actions and interactions.

This is a special meaning of 'plan' that draws on Clarke's embodied expertise in a way that is similar to a jazz musician's skilled encounter with sheet music. Clarke's advanced skills in making meaning with movement meet what she says is 'happening'[30] in people's rhythms and impulses. Like jazz musicians, each key person in the cast and crew is bringing themselves to the ensemble. Clarke directs them towards a coherent interaction and creative outcome. This outcome may have its narrative basis in a script or in those people's lived experience. Through a long, slow, deliberative process of developing the plan, Clarke comes to an understanding of the plan and her own intentions that allows her to all but abandon it. Because she knows it well in *The Connection*, or knows Jason Holliday well in *Portrait of Jason*, she can direct everyone's efforts towards a participatory act of creative 'fabulation'.[31]

2. Improvise

As Clarke notes 'Art is always improvised and always planned'.[32]

One thing that is improvised is what Michele Merritt (2013) calls 'social cognition'.[33] Merritt writes: 'our thinking is arguably socially interactive ... when we are cognizing socially, we are doing so in dynamic, transformative, and interactive ways, such that other persons involved are participants in the cognitive process just as much as we are'.[34]

Another way to describe this kind of social interaction when it occurs in a filmmaking process would be as a 'creative methodology' that, as Millard describes it: 'is process-orientated and privileges collaboration'.[35] Directing collaborators and the dynamics of interactions between people, the camera and cuts requires, as Millard notes, 'skill and expertise ... improvisation involves interacting with a given environment and other people'.[36] For noting, it is the *interaction* between people and environment that generates the movement through time and space, that becomes a film's style. It is not one person who gives orders. Thus, improvisation is a method through which collaborators imprint their own signatures on a film's style.

De Jaegher and Di Paolo have a nice metaphor for this kind of social sense-making that is particularly salient to Clarke. They write:

> our emphasis is on the autonomy of the interactors throughout their engagement with each other in order for the interaction to be considered properly social. For example, couple dancing involves moving each other, making each other move, and being moved by each other. This goes for both leader and follower. Following is part of an agreement and does not equate with being shifted into position by the other. If the follower were to give up her autonomy, the couple dancing would end there, and it would look more like a doll being carried around the dance floor.[37]

Clarke's films do not involve dolls being carried around dance floors, they are social dancing where each 'dancer's' autonomy is an imprint on the film's style. When Clarke is liberated by being forced to improvise, she is liberated to, as she says, 'react

Figure 5.1 Shirley Clarke on the phone circa 1960, presumably finding a way to get a film made. Photographer unknown. WCFTR film title photograph file, PH 7162, *The Connection*, Box 107, Folder 3, Wisconsin Center for Film and Theater Research

emotionally to the actors and what was happening.'[38] Or, as De Jaegher and Di Paolo might describe it, she and the actors could participate in 'moving each other, making each other move, and being moved by each other.'[39] Clarke's dancerly ways of being in the world make her especially adept at finding a way to say what she has to say in this process, which becomes a social dance of different tempi and dynamics in her different collaborations and productions.

3. Find a way

For independent filmmakers, finding a way to get a film made demands creativity, perspicacity and endless problem-solving.

Clarke's notes and written documents describing intentions and plans, script drafts, schedules and budgets, are a kind of paper trail that reveal how she finds her way through some of the challenges.

The notes are illuminating in two ways. In the first instance, looking at them sheds light on the intentions as they become articulated/known to Clarke herself. They also shed light on the ways that intentions become form and style – sometimes as planned and sometimes differently.

The notebook I look at here is one Clarke had while preparing to shoot *The Connection*. Its pages contain a mix that I often found in Clarke's notebooks: the notes bounce between the conceptual, such as ideas for shots or character qualities, and the logistical or 'technical' problems to be solved. However, when looked at as the embodied, embedded and enactive cognising that is necessary to 'find a way'[40] to make her films, it is evident that the conceptual and the logistical are actually a continuum of thinking through creative problems and possibilities. The technical is not 'just' technical.[41] It shapes the ideas by being part of finding a way to enact them with images, people, tools and the world.

One of many, many examples of how the conceptual entangles with the practical can be seen in in Clarke's notes on *The Connection* found in WCFTR, Box 14, Folder 2.

A sentence on the first page of this set of papers on *The Connection* reads: 'Opening of film – slow – conscious of camera's difficulty in know (*sic*) which way to turn – don't know what's going to happen next – c.man is good but just starting'.[iii][42]

This is clearly an idea about how the film should look and feel, how it should move in space. Clarke knows that the camera is not just an inert machine in this film, but the extension, the 'kino-eye'[43] if you will, of the camera person. In fact, the camera operator is a character in this film, J. J. Burden (Roscoe Lee Browne), but that character is often referred to in the script not as a man, but as the camera.

The notes, stapled together and written in pencil continue in this vein of annotating Clarke's aesthetic or dramatic intentions. There are scraps of ideas for shots, lights and cuts through to page 2 which begins with 'Find moments for talk over talk'[44]. This is an idea about sound and the rhythms of a room crowded with increasingly antsy men, more and more unsettled as they wait for their dealer to arrive with the junk they need. It is also, of course a technical note to do with positions of microphones and how the sound will be balanced in the final sound mix.

[iii] It is interesting to me that Clarke takes the trouble to write down that the 'c.man is good but just starting'. With this note, I think she is already trying to soothe the ego of a cinematographer that she will ask to move outside of his comfort zone of creating smooth, artfully lit shots. Clarke had some trouble with the cinematographer on *The Connection*. The art director of the film, Albert Brenner, reports that everyone on the crew thought she was 'too bossy' (DVD extras, Milestone collection). Clarke sees it differently and as a woman who has struggled for authority on set with male cinematographers who think they know better than I, I am sympathetic to Clarke's perspective. It seems that what she was after in *The Connection* was something we would all recognise now as a shaky-cam style that is designed to signal a kind of documentary realism when placed inside a fiction. Clarke was obviously way ahead of her time with this idea, and she speaks about the cameraman's reluctance to take this direction because he thought it would make him look bad. See *Rome is Burning (Portrait of Shirley Clarke)* (Burch, Labarthe, et al.), 1970, at approximately 6 minutes. https://www.youtube.com/watch?v=6etkUKAGCpI&ab_channel=joucy.

After this note about sound, a blank space, then a mysterious set of numbers: '9 – 5 – 1',[45] and then a note about rehearsal pay and different rates for actors working towards a film v. working towards a play off Broadway v. working towards a play on Broadway. This seems to be a logistical note, but I argue that it sits somewhere between the amorphous notion of vision and the harder-edged substance of logistics. How is this about vision? It is about the way that Clarke wants to work with the actors. She wants a rehearsal period that pays actors as though they are developing something for the theatre, a slow steady build, not a few minutes grabbed before calling 'action'. Clarke's vision will be articulated through this enactive process wherein director and actor come to understandings of what is being sought. The improvisations in rehearsals will give rise to plans for the shoot which, in turn, will give rise to new forms of adaptation and improvisation on set, and so on through the edit to the scoring and the final film.

By the third page of this stapled set of papers, it is possible to see the gears of the mind shifting towards the harder edges of logistics. 'Call Freddie'[46] sits at the top of this page. It is a 'to-do list' with numbers for the Living Theater, notes about the union, assistants, lighting gear. And yet, it is clearly part of planning in that it will structure the improvisation that will create the art. It is still about the vision because Clarke is a pragmatic filmmaker. She stays abreast of how things work – gear, schedules, budgets – and this folds into her vision. The art of the possible. The art of what-is-to-hand-meets-what-is-on-her-mind. The art of finding a way to say what she wants to say.

4. Respond

I consider the notion of responding to be the most egregiously under-recognised aspect of theorising filmmaking and film authorship. Creativity is responsive. It generates novel outcomes by responding to need, or problems to be solved.[47] Responsiveness is under-theorised, my collaborators and I have argued, because of the wide-spread 'misapprehension of filmmaking processes based in part on dubious individualist assumptions about creative minds'.[48] Because of the 'dubious'[49] assumption that an individual brain is an individual mind, film theory tends to see a director's vision as the exclusive property of their brains and attribute genius to them individually.

My aim here is to position Clarke (and other brilliant directors) as responsive. To do this I reiterate that a director's vision does not 'leap fully formed from her head'.[50] It is brought forth through responsive improvisation and participatory sense-making. This does not diminish Clarke's genius, it just moves it outside of her skull, and into the context she creates and to which she responds.

Responding is where skill arises in improvisation. Improvisation is not just making things up on the spot, it is reading the room, knowing the plan and having, in fact, a deep enough insight into the intentions and ideas behind the plan to be able to make multiple on-the-spot variations in response to the vicissitudes of an actual working process, and still come away with something that is the idea. As I wrote in Chapter 2, 'A filmmaking process is what Kirsh might call an "enactive landscape"'.[51] It is 'the set of possibilities that can in principle be brought into being when an agent interacts with an underlying environment while engaged in a task or pursuing a goal'.[52]

Responsiveness is a creative and intellectual skill in which expertise can accrue. Expertise in responding manifests as things like listening, observing, assessing, combining, visualising, interpreting and problem solving. In this case we might think of the vision, as amorphous and ephemeral as it is, as a kind of puzzle or problem to be solved. Film crews and actors in turn respond to the vision's knowns, unknowns, affordances and limitations. We might say that filmmaking is, in fact, a process of solving the problem of what the vision is, by responding creatively with offers that define it through the images, sounds, performances, cuts and so on that eventually comprise it as a manifested entity.

The director, in this case Clarke, has the vision. She directs the crew to manifest the vision. As director, she is ultimately held responsible for all decisions that relate to executing it.

Decisions are what directors make. Not shots, not designs, not performances. These things are all made by crew members and actors. Their work is shaped by the director's decisions about their offers, and by the direction the director gives.

Everyone on the crew *responds* to the director's articulation of their vision, and their skilled responsiveness is what generates the film. As such 'realising a vision' or making a film is the definition of enactive cognition and the site of profoundly, complexly, improvisationally and iteratively responsive creativity.

I turn now to some analysis of the feature films directed and edited by Shirley Clarke in the 1960s, to see how she plans, improvises, finds a way and responds to people, place and cultural context in unique and compelling ways.

Figure 5.2 Some of the cast and crew of *The Connection* on set. Photo by Gideon Bachman, 1960. WCFTR film title photograph file, PH 7162, *The Connection*, Box 107, Folder 1, Wisconsin Center for Film and Theater Research

The Connection

The first feature-length fiction film directed and edited by Shirley Clarke, *The Connection* follows a few hours in the lives of eight men as they wait for their dealer, 'Cowboy' (Carl Lee), to show up with the fixes they have all been promised in exchange for their participation in a 'verité' documentary being directed by Jim Dunn (William Redfield).

The film was considered shocking. It precipitated a long censorship battle over a shot from a porn magazine and the use of the word 'shit' (as slang for heroin). But it was probably more alarming to conservative sensibilities for its non-judgemental gaze at drug use. The hero, dressed in white, is the dealer, a languid preacher of the poetics of staying cool played by with measured menace by Carl Lee. I will return to Carl Lee in discussion of each of the films in this chapters, since his presence becomes more and more influential on the works directed and edited by Shirley Clarke and the ways they come into being.

The Connection unfolds a bit like a beat culture hybrid of *12 Angry Men* (Lumet et al. 1957) and *Waiting for Godot*[53] with a choreographic sensibility. It is a musical with monologues (not songs). These tirades unfurl as performances, set pieces, with scores. Their rhythms are individual, but, woven together over the arc of the film's story, they manifest a rhythmic dynamic of alienation–connection–alienation. As Clarke notes 'Everybody thought the film – like the play – was mainly about drug addiction. But I do not think that is what the play is about, nor do I think the film is about that. I think it's about alienation.'[54]

Alienation is one of a handful of themes that can be expressed as powerfully in abstract/choreographic movement as it can be in dialogue-driven drama. This is because the dynamics of groups-versus-individuals are spatial, temporal and energic dynamics. They can be seen in people's proximities to each other and the ways they form sub-groups that harmonise or jitter or enact other qualities of movement dynamics. The staging of monologues and interactions in *The Connection* is mostly jittery. Movement dynamics harmonise only once everyone has had their fix, and then only briefly. In this sense, time, space and movement are Clarke's expression of theme, and they are framed and enacted cinematically through the bodies in motion of actors and crew.

The performances of alienation, as framed by the fluid camera work, move first with angsty impatience, then with the tempi of semi-disembodied heroin highs, then with the tensions of a near-death from overdose and then get back to the endless cycles of waiting, stressing, getting high, coming down and waiting.

The film starts with a note from the character of the cinematographer, J. J. Burden, that says:

> Jim Dunn, the documentary film-maker, titled this film 'The Connection' and turned all of the footage over to me before he left. I worked with him as cameraman and we shot the whole thing in a drug addict's apartment early one evening last fall. The responsibility of putting together the material is fully mine. I did it as honestly as I could.
>
> J. J. Burden[55]

Over the next hour and forty-eight minutes, four of the characters, Leach, Sol (Jerome Raphael), Ernie (Gary Goodrow) and Sam (James Anderson), are each goaded into telling their stories, which mostly unfold as diatribes about the other characters. They shed light on their own world views and, at the same time, each in their own way, accuse the filmmaker, Dunn, of mocking or pimping them and their lives for his own glory.

Early in the film, after Leach's opening monologue, which sets a tone of complaint and irritation at Dunn, a man comes in with a portable record player. He circles the room before finding a spot for the machine, and everyone goes quiet. The man plugs in the record player and puts on a jazz record. But it quickly malfunctions and starts skipping, and the ritual of music that has mesmerised the characters is broken. The complaints start up again (a moment of 'talking over talking' as per Clarke's notebook[56]) and the unexplained, unintroduced man, who came in for no apparent reason other than to circle the room and start the music, leaves.

The animosity towards Dunn then picks up again and continues throughout the film. Dunn has paid for their fixes, which are slow to arrive, and the characters resent him for exploiting them, resent each other for being there and being involved in this, and resent themselves for their own complicitly. Worth noting about the monologues is that while all are bitter towards someone, none of the vitriol is ever directed at Black characters or musicians, or their dealer. Contempt is reserved for the white men, themselves and Dunn.

The filmmaker Dunn, who is presumably also, at least to some extent, an avatar for Clarke's own misgivings about herself and directors in general, gets the worst of it. The nastiest of accusations to Dunn come from Sam, a Black man, who says, directly to the camera: 'what do you want Jim Dunn? A soft shoe dance? I don't need burnt cork y'know'.[57] Clarke may also be talking to other filmmakers through Sam's accusation, but the delivery down the camera's barrel, by the man who is probably the most credible, certainly the most graceful, of the drug users, is almost certainly directed at herself, too. A warning? A reminder? A moment of recognition? All of the above, and more than that, a signal to the audience that she, like us, is complicit. She knows it, and wants us to know it, too.

The film opens with music. The camera follows Leach into the kitchen. Sol comes out of the room marked 'toilet', raises an eyebrow at the camera, and says something to Freddie (Freddie Redd) who is playing the piano. Freddie stops and glares at the camera.

The glaring at the camera, and by extension the filmmaker Jim Dunn, the filmmaker Shirley Clarke and the film viewers, us, is an important part of the dramaturgy of *The Connection*. It is also a part that Clarke suggests was largely improvised during the shoot.

> the actors, while turning toward the camera and speaking to it, are part of the game which is played out in the audience. And there are also moments of reality where the game isn't played, moments which are just as organised and manipulated but in

a completely different way. These two levels of the film were the result, in any case, of one set of instructions that the actors were given once and only once: they had to be conscious at all times of the fact that the camera was on them, and they had to deal with that fact when and how they wanted. At each moment of the process, there could have been an improvisation or a reaction from the actors which would be quite spontaneous, and these moments are very effective because they add another dimension to the game that's being played.[58]

Although there are numerous references to looking at the camera in the scripts that I saw at the Wisconsin Center for Film and Theater Research, the scripts, as noted above, could not be shot as they were written. So, as Clarke says, this improvised interaction between actors and camera adds a layer of questions to this film that caused some audiences to mistake it for documentary.

The camera work, as noted above, was also intended to give the impression of documentary shooting 'on-the-fly'. It does not really do this because of its smooth professionalism, but that smoothness of choreography and camera does in its own way contribute to what Richard Rushton calls the 'reality effect'[59] of the film. Takes are long, often lasting several minutes. The framing gives the impression of chasing the paranoid junkies around the room, provoking irate reactions that seem to be unfolding in real time, in part because they are uncut, and in part because they repeatedly corner the characters, forcing them to dodge or attack (through the rhythms and directions of their blocking) to evade its persistent gaze. This is Clarke's 'choreographic' mode of directing, and it keeps the film's drama taut. Even though not much happens narratively, a lot happens choreographically, and drama is conveyed by the relationships of character and camera in space over time.

When Cowboy finally arrives, the shooting and cutting change. Musicians get their fixes first, and as each one comes out of the toilet, they join a jam with a cooler jazz than we have heard before. Cuts and shots swing around, more breezy, jaunty, mobile, the sound relaxing into the smoothed edges of the men's tempers and moves once they are high.

That is, until it is Jim Dunn's turn to be confronted with pressure to get a fix himself. Dunn, who the others have challenged throughout the film to try drugs, argues with Cowboy. Dunn hesitates. Says he doesn't know about drugs but knows there is something dirty about just 'peeking' into people's lives.[60] Cowboy takes offence at his hesitation. Stabs a knife into the table. Swaggers past him and holds the door to the bathroom open. A challenge. Dunn picks up a camera as though about to threaten Cowboy with it. But it isn't the weapon for this situation, and he lets it drop back onto the table. Strips off his long-sleeved, button-down shirt and heads into the toilet in his t-shirt and (off-screen) shoots up.

Once high, Dunn forgets, for a while, about making the film, and the camera work and cutting change again. The camera is Burden's now, more musical and intimate than it has been. Burden, a Black man and friend of the musicians, enacts the fluidity of music and the mood. He participates in these by sliding the camera over and around the keys, the strings, the drumsticks all in congruent motion. The *mise en scène* evolves, figures slide in and out of frame, the camera up and down. A unique and creative moving image of participatory-sense-making-when-high, generated by the cast and crew's embodied rhythmic responses to music and Clarke's choreographic direction.

As the music of the sweetest moments of the high unfolds, Cowboy enters, sits and snaps his fingers, turns his head to his left and there is Sam, who has been lost in a kind of dance with a teacup, crouching to land his cup on the floor, tea unspilt. Sam's move downward motivates the shot to pan across the band's feet and land on Jim Dunn, sitting defeated, head lowered down. The music ends. Dunn looks up at the camera. He's out of it, but tells J. J. Burden to keep shooting, and goes in search of his own camera. Dunn's stoned eye is more elliptical and poetic than his straight one. Shots in his point of view find objects, moments, a match burning a dozing junkie's fingers, a clock, a woman's ass in a magazine, the teacup just as it finally breaks. The poetics of these montages feel distinctly 'Shirley-ish'[61] in their rhythms and preoccupations. As though her own gaze is finally given a reprieve from the strictures of drama shooting to indulge in more abstract, dancerly patterns.

Each of these qualities of camera and editing form, in a sense a 'movement' in the structure of this film's *mise en scène* symphony. The restless, argumentative allegro yields slowly to the stoned minuet, which gives way only briefly to an upbeat andante, which is interrupted by a flurry around Leach's overdose, which in turn is counterpointed with Priest's competent, business-as-usual, rescue of him from death.

As Priest is administering a form of CPR to Leach, the musicians and Ernie drift out, heading off to gigs, leaving Sol, Sam, Dunn, Priest and the now sleeping Leach sitting and staring as the man with the record player comes back in. This time he is seen from the opposite side of the set, but he makes the same deliberate circle around the room and plugs in his portable record player. Unlike the first time, the disc now spins uninterrupted. The characters left in the room sit still, staring blankly, mesmerised by the music, and creating an image of the repetitive cycle of alienation from each other and the world in which they are stuck. This structural framing device of the man with the record player is one of the most explicitly choreographic moments in the film.[iv] It references a very common way of designing dance wherein the dancers start and end in basically the same patterns, no matter what their exertions have extracted or depicted in the interim.[v]

The repetition of the inexplicable man with the record player is a musical/choreographic restatement of themes that makes this drama into a dance – a story of human action and interaction[62] told in time, space and movement more than narrative event or causal change.

[iv] The other one is the dance that Sam does with a teacup, a couple of slow motion turns from one side to the other that are choreographed into a playful phrase by being cut into shots of the sax player's moves and the drug dealer's gaze.

[v] See Chapter 3 for discussion of an example of this in Clarke's first film, *Dance in the Sun*, which follows a similar pattern of starting and ending with the source of music.

This depiction of a theme is planned, of course, but its feeling and ideas are experienced through actor and camera movement as directed by the choreographic sensibility of Clarke. By enacting the moves and moods as they understand them, the actors and crew make a creative incursion into the vision. By editing the movement and moods of the shot material into its final form, Clarke takes more 'control' of the story experience than most directors do. However, like all editors, she is enacting a responsive, embodied and embedded process in the edit suite. She continues, through editing, to labour and collaborate, with actors, camera, sound, script, music and herself as director, to enactively generate the vision.

Figure 5.3 Directing *The Cool World*, with Baird Bryant, cinematographer, using a wheelchair as a dolly. Carl Lee and Bryant's first assistant, and wife, Jane, also pictured. Photo by Leroy McLucas, 1960. WCFTR film title photograph file, PH 7162, *The Cool World*, Box 108, Folder 32, Wisconsin Center for Film and Theater Research

The Cool World

The Cool World is based on a then-popular 1959 novel by Warren Miller of the same title. However, as a film, it owes as much to Clarke's skills with improvisation and choreographic ways of working, and her collaborator's embeddedness in place, as it does to the book.

The story of *The Cool World* unfolds across a few days in Harlem as teenager Duke Custis (Hampton [Rony] Clanton) tries to raise money to buy a gun, so he can gain authority within his gang, and respect on the streets. He watches the world around him, judging who is cool and what is not. The camera watches him watch but, unlike Duke, the camera doesn't judge. It is patient, fluid, curious and ultimately inflected with the mood of the place in the moments of the drama.

Clarke says that *The Cool World* is the first time a film was shot in Harlem as Harlem, rather than a fictionalised or glamorised version of the place as seen by people who did not live or work there. She remarks that filmmakers didn't make films there 'because they thought it was dangerous. They didn't even think it was necessary'.[63] Clarke did think it necessary, and as a result, *The Cool World* creates an experience of place telling its own story. As Clarke reports it, Harlem plays itself, documentary-style, in *The Cool World*.

> The exteriors were all shot on location in Harlem. For the interiors, the New York Housing Authority gave us the use of a whole tenement building which was about to be demolished. For each set, we used a different floor of the building. We didn't have to buy a stick of furniture – we just used what was there. Our interiors were all pre-lit, so we could move the camera freely. Throughout the film, the camera was hand-held. For sound, we used radio microphones, so we didn't need a boom.[64]

This use of extant buildings, furniture and streets, and Clarke's 'observational' gaze on them, is part of what gives the film its hybrid status. The dogs that wander across the streets, the pedestrians that pass through the frame, are not extras, they are, usually, the people that live there. Though, as Clarke says in the interview in *Rome is Burning*, 'Even the documentary shooting on the street was done to a preconceived style'.[65] This style, with its intensities of the black-and-white cinematography, are strongly reminiscent of the Italian Neorealist work that Clarke admired.

The influence of Vittorio de Sica is palpable, and there is a distinctive fluidity of camera work as *The Cool World* improvises with and responds to the place and its qualities. The *mise en scène*, particularly the movement of characters in and through the frame, is signature Clarke. Its restless, contrapuntal, or fluid changes of direction and energy tell a story through motion. Clarke's 'style' is visible in this motion. Her authorial voice manifests by responsively composing the movement offered by actual people and places.

Figure 5.4 Clarke has written in pencil on the back of this photo: 'Setting up C.U. frame for opening shot of "The Cool World", Carl Lee – leading actor and co-author with Clarke, street speaker – Richard Ward –, photo by Leroy McLucas, p.s. I love this photo – looks like I'm about to "pee"'. Shirley Clarke collection, M91-052, Box 25, Folder 9, Wisconsin Center for Film and Theater Research

Given the importance of embeddedness in place, I pause here to return to an important aspect of my thesis: the significance of the collaborators. On this film, there are key collaborators from, and living in, Harlem. Clarke directs these collaborators with a deft, creative sensibility that uses movement to weave together ideas, personalities and pressures and their unfolding. But the collaborators are also experts. They include cast members; casting and dialogue director, Carl Lee; Madeleine Anderson in a role identified as assistant, but which we might now call cultural liaison; and composer, Mal Waldron. These experts respond to direction and context by participating creatively and intellectually in the making of the film through their own forms of expertise.

Through their generative and responsive enactive cognising with Clarke, these and other key collaborators are, I propose co-authors. Clarke is the 'first author', the instigator of the work and its director. She has pointed in the direction that she thinks the cast, dialogue director, cultural liaison and composer should go, but they are also, within their areas of expertise, generating maps or directions for how their roles will be fulfilled. They are not dolls being 'carried around the dance floor'.[66] They have autonomy and are 'moving each other, making each other move, and being moved by each other'.[67]

As I propose in general, by positioning filmmaking as an instance of distributed cognition, these collaborators' work of manifesting the vision in material form is not 'merely' the work of hands. It is creative and intellectual labour. They are authoring the actual images, movements, interactions and ideas that will comprise the final film by creating them, enactively, with place and each other. I turn now to brief descriptions of how Clarke and selected collaborators cognise together in the process of creating the film *The Cool World*.

Cast

The cast is dominated by a group of kids, Harlem residents, who were identified through a long exploratory process. Their expertise in navigating place and their easy familiarity with each other, the spaces and the culture of their place is imprinted on-screen. They 'author' their own performances and own their own connection to the 'practice and knowledge'[68] of their community.

Clarke says, 'We never did a scene without checking with the kids first to see if the action seemed believable to them.'[69] If a scene didn't seem believable to the kids, Clarke and Lee changed it or cut it. As Clarke says:

> A great many scenes were improvised. The kids were given a lead-in as to what they were to accomplish in general in the scene. At all times they were asked if this was something they would do, or wouldn't do; if they believed it, or if they didn't believe it. If they said 'no', we didn't do it.[70]

Through this consultative process, Clarke (and Lee and Anderson) create space for the cast to imbue interactions with their own ideas in a context they could relate to. This is an instance of Clarke directing them well, and of Clarke and the actors doing the enactive cognising that De Jaegher and Di Paolo describe as 'moving each other, making each other move, and being moved by each other'.[71] This responsive, enactive process gives the film, and us, access and insight we could not otherwise get. It is also, on this enactive cognition account, creative and intellectual work, with the resulting images, gestures and expressiveness being the articulation of the vision.

Co-authors

Clarke also directs Carl Lee and Madeleine Anderson's expertise well. Without minimising the skill and insight she brings to doing this, it is important to acknowledge the participation of each of them in creative authorship in the making of *The Cool World*.

Carl Lee gets a top-line credit as Casting and Dialogue Director in the film. Here Clarke is acknowledging that the language of the dialogue in the film, with its nuances, vocabularies, subtexts and inflections of Black Americans is not hers. The language and dialogue belong to Lee, to the kids he finds to perform in the film and to the community. Clarke recognises Lee's authorial input with the Casting and Dialogue Director credit, and says:

> I would not have been able to make The Cool World had I not been living with Carl Lee at that time ... It took Carl three months of going up to Harlem all the time, gathering kids, and bringing them down for us to interview. For a while, we really thought we weren't going to be able to cast the film because we were getting all the 'good' kids in school, and they weren't giving us believable readings. When I finally persuaded Carl to try to get to the gangs and bring some of those kids downtown, most of them couldn't read scripts. What we would do was improvise with them. It was very exciting because the 'real' kids started to improvise the script we had written right back to us.[72]

I will return to the improvisational methods in a moment. But first, another person who made it possible to improvise in Harlem was Madeleine Anderson, about whom Clarke says:

> Madeleine was this amazing lady who wanted to make a movie herself and subsequently made a film for WNET and the Children's Workshop.[vi] She agreed not only to be my assistant but to stay with me through the whole film. Eventually she became my assistant editor. She would go out on the street, and it was her job to explain to the people in the street who were upset by the filming why we were doing the movie and what it was all about. For the most part, that cooled the street ... She did it wonderfully.[73]

The word 'assistant' is unfortunately one of those words that tends to get associated with 'just' helping, and helping has, in my experience, been pejoratively misunderstood as unskilled and

---

[vi] Anderson, like Shirley Clarke's daughter Wendy, also deserves a book of her own. For more on her remarkable achievements and insights see: https://nmaahc.si.edu/explore/stories/filmmaker-madeline-anderson

minimised as insignificant in creative and intellectual labour.[74] I cannot remove the word 'assistant' from Anderson's credit, but, drawing on research-informed knowledge and experience of creative practice, I argue that this work is more than 'just' helping, it is vital. How you work with people, schedules and logistics matters. In the case of *The Cool World*, they matter to the extent that the film's style and impact would have been completely different if this work had been done by someone else. Anderson's skilled expertise with the communities and places of *The Cool World* materialises the film's style.

One more set of collaborators that 'make' this film with Clarke are the musicians who come in at the end of the process. The jazz score, written by Mal Waldron and performed by the Dizzy Gillespie Ensemble with Yusef Lateef, manifests the sound of place, the rhythms of life within it and the connections between places and people that are unspoken.

The score of *The Cool World* is as hard to describe as it is to overestimate in importance. The musical passages dynamise the phrasing of the edit's visual flow. Together, movement of image and sound imbue the film with complex, sensual, contrasting dark and light tones, moods and fluidity of motion. Directing of the music composition process and collaboratively deciding where music belongs, how it should feel, how long it lasts, are part of Clarke's visionary authorial work. No one else would have had the particular insight, perspicacity, authority, accrued cultural and technical expertise, access and sensitivity to do it in the way that she did. At the same time, and without minimising the importance of Clarke's directorial imprint, the composing and improvising of Mal Waldron and the jazz musicians is easily recognised as part of authorship in the whole that is *The Cool World*.

Movement structure in *The Cool World*

Turning to look at the film itself, and its flow as a whole, it is possible to see that Clarke directs and edits three kinds of movement scenes through *The Cool World*. These are: montages of place; inner monologues of Duke; and the interactions of young men looking for position, vying for power and living in motion – motion of fights, games, negotiation or play. These three kinds of movement – call them montages, monologues and living in motion – interweave and sometimes overlap through the film's structure into patterns that tell story.

Montages

The montages tell a story by creating the rhythms and pressures of the cool and not-so-cool world swirling around Duke. Clarke's eye for the phrasing of movement composes the shots by Baird Bryant into dynamic 'dances' of human action and interaction unfolding through and within the complex counter-rhythms of place.

For example, a 'Saturday Night' montage (approximately one hour and ten minutes in) begins as the character of Luane (Yolanda Rodriguez), who is dreaming of seeing the ocean, turns her head towards the darkened window. A piano that sounds a bit like a toy plunks out a little melody and a police car siren wails across it. The piano gets nudged aside by a smooth saxophone. The world outside the window unfurls in a series of shots punctuated with neon, headlights, jazz and silhouettes of figures dancing, arguing, negotiating street deals.[vii]

Clarke uses movement to drive associations and connections of images and ideas. In this montage she conducts movement through shots by cutting together the punctuations of lights, the volumes of dark, the motion of the camera and the people framed

---

[vii] The montage is reminiscent of Esfir Shub's masterpiece of creative editing in *Segodnya* (*Today*, 1929). It, and all of the montages in *The Cool World*, build on the influence of the vibrant movement style of Shub and the other great documentary editor/directors of the Soviet era, Elizaveta Svilova and Dziga Vertov.

by it, to make a composition of the world that resists intimacy but invites action. Duke's voice-over is an intermittent montage piece. It doesn't move the story forward so much as pressurise it. He notices time is rushing past. He notices himself driven to make his mark in motion. 'What I want, and what I need, is to go down burning',[75] he says, and then he runs through the streets – not to or from anywhere in the narrative chain, just for the running-through-the-streets feeling of the moment.

Many other sequences like this punctuate the film: including the opening montage around the street speaker (described in Chapter 4); a montage of the white neighbourhoods and edifices of Manhattan seen through a bus window; a montage of kids – playing, scrabbling, digging and squabbling as Duke's voice-over ruminates on the pennies he never saved; and an early morning montage – one of many that reveal place as both obstacle and opportunity to Duke, as he has to find the money to buy the gun.

On this morning, Duke comes out the door and a trumpet player in the street starts a riff that slides over a phrase of images in motion – newspapers, bikes and the street on the go. People working through their lives, sweeping, discussing, wrangling. Some women outside a record shop are dancing. A checkers game. An argument. Some laughs. A woman in white gets in a car. The car drives by Duke. Clarke cuts to a shot of Priest driving. Then cuts to a two-shot that reveals Duke is in the car with Priest. The car drives us into another kind of scene. This is a choreographic transition that connects Duke from a montage rumination into the world of interpersonal drama.

Monologues

Duke's inner monologues are another strand of the film's design. They are, it seems, a kind of inner coaching, that evolves over the course of the film from naive ambition to a more cynical outlook on his own growing violence, and whether it really matters if he pushes people around the way he himself has been pushed.

Duke's inner monologues paint a picture of narrative energy and need for the gun, but in them he does little – he looks, he thinks, he decides on yet another course of action that he seems to know is unlikely to lead him anywhere.

One inner monologue starts up at about forty-seven minutes into the film. Duke walks away from a confrontation with the Wolves at the playground. His voice-over is a Noir scenario. *'I'm standing on the street. Its dark. I hear the sound of wolves ... I pull out my piece and put three holes in him ... he looks up and says you got me fair, Duke'*. In a nice sleight of hand, Duke's Noir fantasy actually ends on that line, but it doesn't seem to. He says: *'I look down the street and suddenly I feel cold all over. I see death everywhere.'* This line seems like it is being voiced from within Duke's imaginary persona of a jaded detective. But in fact, he has switched perspectives to the present and his real life, where he cannot get the gun he craves. He ruminates: *'Priest is laughing at me'*. Then he realises where his mind has taken him and he snaps out of it: *'what's the matter with you, Duke, it is broad daylight. You just had a bad minute. Just a bad minute.'*[76]

Living in motion

Duke's self-conscious inner voice is a counterpoint to his more active, but less verbal, embodied presence in the third strand of the film's movement structure, the scenes I'm calling 'living in motion'.

These unfold when Duke is in negotiation with his gang, with Priest (Carl Lee), with his rival, the junkie Blood (Clarence Williams), or with Blood's straight-arrow brother. These scenes always seem to fracture into a kind of rhythmic chaos. They move just ahead of the speed at which we can grasp who wants what or even exactly who is speaking. The camera is always on the move, and rarely focussed on the face of the person talking, which leaves dialogue bouncing around the room with the same fractious energy as the kids.

A scene like this one unfolds just before the Saturday night montage.

In the apartment Duke's gang has designated as their clubhouse, three guys are dancing. Others are hanging around. The restless camera and jazz trumpet take a spin around the room. Duke comes in and they discuss what to do about their junkie club president, Blood. Duke stays loyal and, like his performances in other similar scenes, his presence seems to be an anchoring force. His strength as a leader derives from his relative stillness. Blood comes in, nodding, full of plans, full of drugs. Blood is caught in Duke's stare. The others shift around dynamically, closing off or opening space for action. Duke and Blood start to fight. It doesn't go far before an off-screen voice comes in with the news that Duke's friend Littleman has been killed. These random events overlap, crash into each other. Duke tries to cool things down, tells everyone to stay off the street, gets rid of Blood, appoints his cabinet, climbs into bed with Luane and tells her about the ocean.

Were any of these narrative events momentous? In a way all of them are. Inside the gang there's been a coup. Out in the world a man has been killed. Duke will ruminate on these events later in voice-over monologues, but in the moment, they have a feel of scuffles – chaotic, consequential but unresolved, maybe unresolvable.

Resolutions are scarce in *The Cool World*, which focusses instead on the susurrations of people and place. It leaves questions everywhere. For example, what to make of the scene near the end of the film where Duke takes Luane to Coney Island and she disappears? Duke has made good on his promise and brought Luane to see the sea that was readily accessible to her, except that no one had ever told her it was there. Duke is blasé about the ocean and pulls Luane towards the Coney Island carnival games. She doesn't want to go. He shoots arrows and guns, and throws things while she watches. And then she disappears. Does she drown? She just isn't there. Does she run away? The shot of Duke looking for her on the now-deserted beach is one of the widest, brightest and stillest shots of the film. The camera doesn't move, and for a moment, Duke stops. Looks. And then gives up. 'Aw fuck it'. He moves off-screen. Cut. Coney Island looks a lot like Harlem now, except the vendors are white. The streets are dark.

Montage, monologue and living in motion

Back in Harlem, *The Cool World*'s climax compresses its three modes into one sequence. A montage of Harlem reminiscent of the opening unfolds along with an inner monologue in which Duke turns over meaning and meaninglessness in his life until he is roused to get to the rumble by the influx of his gang into the clubhouse apartment. That sense of living in motion, in barely managed chaos, ensues as the kids liquor up their courage. Just as they are about to head out to the fight, Priest shows up.
    Music stops.
    Priest and Duke talk.
    Music starts.
    Duke lets Priest stay in the clubhouse, but Priest doesn't give him his gun.
    Music stops.
    Duke leaves. Argues with himself in the hallway. Decides to go on without the gun.
    Music starts again.
    Duke joins his gang outside.
    Music stops.
    It stays stopped.
    The almost silent geometric ballet of the final fight crosses the frame in the diagonals and curves of a playground. Swings are thrown and dodged. The arch of the climbing frame supports some kicks and jabs, a scramble then a tumble. The planks of the seesaw rise up to a tipping point and hover, dodging back and forth before throwing combatants to the next frame. The

geometric shapes define the tussle of the Pythons' white jackets against the dark ones of the Wolves. Duke runs down the slide to grapple with Angel, the leader of the Wolves. They roll, dodge and pursue, until Angel gets a knife in the back.

The music comes back in. With the cops.

Duke and his accomplice run in opposite directions.

Back at the apartment Duke finds Priest dead. No help there.

He runs through whip pans across Harlem. No one pays much attention to him. He is not the king of the streets, he is just a running kid. Until he isn't. His inner monologue of glory starts up again as he is apprehended, and the cop car takes him off the streets.

The feelings and ideas of *The Cool World* are made by place, performers, camera, sound, edits and music perpetually in motion. Clarke conceives of the film this way and directs it with her signature choreographic fascination with movement. Of course, she does not generate the movement or place herself. She *directs* them, by which I mean she negotiates and responds to the people who generate them. This is how her 'vision' or 'signature' comes into being.

Film directing is, by definition, always already reliant on the interaction of distributed creativity of people and place. This creativity is what a director directs. In *The Cool World*, Clarke's distinctive directorial approach interacts with the creative and intellectual work of Lee, Anderson, Claxton, Bryant, Waldron and other members of the cast and crew, to manifest a film that instantiates Clarke's distinctive ways of distributing authorship through and with particular people, places and movements.

The name 'Shirley Clarke' thus, as I argued in Chapter 2, stands not just for the individual brain of the film's director/editor, but for her dynamic creative weaving of practices and concerns. *The Cool World* is what she directs, and her directing is a skilled and choreographically inflected distribution of the creative cognitions and authorship incursions of the people with whom, and places within which, she enacts the filmmaking process.

Figure 5.5 Carl Lee and Shirley Clarke at a press conference for *The Cool World* at the Venice Film Festival. Photo by Giacomelli, 1963. WCFTR name photograph file, PH 7163, Box 52, Folder 1, Wisconsin Center for Film and Theater Research

Portrait of Jason

> Most of my films are messages to other film makers about things they are doing that I question. Things I would like them to take a look at. A very good example and the clearest one is *Portrait of Jason*, which was made to show Ricky and Penny [Leacock and Pennebaker] the flaws in thinking about cinema verité. If you take twelve days of shooting and edit only the climax points you get crap. My theory was that you don't take out the 'boring parts' – the way someone reaches those climaxes or ideas or whatever. *Jason* is two hours of real time, not film time.[77]

If *The Connection* is a tightly scripted plan on which Clarke and crew and cast extemporise, and *The Cool World* is a more loosely scripted structure that catalyses improvisations and polyrhythmic enactions, *Portrait of Jason* seems to almost reverse the idea of improvising with a plan. There is no written plan for how the story will unfold, no agreed script, outline or choreography. There is a man, in a room, drinking, smoking cigarettes and weed, talking, singing, sighing, crying, laughing, smirking, flirting, confessing, lying and more. And that, plus the occasional prop from a cabaret show or prompt from off-screen provocateurs, is all there is for nearly two hours. Or is it?

The shoot is an extended improvisation, and yet everything Jason Holliday is doing on-screen, possibly even the controversial ending where he cries with shame, then smiles impishly, then cries again, is always already a schtick, a bit, a story Holliday has told a hundred times before, a number in the great cabaret act he lives within. Holliday has told these stories, you could even say rehearsed them, at cocktail parties, bar pickups and late-night alcohol-infused encounters. He has calculated the rhythms and beats of the words he will use to describe the dowagers that he can tell are good tippers but '*need some recognition*'; or about his mother who was '*a nice coloured lady*' (he laughs and laughs) '*... I mean white folks was proud of her, cause she knew her place*'; or about himself, '*yeah, I'm the bitch. You amateur cunts, take notice* (laughing). *I'm the bitch.*'[78]

Clarke didn't generate a script for this film. It may be, however, that Jason Holliday has a plan in mind. At about twenty minutes into the film, Holliday describes the structure of his long hoped-for cabaret act – the one for which he has borrowed money from everyone but which he had never yet managed to create. In the act he will, he says, start off like '*a real hip cat that's been around ... dance, sing, go crazy.*' Then there will be a '*Bitchy bag*' persona where he tells his '*house boy stories and what have you*'. Finally, he says he will '*end up as a Clown – and all clowns are happy and sad ... So I figure if you can sell sex, comedy and a little bit of tragedy – people love to see you suffer.*'[79]

Cool cat, bitch, tragic clown.

That is the structure of this film. And it is Holliday's plan. He could, on the basis of it, be declared the writer of this portrait.

In fact, self-portrait may be more accurate. Or hybrid, portrait/self-portrait, which may, in fact, be what all documentaries about characters are. *Portrait of Jason* is certainly what documentary theorist Ilona Hongisto would call 'fabulation' in which the act of making the documentary co-creates the reality it documents. *Portrait of Jason* creates Jason Holliday, and while the film's director is Shirley Clarke, the character of Jason Holliday, and this performance of him, is authored by Jason Holliday.[viii] Thus, between Holliday, Clarke and Carl Lee, authorship of the film's story is a definitive act of participatory sense-making – the three of them make sense of Jason, of each other and of the filmmaking process.

Holliday enacts his stories, creating his own on-screen persona. Clarke enacts the role of director by responding. She responds in the moment, cueing the cameraman to go in and out of focus as she feels Jason bring an anecdote to a close or descend into a less engaging moment of reflection. Clarke directs by giving Holliday some feedback and prompts, too. As she says: 'I'm very much in this film. I think I'm as much in the film as Jason is.'[80]

For example, just after twenty minutes in, when Holliday finishes a story and Clarke, off-screen, says: '*That was nice. Very good.*' Holliday replies: '*Thank you*'. Or at another point, late in the night, Clarke checks in with Holliday, then gives him some more direction:

(at one hour, seventeen minutes)
Shirley: *How do you feel?*
Jason: *I feel marvellous, fresh.*
Shirley: *OK, tell us about your mother.*[81]

So, Clarke is present giving direction, she created the space for the story to create itself, and she gives direction to the camera throughout the film. As a director-editor, she keeps herself in the

---

[viii] Holliday's birth name, he tells us early on in the film, is Aaron Payne. He took on the name and persona of Jason Holliday in San Francisco, which he tells us is a good place to invent yourself.

final film, though as Irene Gustafson, who listened to the unedited sound recordings of the night, notes:

> she did excise several small but significant portions of Jason's performance. Most notably, she edited out his most direct critiques of Clarke and of the filmmaking process itself. Specifically, he jokes about Clarke's own use of black maids and compares the filmmakers to 'cops'.[82]

Clarke reports that it took her seven months to cut the material down from four hours to just under two. What she does in this editing time is act as a dramaturge to Holliday's script/design of his on-screen presence. She finds the film's form by shaping the raw filmed material to the structure Holliday has devised. While it appears to unfold with minimal intervention, the directing-by-editing of *Portrait of Jason* is evident in its narrative and dynamic shape, the rhythms of the release of information, escalation and reversal of emotion, and patterns of focus, out-of-focus and black. Clarke has directed and edited the dynamic of entertainment and pathos, recognition and alienation, bemusement and self-pity, that unfolds and entrains us with Jason Holliday.

However, this film is also made by someone else besides Jason Holliday and Shirley Clarke, and that is Carl Lee. While Holliday creates his performance. Lee provokes and stings Holliday to try to get to some reality of Holliday that Holliday either doesn't want to reveal, or doesn't know is there, or which may not even be there at all. As Gustafson notes: 'His influence on the film is profound – Jason directs much of his energy, most of it flirtatious, toward Carl, and it is his off-screen voice that we most often hear, either encouraging or deriding Jason throughout the film.'[83]

Carl Lee is an important part of the filmmaking team with these incursions, though it is harder to fit his participation into a clear category. You could say he is doing some writing in the sense that he is demanding certain stories, acts or feelings. For example, at thirty-nine minutes he says:

> *Hey Jason, do one of your nightclub numbers.*[84]

Here it is clear that Lee has knowledge of Holliday's life and stories and wants to get the full array of Jason Holliday-ness on the screen. This is one instance among many where he prompts Jason to run a 'script' that he knows Jason already has ready to go in his repertoire. Interestingly for the tone, journey and eventual reception of this film, this is one of the most benign of Lee's prompts. As the film goes on, Lee pushes Holliday for stories of his father ('Brother Tough'), of hustling, and of the first time he was forced to have sex. These prompts get grimmer and grimmer and Lee gets nastier and nastier. He is giving direction in a style is very different to Clarke's. He is pushing, not responding. He directs, or co-directs, or redirects Holliday by insults throughout the night.

After doing his impersonations of Mae West, Scarlett O'Hara, et al. Holliday pleads with Lee (not Clarke) for affirmation, saying:

> Carl, please turn around and smile at me. Come back in and smile at me. I mean, give me that credit.

This audio exchange unfolds over a black screen.

> Carl: *All right, so we all know you're a great actress. Played all the parts...*
> Jason: *Right?*[85]

Lee switches into being something like a producer next. He articulates strategic thinking about the film's success at the same time he tries to get more out of Holliday when he berates him about not yet doing everything he can to make the film work:

> Carl: *I know you're a big con artist. And I know you don't really give a shit about nothing and nobody. But ah, you are still not coming down front and that's what makes this thing work.*
> Jason: *Truth.*
> Carl: *You come down front.*
> ...
> Carl: *There's only one role you can do Jason, and that's you.*
> Jason: *All right, I know where that's at. Thank you. Give me the bottle.*
> Carl: *You can do that role better.*
> Jason: *Shut them bitches up.*[86]

Lee's directing, producing and scripting are generally overlooked in either praising or damning the film and the story it tells, and it would be remiss of me not to speculate as to why. It could be because the film's behind-the-scenes stories are more conveniently/efficiently told when one person is singled out as the genius behind them. But this is the excuse that has, in various ways, buoyed up the authorship industry since the beginning. So, I can't, in good conscience, perpetuate that damage to understanding how filmmaking works, even though it would save me words and time.

It may also be that in the cancel culture of the 2020s, it is more convenient to blame a white woman of a certain generation for what could be seen as exploitation of Jason Holliday, than a Black man. However, Jason runs eagerly towards the opportunity to perform himself, and if there is anyone in the room who wants to unmask or shame him, it is clearly Carl Lee.

Another reason Lee's participation in shaping the film may be overlooked would be that it suits a feminist agenda more squarely to find a female-identifying individual and elevate her to the status of control. This is problematic because it again obfuscates how films are actually made, and it perpetuates a film-studies method that has excluded women for over a century. Simply reversing the erasure of women by uplifting Clarke and obfuscating Lee creates an exception to the rule scenario, not a change that would benefit culture more widely. Since much of my own work has been to recognise the work of women who have been in positions of 'helping' great men to realise their visions and then excluded from the stories of their genius, it now feels like a responsibility to consider Lee as a significant agent in the filmmaking process here, as he was in the making of *The Cool World*.

Lee's style is to goad and push. Clarke's is more patient, it seems. She is watching, responding, cueing the camera, keeping the sound rolling and thinking, perhaps, about how she will be able to put this all together in the edit suite. Jason's style is also responsive, but the person he wants to please, entertain, seduce and win over here is not Clarke, but Lee, and this makes the 'social cognising' that is going on here a trio, at least, not just the participatory sense-making of a *pas de deux*.

In the struggle between Clarke, Holliday and Lee to get 'Jason' to reveal his 'real' self, something much more important about documentary film and even people is revealed, which is that there may not be a 'real' self. Certainly, there is not a single 'real' that can be pinned down by documentary, no matter how rigorous the restrictions and boundaries on artifice are in the filmmaking process. Clarke set out to make a film that would show her contemporaries what observational documentary really is, what really happens if you don't chop reality up into tiny pieces and make it a designed composition. But in the end, *Portrait of Jason* reveals that observation has no such power to simply record the real. It always already creates it. In this particular documentary, we get to witness Jason Holliday 'really' creating his real fictional self, and Carl Lee pushing and pushing to try to get beneath the performance, and, in the end a very nearly convincing breakdown into tears and moans that seem to be the real Jason. But the tears are performance, too, and the camera, along with Clarke, Lee and Holliday, has co-created them. The documentary film is the enactive thinking through and with all of them, their tools and their world.

Ultimately, Clarke says Jason 'wins' the struggle:

> He cries, and then in the middle of his sobbing, he turns it off. I tried to make a good ending, but each time I thought it was over, he would pull back and do another trip on us: 'I'm not lying.' 'Yes I am.' . . . Somehow, he ends up the victor. I was perfectly willing for him to win . . . I will not allow people to exploit themselves if they don't win in the end . . . it's Jason himself, his charm, his sense of humor, and he is also laughing at himself. I didn't take somebody who was easy to destroy. I picked somebody who was going to win. Jason ends up winning in that film.[87]

Conclusion

Making *Portrait of Jason* was Clarke's solution to the impossibility of getting enough money to make a film any other way. Frustrated by endlessly not working, she devised the shoot of

Jason to be done with donated film all in one night. The film was self-funded and possibly still has not made Clarke's investment back, despite being the film for which she is best remembered. After *Portrait of Jason*, Clarke stopped making anything for a while.

> I don't have the money or energy anymore to do what we used to do to raise large sums of money or find a producer. To get anything made is just incredible. And I was tired. I had been really depressed for quite a while, because after doing Jason [1967], it was clear that I wasn't going to do bigger and better films, that I was lucky if I ever made another one.[88]

Much later, in this interview with Vevé Clark, after discussion of: women and that things have changed 'zero, my dear, zero' (p. 3); of men, especially Stan Brakhage being patronising about her work, asking why she didn't go back to making her 'nice little films' and saying she was not an artist; of the cessation of tax concessions that made it possible to raise money for filmmaking; an interesting discussion of recognition of herself in *Jason*, Clarke finally comes to discussion of the issue of making films about Black people.

> Now I would never do another piece of work, film or video, that does not concern me. Nor will I ever direct a black film, though I've been asked to many times. They must be directed now by black people. Period. It's over. It's another time.[89]

Notes

1 Thompson, E. (2011). 'Living Ways of Sense Making'. *Philosophy Today*, 55, 114–23; p. 114.
2 See: Pearlman, K. (2023). 'Distributed Authorship: An et al. Proposal of Creative Practice, Cognition, and Feminist Film Histories'. *Feminist Media Histories*, 9(2), 87–100. Also Pearlman, K., and Sutton, J. (2022). 'Reframing the Director: Distributed Creativity in Filmmaking Practice'. In M. Hjort and T. Nannicelli (Eds.), *A Companion to Motion Pictures and Public Value*. Wiley, pp. 86–105.

3 Shirley Clarke, as quoted in the interview transcript, 'My life is one long electrical cord (with me crawling around on the floor trying to make a connection)'. Interviewer unknown, circa 1975. (Wisconsin Center for Film and Theater Research, Box 12, Folder 2).
4 Shirley Clarke, as quoted in de Hirsch, S. (1968). 'A Conversation – Shirley Clarke and Storm de Hirsch'. *Film Culture*, 44–55. https://cinefiles.bampfa.berkeley.edu/catalog/9681; p. 47.
5 See: Millard, K. (2014). *Screenwriting in a Digital Era*. Palgrave Macmillan. https://doi.org/10.1057/9781137319104.
6 See: De Jaegher, H., and Di Paolo, E. (2007). 'Participatory Sense-making: An Enactive Approach to Social Cognition'. *Phenomenology and the Cognitive Sciences*, 6(4), 485–507. https://doi.org/10.1007/s11097-007-9076-9.
7 See Thompson, 'Living Ways of Sense Making'.
8 De Jaegher and Di Paolo, 'Participatory Sense-making', p. 487.
9 Ibid., p. 487.
10 Thompson, 'Living Ways of Sense Making'.
11 Sutton, J. (2023). 'Individuals for Anti-Individualists'. *Constructivist Foundations*, 18(3), 374–6. https://philarchive.org/archive/SUTIFA
12 De Jaegher and Di Paolo, 'Participatory Sense-making', p. 488.
13 See, for example, film industry blogs such as 'The Independent Film School' (https://theindependentfilmschool.com/film-directing-directors-vision/) or 'Good Guys Productions': https://goodguysproductions.co.uk/uncategorised/directors-vision-influence-filmmaking-techniques/.
14 De Jaegher and Di Paolo, 'Participatory Sense-making', p. 488.
15 Williams, R. (1981) *Culture*. Fontana Paperbacks. p115.
16 Torrance, S., and Schumann, F. (2018). 'The Spur of the Moment: What Jazz Improvisation Tells Cognitive Science'. *AI and Society*. https://doi.org/10.1007/s00146-018-0838-4.
17 See: Nagrin, D. (1994). *Dance and the Specific Image*. University of Pittsburgh Press.
18 Shirley Clarke, as quoted in Berg, G. (1967). 'Interview with Shirley Clarke'. *Film Culture*, 44.
19 Clarke, S. (circa 1963) typescript. 'Statement by Shirley Clarke of the Whys and Wherefores of *The Cool World*' (Wisconsin Center for Film and Theater Research, Box 5, Folder 1), p. 2. A note in this typescript indicates that the interview was later 'Published in "Jeune Cinema", Prague Czechoslovakia 1964 – recorded interview'.
20 Ibid., p. 2 (my emphasis).
21 Ibid., p. 2 (my emphasis).
22 Ibid., p. 2 (my emphasis).
23 Ibid., p. 2 (my emphasis).
24 Millard, *Screenwriting in a Digital Era*, p. 99.

25 Ibid., p. 99.
26 Ibid., p. 93.
27 Ibid., p. 93.
28 Shirley Clarke, as quoted in Rabinovitz, L. (1983). 'Choreography of Cinema: An Interview with Shirley Clarke'. *Afterimage*, December, 8–11. https://www.vasulka.org/archive/4-30c/AfterImageDec83(300).pdf., pp. 9–10.
29 Ibid., p. 9.
30 Ibid., p. 9.
31 See: Hongisto, I. (2016). *Soul of the Documentary*. Amsterdam University Press. https://www.aup.nl/en/book/9789048525294/soul-of-the-documentary.
32 Clarke, 'Statement by Shirley Clarke of the Whys and Wherefores of *The Cool World*', p. 2.
33 See: Merritt, M. (2013). 'Instituting Impairment: Extended Cognition and the Construction of Female Sexual Dysfunction'. *Cognitive Systems Research*, 25–6, 47–53. https://doi.org/10.1016/j.cogsys.2013.03.005.
34 Ibid., pp. 48–9.
35 Millard, *Screenwriting in a Digital Era*, p. 99.
36 Ibid., p. 99.
37 De Jaegher and Di Paolo, 'Participatory Sense-making', p. 494.
38 Clarke, as quoted in Rabinovitz, 'Choreography of Cinema', p. 10.
39 De Jaegher and Di Paolo, 'Participatory Sense-making', p. 494.
40 Clarke, 'Statement by Shirley Clarke of the Whys and Wherefores of *The Cool World*'.
41 See: Pearlman, K., MacKay, J., and Sutton, J. (2018). 'Creative Editing: Svilova and Vertov's Distributed Cognition'. *Apparatus. Film, Media and Digital Cultures of Central and Eastern Europe*, 0(6). http://www.apparatusjournal.net/index.php/apparatus/article/view/122/306.
42 Clarke, S. (circa 1960). Handwritten note on *The Connection*, in an undated collection of notes stapled together and found in Wisconsin Center for Film and Theater Research Box 14, Folder 2.
43 Vertov, D. (1984). *Kino-Eye, The Writings of Dziga Vertov* (ed. A. Michelson; trans. K. O'Brien). University of California Press.
44 Clarke, S. (circa 1960). Handwritten note on *The Connection*.
45 Ibid., p. 2.
46 Ibid., p. 3.
47 See: Boden, M. (2004). *The Creative Mind: Myths and Mechanisms* (2nd edn). Routledge. Also Csikszentmihalyi, M. (2014). 'Society, Culture, and Person: A Systems View of Creativity'. In *The Systems Model of Creativity: The Collected Works of Mihaly Csikszentmihalyi* (M. Csikszentmihalyi, Ed., pp. 47–61). Springer Netherlands. https://doi.org/10.1007/978-94-017-9085-7_4.

48 Pearlman and Sutton, 'Reframing the Director', p. 86.
49 Ibid., p. 86.
50 See: Pearlman, 'Distributed Authorship: An et al. Proposal'. Also the original poem from which this quote comes: Allen, R. J. (1995). 'Tigers.' In *The Air Dolphin Brigade*. Paperbark in association with Tasdance, p. 40.
51 Kirsh, D. (2013). 'Embodied Cognition and the Magical Future of Interaction Design'. *AVANT*, 2, 124–66. https://doi.org/10.12849/4020 2013.0709.0008, p. 138.
52 Ibid., p. 138.
53 Beckett, S. (1952). *Waiting for Godot* (1st edn). Les Éditions de Minuit.
54 Clarke, as quoted in Rabinovitz, 'Choreography of Cinema', p. 10.
55 Clarke, S., Gelber, J. et al. (1961). *The Connection*. https://www.imdb.com/title/tt0054763/.
56 See: Clarke, Handwritten Note on *The Connection*, p. 1.
57 Clarke, Gelber, et al., *The Connection*.
58 Shirley Clarke, as quoted in *Les Cahiers du Cinema*, October 1968, translated by Janice Bergstrom in The UCLA Film Archives Presents The Connection, 2pm Friday October 8, 1976. Filmography and programme notes compiled and translated by Janice Bergstrom, accessed in Wisconsin Center for Film and Theater Research, Box 14, Folder 6.
59 See: Rushton, R. (2011). *The Reality of Film: Theories of Filmic Reality*. Manchester University Press. https://academic.oup.com/screen/article-abstract/53/3/323/1695225
60 Clarke, Gelber et al., *The Connection*.
61 Gurian, A., in email correspondence with Wendy Clarke, 13 February 2021.
62 See: Nagrin, *Dance and the Specific Image*.
63 Clarke, as quoted in Rabinovitz, 'Choreography of Cinema', p. 11.
64 Shirley Clarke, as quoted in Polt, H. (1964). 'Interview: Shirley Clarke'. *Film Comment*, Spring. https://www.filmcomment.com/article/interview-shirley-clarke/ pp. 31–2.
65 See: Burch, N., and Labarthe, A. (1970). *Rome is Burning (Portrait of Shirley Clarke)*. At 8 mins 50 secs approx.
66 De Jaegher and Di Paolo, 'Participatory Sense-making', p. 494.
67 Ibid., p. 494.
68 Millard, *Screenwriting in a Digital Era*, p. 107.
69 Clarke, as quoted in Polt, 'Interview: Shirley Clarke'.
70 Clarke, 'Statement by Shirley Clarke of the Whys and Wherefores of *The Cool World*', p. 2.
71 De Jaegher and Di Paolo, 'Participatory Sense-making', p. 494.
72 Clarke, as quoted in Rabinovitz, 'Choreography of Cinema', p. 11.
73 Ibid., p. 11.

74 See Pearlman, MacKay and Sutton, 'Creative Editing: Svilova and Vertov's Distributed Cognition'.
75 Clarke, S., Lee, C. et al. (1963). *The Cool World*. https://www.imdb.com/title/tt0056952/.
76 Ibid.
77 Shirley Clarke, as quoted in Rice, S. (1972). 'Shirley Clarke: Image and Images'. *Women in Film*, 3, 20–2 (print typescript accessed in Wisconsin Center for Film and Theater Research Box 12, Folder 2), p. 22.
78 Clarke, S. Lee, C., Holliday, J., et al. (1967). *Portrait of Jason*. https://www.imdb.com/title/tt0062144.
79 Ibid.
80 Shirley Clarke, as quoted in Jones, W. (1967). 'Her Job Was Not to Keep Out of the Way'. *The Minneapolis Tribune*. 22 November. pp. 1, 12.
81 Clarke, Lee, Holliday, et al. (1967). *Portrait of Jason*.
82 Gustafson, I. (2011). 'Putting Things to the Test: Reconsidering *Portrait of Jason*'. *Camera Obscura*, 26(2), 1–31. https://doi.org/10.1215/02705346-1301521, p. 29.
83 Clarke, Lee, Holliday et al., *Portrait of Jason*.
84 Ibid.
85 Ibid.
86 Ibid.
87 Clarke, as quoted in Rabinovitz, 'Choreography of Cinema', p. 11.
88 Shirley Clarke, as quoted in Clark, V. A. (1977). 'Interview: Shirley Clarke. 15 July. Hollywood', p. 2. Typescript with accompanying cover letter of 8 December 1985, expressing intention to publish the interview in *The Legend of Maya Deren, A Documentary Biography* (Wisconsin Center for Film and Theater Research Box 22, Folder 51).
89 Ibid., p. 11.

6

Conclusions and Continuances

So many things left to write about. I've made a case, in this book, that filmmaking is an instance of distributed cognition at work in bodies, cultures and contexts of filmmakers. A core premise has been that:

> cognition includes emotion and motivation, and is not located in the individual brain alone ... mental life is *embodied* rather than restricted to the brain alone, *embedded* in rich material and socio-technical settings, *enacted* in histories of flexible engagement with the environment.[1]

I've used this premise to illuminate some of the key works in Shirley Clarke's oeuvre, and the ways that she directs and edits films as a process of embodied, embedded and enactive[2] creative thinking.

I've also discussed these films as her thinking through and with her collaborators and context in order to offer a way of understanding film authorship as at once singular and multiple. In this process, I have been thinking through Shirley Clarke herself as both singular and a 'self that is relational', with the aim of making it possible to recognise her voice and vision as something arising from her 'self'; but also, as philosopher Kathleen Wallace writes: 'that temporality or historicity is constitutive of the self, that the self is a process, not a static three-dimensional thing . . . the self is a cumulative network'.[3]

I come now, however, to the problem of finishing a book about a 'cumulative network'[4] and yet having failed to mention so many significant branches and entanglements of that network.

In Chapter 3, I covered some of the dance and experimental early works; but what about the controversial *Scary Time* (1960) made for, but rejected by, UNICEF? I have not touched upon the ways that this early foray into social justice filmmaking, and the hostile response to the film, may have fuelled Clarke's rebellion and commitment to making confronting films. Or perhaps damaged her trust in major institutions and turned her away from working in contexts where there may have been more money, but also less creative agency.

I also did not write about *Bullfight* (1955) or *Rose and the Players*,[i] the collaborations with dancer/choreographer Anna Sokolow through which Clarke explored cinematic devices for moving into and out of subjective perspectives and working at the edges where performer and character overlap. These works are significant seeds for Clarke's major works in video in the early 80s: *Tongues* (1982) and *Savage/Love* (1981) with Joseph Chaikin, and *A Visual Diary* (1980) with Blondell Cummings. These 1980s video works are all grounded in the 1950s work with dancers. They continue Clarke's early preoccupation with the problem of how to translate live performance to the screen without killing it off, and they use location, editing and video to bring viewers in and out of subjective experience. They create a screen image of someone inhabiting the vicissitudes of a character who is a version of themselves.[5]

Also never discussed is the time in Los Angeles, where Clarke's forehead (metaphorically) begins to bleed from being hit against the wall of the Hollywood's indifference to her. Her teaching at UCLA and her directing of live theatre have been overlooked, as has her performance in Agnes Varda's *Lion's Love* (1969), where she and Varda tragi/comically negotiate which of them will play

---

[i] *Rose and the Players* was never finished, but one segment, *A Moment in Love* (1956) was finished and, as with *Bullfight* and *Scary Time*, fragments of *Rose and the Players* and many other short works directed and edited by Clarke, are on the Milestone collection, *Project Shirley: The Magic Box*, https://kinolorber.com/product/the-magic-box-the-films-of-shirley-clarke-blu-ray.

the filmmaker who is trying to kill themselves because they can't get a film made. Clarke's network of relationships with Varda, and especially her co-star Viva, stretch from the 60s, when she was adored by artists of the French New Wave, through her activism in the 70s, when she and Viva were arrested together while trying to make a video of a building before it was demolished,[ii] and to the end of Clarke's life.

Viva is just one of Clarke's many artist friends including Sam Shephard, Remy Charlip, Merce Cunningham, Joseph Chaikin, Skip LaPlante, Harry Mann and Ornette Coleman, whose names appear in Clarke's proposal for a project that was never realised, called *A Musical for the 80s*. The aim of this project was to explore the 'themes of maturing and aging' with 'a shared awareness of an idea first articulated by Ernst Lubitsch: "a sense of style must be supported by a group and also essentially comic"'.[6] Themes of maturing and aging are still tricky subjects for women to approach, but for someone known for her 'eccentric Beat girl'[7] persona, they would have even more risky, and, sadly, less likely to be funded. I cannot write about this film (intended to be 'shot by Haskell Wexler and Ricky Leacock'[8]) and can only imagine what this stylish and 'essentially comic'[9] take on this network constellating through and around Clarke could have been.

Fortunately, in this period where Clarke is exhausted by efforts to raise money for films, two things revitalise her: video and video workshop creation. These two are intimately entwined in Clarke's creative and distributed thinking, and both, in a sense, return her to her origins in dance and performance. As a 1973 interview with Clarke in *Radical Software* magazine notes, Clarke's group of collaborators in this phase of her creativity was 'a video troupe to take on the college circuit'.[10] This college circuit is familiar to me – to all modern dancers in the USA then, and still. It is where we earned our daily bread, and there are stories of troupes well

---

[ii] Clarke kept the camera running the whole time, and it is possible to see the arrest and hear Clarke arguing with the cops on tape here: https://archive.org/details/TheArrestOriginal_VCA309

known to history (such as the Merce Cunningham company) and many more who are now pretty much unknown, squeezing themselves and their gear into station wagons to tour these circuits, performing live and teaching workshops. Clarke's use of video is thus a return of her improvisational and choreographic sensibilities to the stage. She frequently notes in her discussion of video that she is interested in it as a 'process art',[11] that what she is doing with it is performance – a live art, a stage art, not a fixed screen art.

Clarke's editing as a key part of her creative toolkit is sidelined in her 1970s video phase, and I can't help but wonder, if it had not been, would her video art have had more lasting value? As it stands the videos left to view are not really for viewing. Or as she says, 'they are of no value artistically'.[12] Other than the completed and distributed works available on the Milestone *Project Shirley: The Magic Box* DVD collection, the videos are mostly endless meanderings with multiple cameras (often pointed at video monitors to create layers of image), the images are fuzzy and only very occasionally arresting, the audio might be whatever music was playing, argument was occurring, or drug was being inhaled.[iii]

However, they are unedited because they are not meant to be viewed on screens, they were in a sense rehearsals or exploratory moments to find techniques, frames, set-ups and ideas for live video-infused performances. They are often tapes made during, and by the participants in, workshops which, as collaborator Andrew Gurian writes, were: 'her most extraordinary use of video . . . The workshops were live and evanescent events; what remains are fragments'.[13] Gurian describes the structure on top of the Chelsea Hotel where these workshops took place, and the unfolding of one of them:

[iii] A number of these extant video tapes have been digitised by the tireless archivists of the Wisconsin Centre for Film and Theater Research, and can be accessed on the WCFTR Internet Archive here: https://archive.org/details/wcftr?query=Shirley+Clarke

Some time ago the pyramid, a permanent structure, was divided into several spaces on several levels. It had windows, furniture, plumbing – and now a network of audio and video cables running to and from each interior and exterior space. It was also Shirley Clarke's home/studio, and on this evening she introduced the group members to each other and to what lay ahead in an eight or nine hour video workshop: video game-playing, portrait painting, tape-making – all to culminate in a grand four-channel playback at dawn.[14]

Clarke draws out the comparison of video to dance performance when she talks about the embodied skills and expertise that she and her collaborators and students were developing in response to this new technology. She also makes connections to the skills I have identified as significant to her creativity in film, when she says that she and her collaborators:

> need to develop better motor connections between our eyes and our hands and bodies – we need balance and control to move our cameras around in space and often as performers as well. We need rhythmic skill to move our images from monitor to monitor or pass our camera to someone else. But mainly we need the skill to see our own Images in our own monitors and at the same time see what everyone else is doing. We need to acquire the ability to see in much the same way that a jazz musician can hear what he is playing and at the same time hear what the other musicians are doing and together they make music.[15]

Balance, control of movement, rhythmic skill, noticing, responding and the improvisational and coordinated skill of jazz musicians. These are not evident in the archived video tapes themselves, but the process of developing and honing them is.

These tapes are not records of thoughts, they are the thinking.

It is worth noting that Clarke does not say 'I' had to develop those embodied and embedded forms of expertise, but that 'we' did. She refers, with this 'we', to the distributed creativity of the members of the troupe and, importantly, the people who were expert with the technology.

192 Shirley Clarke: Thinking Through Movement

Figure 6.1 Shirley Clarke and members of the Video Space Troupe: notes on the backs of photos in this folder indicate that this is the first performance of the Troupe and that it is taking place at The Kitchen, May 1973; and that the photos are 'taken by Margarite Journalist from Caracas Venezuela'. Shirley Clarke collection, M91-052, Box 27, Folder 16, Wisconsin Center for Film and Theater Research

Figure 6.2 A complex set up of multiple video monitors at the Chelsea Hotel, circa 1973. WCFTR name photograph file, PH 7163, Shirley Clarke collection, Box 52, Folder 3, Wisconsin Center for Film and Theater Research

Accounts are mixed of Clarke's own skills with the gear – she was certainly interested, and her notebooks reveal substantive consideration of the ways the wires, monitors, signals, decks, cameras and tapes could be networked and rigged to create possibilities.[16] However, she also relied heavily on collaborators like Wendy Clarke, DeeDee Halleck, Gurian and less well-known or historicised but absolutely vital people such as Shridhar Bapat, who was: 'the tech guy at the pleasure palace'.[17]

Bapat, as Alexander Keefe notes was:

> an expert at managing what they used to call Spaghetti City – the mess of wires that connected cameras to monitors, early video synthesisers and recorders, tape to reel. It wasn't easy in the first place, and almost everyone was stoned, anyway. But Shridhar could keep the video cameras from jamming, the tapes from spooling off the open reels; he could rig up monitors and cameras into complex machines for the production of video feedback.[18]

Bapat was one of what Keefe calls 'a coterie of tech-heads armed with duct tape, Q-tips, and obscure expertise acquired the hard way'.[19] In line with my creative practice and distributed cognition framework I would argue that these 'tech-heads',[20] like the collaborating dancers, choreographers, cinematographers and other associates such as Madeleine Anderson or Carl Lee (discussed in Chapter 5) are manifesting the vision. In doing so, they are imprinting that vision's manifestation with the particularities of their own personalities, priorities and expertise.

Speaking in 1982, Clarke remains both prescient and utopian about the possibilities for video. She is prescient about a time when most households will have cable TV, easy access to video cassettes (instead of reel to reel) and 'videophones'.[21] She is utopian in her idea that she and her video colleagues will 'find ways to use video to Inform the public of their Inalienable right guaranteed by the First Amendment – free speech. And that means free access to the communications media'.[22] Clarke's vision as a director of video is not towards the creation of a work but towards the creation of public access, and public rights over the interests of 'Big

Figure 6.3 Ornette Coleman and Shirley Clarke in Fort Worth for the shooting of *Ornette: Made in America*, circa 1983. Shirley Clarke collection, M91-052, Box 25, Folder 16, Wisconsin Center for Film and Theater Research

Business'.[23] She revels in the easy access she had to production of image through video, often contrasting it to the long waits and expenses of shooting on film. She imagines a time when everyone will have equal access to the tools needed to make their voices and perspectives known through two-way media communication. It probably goes without saying that the prescience was warranted while the utopianism seems to have been less so.

Clarke's appreciation for video notwithstanding, she directed and edited one more feature-length film after 1967's *Portrait of Jason*. It took seventeen years to get it finished. Clarke started shooting it after making *Portrait of Jason*, but the boxes of film, and later video tapes, were tucked into the back of Ornette Coleman's closet until 1981, when producer Kathelin Hoffman Gray instigated a 'three-year collaboration'[24] with Coleman and Clarke on *Ornette: Made in America* (1984).

This final film synthesises most things this book has covered into one film: the enactive directing methods of planning, improvising, finding a way and responding; the embedded editing thinking with the material, the context and the characters; and the embodied rhythms and collaborations where a dancer's physical and cultural training meets free jazz. *Ornette: Made in America* also synthesises all of the media in which Clarke had worked – dance, theatre, drama, documentary, video – and, of course, it continues her lifelong work through and with jazz music and musicians.

Like other feature films directed and edited by Clarke, *Ornette: Made in America* is centred on the life of a Black man. This time it is her friend, Ornette Coleman, who Clarke compares, in her notebook 'ORNETTE' to Krishnamurti, Georgia O'Keefe, Martha Graham, Brecht and Gertrude Stein as she ruminates on who might be, like Coleman, an 'avant-garde cross-over, someone who has done something unique with their life, and can see what may be possible for them.'[25]

Producer Kathelin Gray, who also trained as a modern dancer, writes about her understanding of Clarke's intentions: 'to influence the viewer on a pre-rational or unconscious level, through rhythm and movement'.[26] Gray describes the editing rhythms as '"free dance" in film',[27] and notes from her time in the edit suite with Clarke, that the

> process was to create a cognitive map based on a motor space/time: a kinesphere. To connect with a filming or editing, she would sense the musical score, or the musicality of the scene/dialogue. To test just-completed rough edits, we would sometimes stand and move to the shape and tempo of the images.[28]

Ornette: Made in America mixes re-enactment (semi-fictional bio-pic style interludes of boys playing Ornette as a kid and as a young teen wandering the streets of Fort Worth) with footage of Coleman himself on those same rundown streets in the present. These streets are contrasted with concert footage of the new upscale Fort Worth Arts Centre opening night performance of an Ornette Coleman symphony. The symphony performance footage is a kind of bass line that grounds the film's forays off into different concerts, thoughts and moments, cuts to footage from the recent and distant past, actual and remembered.

In the 1968 proposal for the film she wanted to make then, Clarke writes: 'I also intend to experiment in the visualisation of music through the use of electronic video tape'.[29] It is possible she visualised what she would do with electronic signal and montage as early as 1968, but it may have taken the intervening fifteen or so years before she could actualise these ideas. The technology needed to evolve, as did Coleman's music, which drives the montages.

These montages juxtapose art and artifice, present and memory, audience and performer. Neon colours in crash zooms interrupt the serious gaze of the young Black actor on an empty stage. Is he watching the grown-up white people (including Clarke herself), dancing manically to jazz which is being played in the after-party at the arts centre? Or is that an editing sleight of hand? Clarke cuts fast, letting the kid's gaze lead us to jazz musicians marooned in a tent city sit-in, where it is as though the jazz music we can hear is being dreamed by the white and Black kids playing together against the backdrop of the Washington monument. The montage world shifts again, forward in time, first to a symphony concert in San Francisco in 1969 then to a televised concert in Milan in 1980, then back to the 70s and a concert in Morocco, then forward to the present and an interview that returns us to Ornette Coleman's thoughts about jazz thinking.

Some critics struggled with *Ornette: Made in America*. Their frustrations with the film's free jazz cutting are revealing. They want a simpler portrait of an individual,[30] but what the film offers is a chance to think about editing as choreography of movement in the mode of free jazz. When you experience the editing of *Ornette: Made in America*, you experience a film that, through its editing, abandons certain forms and becomes itself free jazz.

Despite Ornette Coleman's interview statements returning repeatedly to the notion of thinking in rhythms, in music, with instruments, with his collaborators, critics' expectations about form cause them to miss what is really being created here, which is a visualisation of distributed creativity.

In this last film directed and edited by Shirley Clarke, the jazz music, montage and creative cognising with tools and community are all visible in the choices of what to shoot and what to include. There is a chaos and subtextual sense to this film that feels as though it recapitulates some of the chaos and subtextual sense that runs through Clarke's own life and work. Would that I could convey those rhythms here; but if I could, that would defeat the purpose of this book: which is ultimately only to provide an access point to the films themselves, so that they become more possible for filmmakers and philosophers to think through and with.

Notes

1 Sutton, J., and Bicknell, K. (2022). 'Introduction: The Situated Intelligence of Collaborative Skills'. In K. Bicknell and J. Sutton (Eds.), *Collaborative Embodied Performance* (pp. 1–18). Bloomsbury, https://doi.org/10.5040/9781350197725.ch-00i. pp.4-5. Emphasis in original.
2 See ibid., pp. 1–18.
3 Wallace, K. (2019). 'A Theory of the Relational Self: The Cumulative Network Model'. *Humana.Mente Journal of Philosophical Studies*, 36, 189–220, p. 190. https://www.humanamente.eu/index.php/HM/article/view/287
4 Ibid., p. 190.
5 For more on the question of whether a person in a dancefilm or video is portraying themselves, a character or a performer, see Pearlman, K. (2010). 'If a Dancing Figure Falls in the Forest and Nobody Sees Her . . .' *Participations*, 7(2). https://www.participations.org/07-02-04-pearlman.pdf.
6 Clarke, S. (circa 1982). Proposal to Women's InterArts Centre, Statement of Intent (typescript from Wisconsin Center for Film and Theater Research Box 23 Folder 1, 'Women's Interarts Center').
7 Rabinovitz, L. (2003). *Points of Resistance: Women, Power and Politics in the New York Avant-garde Cinema, 1943–71.* University of Illinois Press, p. 9.
8 Clarke, Proposal to Women's InterArts Centre.
9 Lubitsch, E., as quoted in ibid.
10 Shirley Clarke, as quoted in Videoball (1973). 'Shirley Clarke: An Interview'. *Radical Software*, 2(4), 25–7. https://www.radicalsoftware.org/volume2nr4/pdf/VOLUME2NR4_art08.pdf, p. 25.

11 Ibid., p. 25.
12 Shirley Clarke, as quoted in Bebb, B. (1982). 'The Many Media of Shirley Clarke'. In *Journal of the University Film and Video Association* 34(2), 3–8; p. 6.
13 Gurian, A. (2004). 'Thoughts on Shirley Clarke and The TP Videospace Troupe'. *Millennium Film Journal*, Fall (42), 5–31, p. 5.
14 Ibid., p. 5.
15 Clarke, as quoted in Videoball (1973), p. 25.
16 Andrew Gurian reproduces a diagram of the intended set-up for the performance at Antioch College in 1974 in Gurian, 'Thoughts on Shirley Clarke and the TP Videospace Troupe', p. 17.
17 Keefe, A. (2013). 'Aleph Null: Shridhar Bapat's Undergrounds'. *Bidoun*. https://bidoun.org/articles/aleph-null.
18 Ibid.
19 Ibid.
20 Ibid.
21 Clarke, as quoted in Videoball (1973) p. 25.
22 Ibid., p. 26.
23 Ibid., p. 26.
24 Gray as quoted in *Kathelin Hoffman Gray Reminisces* – booklet published by Milestone Films as part of the DVD extras available with purchase of *Ornette: Made in America, Project Shirley*, Volume 3. https://milestonefilms.com/products/ornette-made-in-america. Doros, D., and Zahos, Z. (2012). *Ornette: Made in America, A Milestone Film Release* – press kit. https://milestonefilms.com/products/ornette-made-in-america?_pos=1&_sid=d507dc262&_ss=r.
25 Clarke, S. in notebook ORNETTE, circa 1982–3 (Wisconsin Center for Film and Theater Research, Box 21, Folder 3), p. 3.
26 Gray, K. (2012). *Dancer as Filmmaker: The Cinematerpsichorean World of Shirley Clarke*. In booklet published by Milestone Films as part of the DVD extras available with purchase of *Ornette: Made in America, Project Shirley*, Volume 3. https://milestonefilms.com/products/ornette-made-in-america, p. 6.
27 Ibid., p. 7.
28 Ibid., p. 8.
29 Clarke, S. proposal, 'Unproduced Ornette Coleman Film' (1967–68). (Wisconsin Center for Film and Theater Research, Box 8, Folder 1.):
30 Gary Giddins, for example, writing in *The Village Voice* says: 'Perhaps she edits too much ... As a bio the film is a mess.' Giddins, G. (1986). 'Ornate Coleman'. *The Village Voice*. 25 February, p. 62.

Index

Note: Titles and references to images are in *italics*. All film and video works are made by Clarke and her collaborators unless otherwise noted.

activism, 14, 18, 189
agency, 7, 9, 53, 56, 89, 139, 188
aging, 189
alienation, 156, 157, 161, 178
Allen, Richard James, 25, 47, 50, 97
American Cinema Editors organisation, 110
Anderson, Madeleine, 32, 165, 166, 167–8, 174, 193
'Artistic Accomplishments' narrative, 20–2
auteurs, 5, 33, 45, 52
authorship, 4–5, 9, 33, 36, 45, 46, 48, 180
 and *The Cool World*, 166–8
 and distributed creativity, 51–2, 174, 187
 and editing, 108, 109, 110–14
 and enaction, 140, 145, 153
 and *A Portrait of Jason*, 177
autonomy, 34, 57, 65, 150, 165
avant-garde, 23, 24, 27, 30, 32, 41, 84–5, 103, 195

ballet, 73, 76, 173
Bapat, Shridhar, 193
Barron, Bebe, 114

Barron, Louis, 114
Beat girl persona, 39, 189
Bebb, Bruce, 94
Beck, Julian, 28, 29
Birds (Hinton et al., 2000), 25
Black culture, 15, 59–60
 and *The Cool World*, 122–33, 167
 and enactive cognition, 138
 see also Black men; Harlem; racism
Black Lives Matter movement, 8, 59
Black men, 8, 9, 11, 60, 119–20, 123, 158
Brakhage, Stan, 182
Brenner, Albert, 152
Bridges-Go-Round (1958), 7, 100
 and abstract movement, 113, 114–17
 and rhythm, 75
Bromberg, Ellen, 97
Brooklyn Bridge (NYC), 115–16
Browne, Roscoe Lee, 152
Brussels Loops (1957), 7, 25, 100, 102
 and editing, 113, 114, 117–21
 and rhythm, 75
Brussels World's Fair, 7, 25, 117
Bryant, Baird, *162*, 169, 174
Buckley, Peter, 72, 110
Bullfight (1955), 25, 72, 78, 97, 100, 114, 188

Burch, Noël, 82
Butterfly (1967), 17

Cassavetes, John, 35, 41
censorship, 32, 156
Chaikin, Joseph, 188, 189
Charlip, Remy, 189
choreographic sensibility, 25, 100, 101, 134, 156, 162
choreography, 25, 72, 80, 88, 96, 98–9, 147, 159 176
cine-dance, 23–4
cinematography, 152, 164
civil rights, 14–15, 77
Clark, Vevé, 182
Clarke, Bert (husband), 16–17, 84
Clarke, Wendy (daughter), 17–18, 33, 34, 37, 193
 and *In Paris Parks*, 101
 and *A Portrait of Jason*, 36
cognition, 46, 49–50, 74, 142;
 see also distributed cognition
Coleman, Ornette, 19, 189, 194–7
collaboration, 19, 26, 45–6, 48–9, 57–8, 78, 138–9
 and *The Cool World*, 165
 and improvisation, 149
 and modern dance, 76–7
 and *Ornette: Made in America*, 19, 194–5
 and *Skyscraper*, 101–2
 and vision, 143–5
community, 36, 54, 59, 74, 76, 78, 101, 102–3, 138
 and *The Cool World*, 32, 113, 121, 125, 126, 128, 133, 166–7, 197
Connection, The (film, 1961), 32, 60, 139, 155, 156–62
 and direction, 144
 and drug dealers, 97
 and finding a way, 151–3
 and planning, 148–9
Connection, The (play), 26–30

Cool World, The (1963), 7–8, 19, 30–3, 163–5, 175
 and cast, 165–6
 and co-authors, 166–8
 and Harlem shoot, 120, 162
 and living in motion, 171–4
 and monologues, 170–1
 and montages, 169–70
 and movement structure, 168–9
 and opening scene, 113, 121–33
 and women, 139
creative practice, 1–2, 3, 4–5, 45–6, 51, 61–4
crew, 17, 47, 54, 60, 62, 63, 76, 154–5
 and *The Connection*, 157, 160, 162, 175
 and *The Cool World*, 32–3, 125, 174
 and *Dance in the Sun*, 84
 and participatory sense-making, 144, 145
 and planning, 148–9
 see also collaboration
Cummings, Blondell, 188
Cunningham, Merce, 74, 189, 190
cuts *see* editing

dance, 1, 2, 4, 5–6, 18, 62, 70
 and camera, 99–100
 and character, 24, 81, 96–7
 and college circuit, 189–90
 and community, 74, 77
 and *The Connection*, 161
 and context, 71, 72
 and *Dance in the Sun*, 80, 88, 89, 90, 91, 93, 94
 and education, 16
 and embodied cognition, 54, 72, 74
 and improvisation, 146–7
 and jazz, 19
 and Kuleshov, 94–5
 and mind-reading, 62–3
 and training, 72–3
 see also dancefilm; modern dance

Dance in the Sun (1953), 6, 24, 71, 78–86
 and documentary, 95–7
 and phrasing, 87–94
 and videodance, 100
dance thinking, 71, 73–9
dancefilm, 5–6, 9, 14–15, 23–5, 37, 71, 78, 95, 97–8, 100–1; *see also Dance in the Sun* (1953); *In Paris Parks* (1954); *Skyscraper* (1959)
dancing cognition, 5–6, 70–107, 146
Dargis, Manohla, 41
De Jaegher, Hanne, 48, 58, 142, 150, 151, 166
De Mille, Agnes, 85
De Sica, Vittorio, 164
Decroux, Etienne, 101
Deren, Maya, 24, 38, 39, 79, 85, 94
 A Study in Choreography for Camera, 90
 and narrative, 82, 84
Di Paolo, Ezequiel, 48, 58, 142, 150, 151, 166
direct cinema, 25–6
directors, 2, 7, 45–7, 140, 158, 162
 and collaboration, 57–8
 and editing, 108
 and responding, 154–5
 and vision, 143–5
distributed cognition, 1–2, 4–5, 7, 45–9, 50–3; *see also* embedded cognition; embodied cognition; enactive cognition
diversity, 62, 76–7
documentary, 4, 14–15
 and *Brussels Loops*, 113
 and *Dance in the Sun*, 95–7
 and Robert Frost, 140–1
 and *Skyscraper*, 101–2
 see also Ornette: Made in America (1984); *A Portrait of Jason* (1967)
Doros, Dennis, 33, 35
Downey Sr, Robert, 35

drama, 96–7
drugs, 19, 36, 97
 and *The Connection*, 156–7, 158, 160, 161
Duncan, Isadora, 73
Dundy, Elaine, 4, 14, 15–16, 36–7
 and theatre, 26, 28

editing, 1, 2, 3, 6–8, 9–10
 and authorship, 110–14
 and *Bridges-Go-Round*, 116–17
 and *Brussels Loops*, 118–21
 and *The Connection*, 157, 159–62
 and *The Cool World*, 122–33
 and *Dance in the Sun*, 82, 83–4, 85–6, 89–94
 and decision-making, 63–4
 and embedded cognition, 55–7
 and form of choreography, 6, 55, 79, 86, 87, 133, 196
 and phrasing, 71, 86, 89–90, 94, 102–3, 125–6, 133, 168–9
 and *A Portrait of Jason*, 177–8
 and *Skyscraper*, 102
 and trajectory phrasing, 80, 87, 89, 111, 125
 and vision, 144
embedded cognition, 55–7
embodied cognition, 6, 54, 71–3, 146
enactive cognition, 9, 57–61, 138–40, 142–3, 144–6
 and *The Cool World*, 165, 166

Felix the Cat, 13–14
femininity, 3, 39
feminist, 1–2, 5, 7, 8, 24, 33, 38–9, 45, 85, 180
Fennell, Emerald, 144
Film-makers Cooperative, 35
finding a way, 151–3
First Nations people, 59
flow of movement, 110–11
Fosse, Bob, 74

Four Journeys into Mystic Time (1979), 99–100
French New Wave, 189
Frost, Robert, 37, 140

Galentine, Wheaton, 101
Gelber, Jack, 27, 148
Gillespie, Dizzy, 133, 168
Gornik, Vivian, 18
Graham, Martha, 77, 78, 85
grant applications, 20–2, 26–31
Gray, Kathelin Hoffman, 194, 195
Guggenheim Foundation, 20–2, 26–31
Gurian, Andrew, 35, 108, 190–1
Gustafson, Irene, 178

Halleck, DeeDee, 193
Harlem (NYC), 15, 97
  and *The Cool World*, 120, 121–33, 163–4
Haryse, Mary, 18
Heersmink, Richard, 52, 55–6
Heller, Amy, 33, 35–6
Hinton, David, 25
Holder, Maryse, 39
Holliday, Jason, 35, 149, 176–9, 180–1
Hollywood, 23–4, 33, 82–3, 108
Holm, Hanya, 78, 85
Hongisto, Ilona, 177
humour, 37, 39–40, 75, 99–100
Humphrey, Doris, 78, 81, 86–7
  The Art of Making Dances, 73, 76, 77

image theatre, 29–30
imagination, 2, 6
  and *Bullfight*, 97
  and *Dance in the Sun*, 84
  see also kinaesthetic imagination
imagined geographies, 79–80, 90, 94
improvisation, 9, 15, 52, 76, 134, 141–7, 148, 149–51, 154, 190–1
  and *The Connection*, 153, 158–9
  and *The Cool World*, 31, 163, 166, 167

and dance, 146–7
and jazz, 145–6
and *A Portrait of Jason*, 175–6
and responding, 154
In Paris Parks (1954), 17, 24–5, 75, 100–1
intuition, 111

Jacoby, Irving, 101
Jason and Shirley (Winter et al., 2015), 35–6
jazz, 3, 13, 18–20, 77, 149
  and collaboration, 76, 148, 191
  and *The Connection*, 19, 157
  and *The Cool World*, 168, 169, 172
  and dancing, 75–6, 111
  and editing, 116
  and improvisation, 15, 52, 76, 142, 145–6
  and *Ornette: Made in America*, 19, 195–7
  and rebellion, 15
Jewish, 3, 8, 15

Keefe, Alexander, 193
Kennedy, John F., 140
kinaesthetic empathy, 6, 82, 111
kinaesthetic imagination, 6, 86, 112, 133
kinaesthetic intelligence, 2, 7, 55, 100
Krueger, Joel, 19
Kubrick, Stanley, 37
Kuleshov, Lev, 94–5, 100

Labarthe, André, 82
labour, 48, 145, 162, 165, 168
LaPlante, Skip, 189
Lateef, Yusef, 168
Leacock, Richard, 25, 35, 118
Lee, Carl, 32, 33, 35, 36–7
  and *The Connection*, 156
  and *The Cool World*, 165, 166–7, 174
  and *A Portrait of Jason*, 178–81

LGBTQIA+, 9, 45
life-dancing, 3
Lion's Love (Varda et al., 1969), 188–9
living in motion, 171–4
Living Theatre, The (NYC), 26–30, 31
Lubitsch, Ernst, 189

Macera, Teo, 114
McLeod, Kembrew, 21, 37, 83
McPherson, Katrina, 97
Malafouris, Lambros, 48, 58
Malina, Judith, 26, 27–8, 29
Man with a Movie Camera (Vertov et al., 1929), 96
Mann, Harry, 189
marginalised communities *see* Black Lives Matter; LGBTQIA+; racism; women
Marshall, Sylvia, 79
Mekas, Adolfus, 35
Mekas, Jonas, 22–3, 33, 34, 35, 41
Merritt, Michele, 149
Michelson, Annette, 34
Millard, Kathryn
  Screenwriting in a Digital Era, 148, 149
Miller, Warren
  The Cool World, 163
mind-reading, 62–3
mind–body split, 48
mise en scène, 148, 160, 161, 164
Modell, Arnold, 112
modern dance, 3, 5–6, 9, 15, 29, 49, 50, 62, 71, 73–5, 79, 103, 111
  and collaboration, 76–7
  and *Dance in the Sun*, 80, 81, 85, 92
Moment in Love, A (1956), 25, 100, 188
Monaco, Paul
  The Sixties, 32
monologues, 156–7, 158, 170–1, 173–4
montage, 14–15, 35, 100, 108
  and *Bridges-Go-Round*, 116
  and *Brussels Loops*, 113

and *The Connection*, 160
and *The Cool World*, 113, 128, 133, 169–70, 172, 173–4
and *Dance in the Sun*, 96
and *Ornette: Made in America*, 196, 197
and *Skyscraper*, 101–3
and Soviet Union, 79–80, 94, 96
Mumford, Gene, 102
music, 4, 7, 18, 19, 76
  and *Bridges-Go-Round*, 114, 115, 116, 117
  and *Brussels Loops*, 118
  and *The Connection*, 157, 158, 159, 160, 161
  and *The Cool World*, 162, 168, 173, 174
  and *Dance in the Sun*, 81, 83, 84, 85, 94
  and *Ornette: Made in America*, 196
  see also jazz
musical comedy, 83, 102
Musical for the 80s, A (unrealised), 189

Nagrin, Daniel, 19, 74, 75, 76
  Dance and the Specific Image, 146–7
  and *Dance in the Sun*, 79, 80, 81–2, 83–4, 88–94, 96
narrative
  and *The Connection*, 157–8, 159–61
  and *The Cool World*, 163, 172–4
  and *Dance in the Sun*, 80–2, 83–5
  and dancefilm, 100
Neorealism, 122, 164
Nevelson, Louise, 18
New American Cinema Group, 1, 3, 14–15, 33–5

Oklahoma! (musical), 85
Olenina, Ana, 95
opposition, 14, 23, 35
Ornette: Made in America (1984), 194–7

participatory sense-making, 9, 57, 59, 60, 64, 141–7, 154, 160, 177, 180
Pennebaker, D. A., 25, 35, 101, 118
phrasing, 86–94, 112–14
   and *Brussels Loops*, 119–20
   and *The Cool World*, 125–6
   and *In Paris Parks*, 101
   and *Skyscraper*, 102
planning, 142, 148–9, 153, 194–5
politics, 1, 2, 3, 15, 32, 33
Pollock, Griselda, 64
Portrait of Jason, A (1967), 19–20, 35–7, 101, 175–82
power relations, 36, 101
protest, 30–2

Rabinovitz, Lauren, 38–9, 82, 90, 99
race *see* Black culture; racism
racism, 3, 8, 59, 60, 103, 119–21, 139; *see also* civil rights
rage, 3, 15, 16, 18, 63, 127, 139
rebellion, 3, 15, 18, 24, 58, 188
responding, 153–5
Reynolds, Dee, 86, 112
rhythm, 6, 7, 15, 17, 19, 40, 62, 70, 73, 78, 87, 103
   and *Bridges-Go-Round*, 116–17
   and *Brussels Loops*, 119–20
   and *The Connection*, 152, 156, 159, 160
   and *The Cool World*, 121, 123, 168, 169, 171
   and *Dance in the Sun*, 79–80, 89
   and editing, 108–13
   and embodied cognition, 54
   and embedded cognition, 56
   and enactive cognition, 58
   and jazz, 76, 77
   and *Ornette: Made in America*, 195, 196, 197
   and planning, 149
   and *A Portrait of Jason*, 176, 178
   and race, 139
   and *Skyscraper*, 101

   and video, 191
   and videodance, 99
Richter, Hans, 22–3, 83
Robert Frost: A Lover's Quarrel (1963), 140–1
Robinson, Lisa, 77–8
Rogosin, Lionel, 35
Rome is Burning (Burch/Labarthe et al., 1970), 82, 164
Rose and the Players (unfinished), 17, 188
Rosenberg, Douglas, 97
Rushton, Richard, 159

St Denis, Ruth, 73
Saltburn (Fennel et al., 2024), 144
Savage/Love (1981), 99, 188
Scary Time (1960), 188
scores *see* music
Scott, Marion, 99
screendance, 25, 95, 97–8, 100
Segodnya (*Today*, Shub et al., 1929), 169
Seidenberg, Robert, 39–40
sense-making, 9, 57, 58–9, 60, 64, 71–2, 138, 141, 150; *see also* participatory sense-making
sexuality, 32, 76–7, 139
shapeshifting, 13
Sheehan, Rebecca, 33, 38
Shephard, Sam, 189
Shub, Esfir, 108, 169
Signals through the Flames (documentary, 1983), 28
Skyscraper (1959), 26, 75, 100, 101–2
social cognition, 149
social justice, 139, 188
Sokolow, Anna, 77, 85, 188
Soviet montage, 94, 96, 108
stock market crash (1929), 15–16
Study in Choreography for Camera, A (Deren et al., 1945), 90
Sutton, John, 48, 49, 53
Svilova, Elizaveta, 169

Tharp, Twyla, 74
theatre, 26–30, 32, 153, 188
   and Broadway, 85
   and *Dance in the Sun*, 80
   thinking body, 6, 53
Thompson, Evan, 57, 138
Todd, Mabel, 53
Tongues (1982), 99, 188
12 Angry Men (Lumet et al., 1957), 156
24 Frames per Second (1977), 99
Tynan, Kenneth, 26

UCLA, 40, 100, 188
Udall, Stewart, 140
UNICEF, 188

Van Dyke, Willard, 7, 25, 101, 118
Varda, Agnes, 188–9
Vertov, Dziga, 169
video art, 9, 14–15, 189–91, *192*, 193–4
videodance, 98–100, 188
vision, 2, 9, 10, 45, 47, 141, 143–4, 193
   and *The Cool World*, 165, 166, 174
   and editing, 134, 162
   and enactive cognition, 57, 58
   and response, 147, 153–5
Visual Diary, A (1980), 188
Viva, 189

voice, 2, 3, 4, 5, 9, 10, 45, 103, 134, 187, 194
   and *The Cool World*, 164
   and enactive cognition, 57, 138, 139, 140
   and *A Portrait of Jason*, 35
voice-over, 101–2, 170, 171, 172

Waiting for Godot (Beckett), 156
Waldron, Mal, 19, 165, 168, 174
Wallace, Kathleen, 52, 187
Ward, Richard, 122
Wheeler, Michael, 60, 61
When We were Kings (Gast et al., 1996), 96
white women, 3, 8
Wieland, Joyce, 38, 39
Williams, Raymond, 145
Winter, Stephen, 35, 36
Wiseman, Fredrick, 32–3, 35, 122
women, 2, 7, 8, 11, 29, 38, 39, 45, 52, 64, 109, 139, 182, 189
   and *Bridges-Go-Round*, 114
   and *Dance in the Sun*, 85
   and editing, 56, 134
   and modern dance, 76–7
   and *A Portrait of Jason*, 180
   see also white women
Woods, Jason, 36

Zippens, Lionel, 34

EU representative:
Easy Access System Europe
Mustamäe tee 50, 10621 Tallinn, Estonia
Gpsr.requests@easproject.com

www.ingramcontent.com/pod-product-compliance
Lightning Source LLC
Chambersburg PA
CBHW071714160426
43195CB00012B/1677